HOW LOW CAN YOU GO?

ROUND EUROPE FOR 1p EACH WAY (PLUS TAX)

Tom Chesshyre

HODDER & STOUGHTON

To Robert, Christine, Edward and Kate

Contents

1

STANSTED, ESSEX

THE UNSPELLABLES

I'm squeezed into a grimy aquamarine seat in a crowded carriage of the Stansted Express, waiting to depart from Liverpool Street Station on a cold December afternoon. The train is packed, standing-room only, with people like me on their way to Stansted Airport in Essex to take a no-frills flight.

It is dirty, expensive and squashed. My train ticket has cost the same as my return flight. But there's a sense of excitement among the passengers; of holiday journeys ahead. Maybe that's why nobody pays much attention to our insalubrious surroundings and is prepared to take this lousy train. Plus, of course, a taxi out into the badlands of Essex is way too dear for us cheapo, low-cost airline types.

Next to me three American female backpackers are loudly discussing boyfriends and how drunk they hope to get over Christmas. 'I'm so glad I didn't get into a proper relationship with him, I think I might have gone a bit psycho,' says a big blonde twenty-something with orthodontic braces. She's wearing a floppy red University of Dallas jumper, and for a moment I wonder whether she's one of President Dubya's daughters. I glance over, and she gives me a death stare before adding: 'I love it when Mom and Dad have their Christmas Eve drinks. Mom gets sooo smashed. So do I. It's just sooo funny.'

The Stansted Express is late. The yellow station clock ticks outside the window. I'm at the point of giving up on all these 'expresses' linking London to its airports. Maybe I've just been incredibly unlucky, but they always seem to be delayed. Be it ten minutes (which I consider not bad) or twenty minutes (fairly standard) or longer (when I start to lose the will ever to catch a plane again, no matter how cheap it is), they almost freakishly never arrive quite when they're meant to.

I remember one occasion when a jam-packed Heathrow Express, supposedly a fifteen-minute service, billed as the 'fastest and most convenient way to get to Heathrow', arrived at Paddington at 1.30 a.m. after a three and a half hour journey. It had suffered a technical problem due to one part of the track not having electricity. So it had to be towed. Except there was no spare train as it was Sunday night and there weren't many drivers on shifts . . . And so on and so on it went in a roll-call of excuses.

It's a damn good excuse this time though – a real corker, a collector's item. 'A table is broken,' a thin, whiny voice announces from the barely audible speakers. It's got that lifeless quality that you only get on British rail announcements. 'We are having it repaired as it is a security risk. We should be moving shortly. Thank you for your patience and sorry for the delay.'

I'm flabbergasted. A broken table: a security risk! Will the table be arrested at gunpoint or just rugby-tackled to the floor? This is new territory, even for an airport 'express', I mutter to myself in disbelief. The Dubya daughters eyeball me suspiciously.

We roll in to Stansted half an hour late. 'Sorry for the delay,' repeats the whining voice. 'We hope you have a pleasant onwards journey.' No thanks to you, I'm thinking. How about some money back? Cold, hard cash—now! Down with anonymous tannoy excuses! But, suckers that we are, we just scoot along inside the airport to catch our planes.

Inside the terminal, Stansted is bedlam. Hundreds if not thousands of people are forming long, shapeless queues for check-in desks for flights to Venice, Bordeaux and Tenerife. There's a roar of excited chatter. Frantic latecomers are using overloaded trolleys as battering rams to get through. Many people are wearing outfits totally unsuitable for the Essex winter: shorts, T-shirts and I can even see the odd pair of flip-flops and sandals. A group of girls who must be on a hen party is wearing matching pink T-shirts and sombreros. There's a manic sense of barely organised chaos. Stansted feels like it's at bursting point, as always.

I am forced to barge through all the queues, body-surfing my way to my check-in. It's on the far side, just beyond bustling lines of holidaymakers waiting for Rome and Verona departures. I finally squeeze through the crowds and find myself at check-in desk 23.

In comparison to the rest of the airport, it's deserted round here: tumbleweed practically blowing across the concourse. Everywhere else, it's every holidaymaker for themselves, in a no-holds-barred stampede for the duty-free. But my check-in queue consists of just two.

The flight hasn't been cancelled. This is the right time and place. The flight is on schedule.

It's just, you see, that my destination is Szczecin. And not many people want to visit Szczecin, Poland's second biggest port, in the middle of December. They want to go to Madrid or Malaga or Faro instead. They want to go to well-known places where it's warm – or at least warm*er*.

So what about me? Why am I going to Poland's second biggest port in the middle of the winter? Am I mad? Have I lost my bearings and my marbles?

It's not that at all. The reason I'm going to Szczecin is precisely because *no one else wants to go*.

As a travel journalist writing for national newspapers and magazines for the past dozen years since my early twenties, I've been lucky to see many of the world's most famous sights: Machu Picchu in Peru, the pyramids in Egypt, Uluru in Australia, the Grand Canyon in America, Petra in Jordan, the Serengeti in Kenya, Table Mountain in South Africa, the Grand Palace in Bangkok and the Great Wall of China, among much else. In Europe I've visited most of the major cities, hopping over regularly on weekends to stay in fancy boutique hotels and write city break guides.

So I've seen the Venices, the Monacos and the Barcelonas. I've flown to many of the farther flung wonders of the world, and it's been great. I've gambled into the night in Las Vegas, I've snorkelled on the Great Barrier Reef, I've gone skiing in the best resorts in Canada.

But so, it seems, has everyone else. Cheap fares have opened up the whole world to mass tourism over the past decade, more or less covering the time I first went out with passport and pen. The south of Spain and France are old hat. So, for many, is America and southern Africa. Now we're off to Thailand, China and Australia, not to mention Laos and Tibet – and thinking ever more daringly for each trip ahead. Will it be the Antarctic or Cambodia next? How about a little visit to the Galapagos? I hear the South Pacific is nice at this time of year.

It's got to the point that Philip Hensher, writing in the *Independent* in October 2006, declared the 'near-total collapse of travel writing' that informs readers about places they have not visited before. This, he says, has come about because we can now go almost anywhere in the world on cheap flights. Travel books, he argues, have 'stopped being bought by people who liked to dream about going to exotic places, and started being bought by people who [want] to find out more about the place they'd just been to, or [want] to be reminded of an enjoyable time.'

This is true, but it's not the whole truth – as I found when browsing the Ryanair website one lunchtime at work.

I'd been trying to book a weekend flight to Dublin, but as I looked at the destination map and clicked on the drop-down menus, I kept being distracted by all the other bizarre-looking destinations dotted among the Aberdeens and Grenobles. Where exactly was Brno? Where or what was Oujda? Balaton was in Hungary, I knew, but Bydgoszcz and Poznan? Not to mention

Wroclaw and, most exotic of all, Szczecin! Travel was my trade, and I couldn't even guess where these places were.

Already I'd forgotten Dublin, and I was staring goggle-eyed at all these seemingly endless mystery routes to obscure parts of countries like Poland, Slovakia, Estonia, Lithuania, Bulgaria, Hungary and Slovenia, offered not just by Ryanair, but also, I soon found, by the likes of easyJet, SkyEurope and Wizz Air.

And they were cheap! Szczezin was available for the elusive 1p fare that never seems to apply to Madrid or Barcelona. Admittedly there were taxes on top, but it was still dirt cheap for somewhere so 'exotic'. Has Hensher been to Szczecin? I'd never even heard of it. These places were right on my doorstep, but I'd never even dreamed of visiting them. So I found myself tapping in my credit card details for a return ticket to Szczezin on a free weekend in December – with no plan of action other than making this the first trip of many, to see for myself all these places I hadn't been to, couldn't pronounce, and would never have heard of, if low-cost airlines didn't fly to them. I wanted to go off the beaten track, and this seemed as good a way as any. God knows what I'd find, but at least it would be more of an adventure, in one way, than going to Bali again.

That was the idea, anyway. So it is with a great sense of anticipation, plus a healthy dose of trepidation, that I make my way, boarding pass in hand, to Gate 46. People are sprinting to make final calls for Venice and Rome: women shedding their high heels for speed, chubby chaps in Nike tracksuits huffing and puffing. A sign says: Failure to report to the boarding gate at least thirty minutes prior to departure will result in the aircraft departing without you. THE PLANE WILL NOT WAIT. Over at the Szczecin gate, our small group of passengers is quickly through. The plane doors shut. We taxi to the runway. And we're off.

I settle in my blue synthetic-leather seat, feeling smug. This flight cost 1 pence. Just 1 pence! With taxes the price admittedly came to £24.63. That's 37 pence less than the Stansted Express. And it's for a 900-mile round-trip. Try beating that for value for money, I think to myself, as the nose lifts upwards and Stansted disappears beneath the clouds.

At the other end of my row is a young Polish-looking chap with a crew-cut. He's clutching a Boots plastic bag from which he produces a homemade sandwich. I fancy a 'Hot Pizza: the authentic Italian taste!' from the Ryanair bar. 'We're all out,' says the stewardess, a bottle blonde. Instead I plump for a ham and cheese ciabatta (£3.95) and a cappuccino (£1.75). Boots Bag stares at me as though I'm some kind of multi-millionaire—£5.70 can probably buy a car or a small apartment in Szczecin. It's food for thought that my Ryanair lunch is costing me more than my flight.

I'm curious to know, is the stewardess familiar with our destination? 'Oh you poor thing, you're away for a whole weekend?' she says sympathetically. 'It's so cold. I can't see many people going. I really can't. I've no idea how long we'll keep on flying there.' In short she knows nothing about it, except that it's cold. I'd guessed that much. It's December and we're going to Eastern Europe.

The cabin is, frankly, dirty. Several crunched-in Cadbury's mini-eggs are on the floor, there are sweet wrappers in my seat pocket, there's an old coffee cup under the seat to the left, and the table is sticky from a spilt drink. A steward comes round with some ragged-looking *Ryanair Magazines*.

I introduce myself to the man at the end of the row. His name is Hubert, twenty-four, from Szczecin, and he's going home to see his girlfriend for the weekend. He's keen to chat. He leaps into the free middle seat and starts telling me about his job working in the kitchen at a pub-restaurant in Victoria Station.

'I cannot understand the behaviour of the English people,' he says, sounding perplexed. 'The whole time they say please and thank you. They put the chair back, you know, tuck it under the table. And then you look at the table: it is a complete mess! There's sugar everywhere, chips all over the table, and some people they smoke the cigarette. And what is that word?' Cigarette butt? 'Yes, yes, the butt. They stick the butt inside the cup. It is crazy!'

Hubert, it transpires, has a degree in marine geography from the University of Szczecin. 'I wish I could find a job that uses my mind, not just my hands.' He hopes to work as a tour guide in Poland, but he can earn five times as much in a relatively unskilled job in Britain. He shares a flat in Bow in the East End with his sister and her boyfriend, which costs them £200 each a month. His sister works as a manager at the canteen for Underground staff at St James's Park station: 'My family is very happy that we are happy. That we can afford to buy what we want—clothes, music—and rent a flat. But I wouldn't want to spend the rest of my life in England. No way. No thanks.'

He's in a talkative mood, perhaps because he doesn't often speak to English people. There are three other Poles at his work, and they stick together most of the time. 'What is it about some young English people,' he asks rhetorically, but as though he really wants to know. 'I see these young people. They are drunk behind my flat. Maybe they have just got children, so the state gives them a flat – so they don't need to work. I don't know. But I spent four months working in Sweden, and you just didn't see people standing around and doing nothing. Everybody does something in Sweden. My friends who come to England, they get jobs easily. Easily. They have jobs taking the fruit from the trees, or in cafes, or in restaurants – easy jobs.'

He could write a thesis on 'The English: why are they so lazy?' I soon realise. I ask about the differences between English and Polish food. It's another favourite topic. 'Oh!' he exclaims. 'In England people eat sandwiches, burgers, cheeseburgers, meat balls and pasta. In Poland it is much better. The bread, for example, is much better. Completely different.' How? He pauses, and scratches his crew-cut. 'Just completely different. You'll see.' Then, as though to kill off any argument about the supremacy of Polish food, he says triumphantly: 'You eat the bacon and the beans.' He pauses for effect. 'But we eat the sauerkraut and the cucumber in the salted water!' QED. It's as simple as that. What more can I tell you, being his implication. OK, OK, Hubert, you got me there. It was the salted cucumbers that did it.

Whether or not Hubert is right about the merits of Polish versus English food, I'm unsure. But I have a feeling that he's right about one thing: if nothing else, Szczecin is going to be something completely different. I can't wait. What will 1p each way to an unspellable place in Poland deliver?

SZCZECIN, POLAND

POUNDS FOR ZLOTYS

It's pitch black. It's cold – the digital display says –6°C. And we're deep in the Western Pomeranian forest.

There's not another car in sight. No rear lights to follow. No cats' eyes marking the way. Nothing but potholes – dreadful potholes. It feels like we're driving across the surface of the moon, being bounced out of our seats, and we're only doing 50 kilometres per hour.

Even though Ryanair called our destination Szczecin we've actually landed at Goleniow airport, 40 kilometres from Szczecin itself. Hubert, my new friend from the plane, is catching a lift into town with me. 'We must watch out for the big pigs!' he says, peering into the forest. It's so dark you can hardly make out the shapes of the trees. What would happen if you broke down out here? How on earth would you, without a Hubert, explain to the authorities where you were? He continues, 'Big pigs! Watch out for them. They are very dangerous.' Before I can ask him to explain, he's answering his mobile phone.

After couple of minutes – me on full 'Dangerous Big Pig' alert and Hubert having an argument with someone – he clicks off, and tells me about the wild boars that roam the forest. It is apparently one of the best places for hunting wild boar in Europe. If you hit one with your car, however, it's not going to be a little dent. There's also, he says, a question of who will come off worse: the wild boar or the people sitting up front (i.e., us). I do not want to find out.

Hubert explains that it was his girlfriend on the phone. She's waiting for him at the bus station in town, and is not pleased that he's taken a lift from a stranger. 'Very angry, in fact,' he says plainly. 'She says to me: "Why do you get in this car with this strange man? Why?"' He chuckles to himself. As the road cuts through even darker forest, he starts telling me about his unlikely plans to go on holiday with his girlfriend to Mongolia next year: 'I hear a lot of good things about Mongolia,' he says, as though he's discussing a trip to the Algarve. 'It will be an adventure!' He's earned enough at the pub-restaurant at Victoria Station to save up for the flights. 'Yes, I've always fancied Mongolia,' he says dreamily.

We clatter through a bad patch of potholes. 'Ah, real Polish roads!' comments Hubert, almost proudly. Then we reach the end of the forest and the beginning of a northern suburb of Szczecin, with smooth, clearly unreal, Polish roads. 'You see! The EU has been good for us! Very good!' The creaking stops and we cruise past Soviet-era buildings down wide Soviet-era boulevards. 'Be careful in the north! It is dangerous! They take your wallet. You must be very careful!' he says, as we pass a vast ghetto-like estate. And soon we're in the Big Smoke itself, the centre of Szczecin, capital of Western Pomerania, in the north-west corner of Poland, just thirty miles from the border with Germany. I've made it to the first of my unspellables.

The guidebooks are not exactly kind about Szczecin. It's a 'gruff workaday place that bares few of its charms to the passing visitor' according to the *Rough Guide*, little more than an 'important transport hub' with a 'tangle of bridges, cranes and dockside machinery.' Wonderful. *Lonely Planet* is equally downbeat. It describes Szczecin as 'a work in progress'. Lovely.

But the history is fascinating – no matter how grim a place this seems. Before the Second World War, Sczeczin was in Germany. At the end of the war, it changed hands and became Polish, and the Germans inhabitants were made to leave. They were replaced by Poles who were shipped in, mainly reluctantly, from lands that had previously been Polish, but became Ukraine and Lithuania after the war.

Back when it was German, the city was called Stettin – which had the advantage of being a whole lot easier to pronounce. Winston Churchill managed it when he gave the city the biggest mention in its 1,200-year-old history in a speech in March 1946.

From Stettin in the Baltic to Trieste in the Adriatic, an Iron Curtain has descended across the continent. Behind that line lie all the capitals of the ancient states of central and eastern Europe. Warsaw, Berlin, Prague, Vienna, Budapest, Belgrade, Bucharest and Sofia . . . all are subject in one form or another, not only to Soviet influence but to a very high and increasing measure of control from Moscow.

He added that this 'is certainly not the liberated Europe we fought to build up. Nor is it one which contains the essentials of permanent peace.' Although the phrase 'iron curtain' had been widely used before – Joseph Goebbels, Hitler's propaganda minister, had even uttered the words – it was this speech that sealed its place in history.

Szczecin had been Germany's main Baltic port. It soon became, and still is, Poland's second biggest shipyard, after Gdansk. Although it handles the most tonnage, it is smaller than Gdansk. Both shipyards saw anti-Communist protests in 1970, when many shipyard workers were killed in clashes with police. And Szczecin became a major hub of the anti-communist Solidarity movement – less famous than Lech Walesa's supporters in Gdansk, but equally effective. The city is predominantly Roman Catholic – tens of thousands filled the square outside the City Hall when John Paul II visited in 1987, and there's now a statue to the great man in its centre. The population is 400,000, the same as it was before the war, with just 1,000 Germans now living in the city. Apparently, one hundred or so very elderly Germans still remain from before the nationality switch.

Since the Communists were finally driven out in 1989, there have been momentous changes, including, of course, the catalytic effect of EU membership since May 2004. Combine this recent history with the rollercoaster of events of their early history, in which Szczecin began as a Slav stronghold in the eighth century, followed by conquests by Danes, Swedes, and Germans – with a proud period in the middle when the Pomeranian Princes ruled the roost, joining the Hanseatic League in the mid-thirteenth century in their heyday – and you've got a place with a whole lot to talk about.

All of which political to-ing and fro-ing strikes me as being well worth investigating. Which is why, early the next day, after my late night check-in to a tower block Radisson SAS, I'm waiting to meet the President. That's right: the President of Szczecin, an ex-docker named Marian Jurczyk, wishes to see me. I made a few calls last week, not expecting much, perhaps a meeting with a city hall press officer, but before I knew it an audience with the President, Szczecin's mayor, had been granted.

His office is in a vast, turn of the nineteenth-century, stone building. I'm led by aides up a curving marble staircase to the first floor, where men in suits are waiting in a grand hallway lit by a chandelier, with a long iron balcony overlooking a large square.

The President is busy, so we will have to wait, says Pawel, my translator. We stand by the window looking out onto the balcony and the square. Pawel has a large face, grey eyes and brown hair in a neat side-parting. He looks a bit like the comedian David Walliams. A yellow scarf is looped over his full length jacket. He's clutching a thin notebook. 'Hitler made a speech here. On this balcony in 1938. There were huge crowds.'

Pawel is full of information. 'The far statue,' he says, pointing into the square, 'is of three eagles, representing Polish independence.'

Each of the three eagles has a particular meaning, but I get confused about which one represents 'building a sustainable future', and which one represents 'the idea of reconquered areas', and which one represents 'reconquering' – and to be perfectly honest, there's a limit to how much I really want to know about this eagle statue. The nearest statue, he adds helpfully, with its back turned to us like we're being snubbed, is the one of Pope John Paul II.

We're called over. The President is ready. Two men with slick haircuts in sharp suits and long black leather jackets slip out before us. What kind of President are we dealing with here? I'm dressed in a dark blue ski-jacket with a hood and brown cord trousers. Everyone else is much smarter. I feel like I've been called in from the docks to strike a deal on behalf of the workers.

For Marian Jurczyk that was how it used to be. Jurczyk was second in Solidarity's chain of command behind Walesa – who was in charge in Gdansk, while Jurczyk was running the show in Szczecin. Now he is first in command of a major Polish city – the seventh largest – sitting in the very office in which Communist party officials once contemplated how to keep shipyard workers under control.

It is a big, dark room, with eight leather armchairs around a large circular coffee table. There is a desk next to a picture of a silver eagle on a red background, a wooden cross hanging on the wall, a ticking grandfather clock, and a model of a ship in a glass case sitting on a cabinet. Past long yellow curtains, blue Christmas tree decorations are alight outside in the December gloom.

Jurczyk, seventy, has thinning grey hair, a brown suit, gold-rimmed glasses, large dockers' hands, but the air of a suburban bank manager. What does he think of the new Ryanair flights? I ask. 'For both the tourists and the businessmen, it is good.

Szczecin is the most attractive city in Poland. It has lots of green spaces, water and forests,' he – or rather Pawel – says. I have to wait for several minutes between each question for Jurczyk to answer, while Pawel scribbles notes. The first answer includes a mention of Parisian-style roundabouts, (which are apparently a good thing), radial streets (also good), two billion zlotys of investment for a water treatment plant, and plans to build another shopping centre and an aqua park.

Jurcyzk looks up every now and then, but mainly gazes down to his large hands, which he squeezes together when he makes a good point. 'Britain has always given a helping hand to Poland,' he says. 'Tourists who come here will get a warm welcome. They will not regret it. But may I also say, and this may not be politically correct, but I think British people should come here to see the brave Polish fighters who fought for the British in the war.'

Not the snappiest of slogans for a series of tourist adverts for Szczecin, I can't help thinking.

It's the old Solidarity days and its aftermath that Jurcyzk really wants to talk about. And with the grandfather clock ticking, he pours forth. As he talks, I realise I'm speaking with a man who risked his life for his cause; it's an unexpected honour. Szczecin has clearly not had the best of things over the years.

'The policy of the Polish state has always been very cautious towards Szczecin,' Jurczyk says. 'There was always a fear that it would go back to Germany. So after the war, the central authorities were reluctant to invest. A lot of the rubble from flattened buildings was taken for construction in other cities in the east. It means that Szczecin is about twenty years behind other Polish cities.'

Being a centre of the Solidarity movement didn't help as it made authorities even less likely to invest. In the 1970s, Jurcyzk was jailed for three years for 'anti-Communist behaviour'. It could have been worse: the death penalty was given to some. In

1980, a deal was struck with the Communists, and Jurcyck still feels deeply let down by the Communist failure to deliver on promises such as freedom of the press, releasing political prisoners, permitting trade unions, higher wages and an end to Party privileges, which were made at the time.

'We were betrayed. It was necessary to have those talks to avoid bloodshed and shooting in the streets of workers. I believe in peace. At the time of the strikes, the USSR was a global superpower, and it had military plans in the Eastern bloc. So the talks were necessary. But we were betrayed – we did not get what we were promised. Yet if we had not had those strikes and if John Paul II had not supported the workers and instilled in them the desire for freedom, then we would not be where we are today. A lot of corrupt people have got away without any penalty for their crimes. I wish that was not so.'

He is full of praise for Pope John Paul II: 'He is the most important Polish person to me. Religion and politics mixed how they should mix. He said he was the son of the nation and could talk for us. Neighbouring states did not have that.'

We spend 40 minutes together, drinking coffee and occasionally eating orange sweets. He presents me with a book entitled *The Sights of Szczecin*. And I take a picture of him standing in front of the white eagle by his desk. Then he says to me, with a glint in his eye, leaning forward, with Pawel leaning forward, too: 'I would like to emphasise the point that the Polish women are very beautiful, eh? And you are a young man, eh? Very, very beautiful.'

The President of the city is offering me its women – definitely not bad, I'd say, for a first morning's work.

Pawel and I go for a coffee around the corner in a gloomy café in the philharmonic orchestra building. There are old music sheets pasted on walls, gilded mirrors, worn armchairs and the feeling that not much has changed in here since 1989. He tells me about his plans to start a tourism business offering hunting, fishing and, curiously, dentistry. He's thirty-eight, with a young family, and he learnt his English on trips to the United States – he has a relative in Florida. This relative used to send packages of food and clothing to his mother and father during the days of communism: chocolates, chewing gum, coffee, jeans.

She also sent cash. It was illegal to have foreign currency in those days. However, it *was* legal to exchange foreign currency for coupons at official currency points. These coupons could then be spent in 'US currency shops'. Pawel said, 'Even Kafka couldn't come up with something like that. Foreign currency was technically illegal, but in practice it was,' he pauses, looking for the right word, '*semi-legal*. There were a lot of semi-legal solutions at the time.'

Pawel kindly offers to show me around as he's got a couple of hours free. We jump in his car, which is squeezed tightly into a tiny space. 'You see, this was never a problem before. We never had so many cars. This is a good sign.' And we head off for the river front. He turns on his stereo and a Churchill speech is playing; I catch the phrase 'barrier and a shield', before Pawel turns it off. 'You don't want to listen to that!' And he puts on a Madonna tape. She's singing 'Borderline' – which seems quite appropriate for these parts.

There are several grand buildings dating from the early twentieth century, including the National Museum and a Maritime Academy, running along the embankment. But it's the view across the grey and polluted-looking river Odra to the docks and the shipbuilding yards that gets you. There are garish advertising boards on a small island, beyond which is the tangle of cranes, along with funnels of cargo ships and grey concrete office blocks. The sky is grey. The river is grey. The trees look grey. It's also very cold – at least minus 5°C. In the foreground a statue of Hercules is covered in graffiti. Okay, this is not the Champs-Elysées, there are no Spanish Steps in Szczecin, but this is all peculiarly intriguing. It just feels nice, for once, to be the only tourist in town.

It's too cold to walk around much. So we drive about the centre to the sound of Madonna singing 'Crazy For You'. There are a lot of rundown-looking 1960s apartment blocks – the type that, no matter how many coats of paint they get, will always look dreary. But there are also Lexus and SAAB car showrooms, and signs for Mercedes, Philips, Tesco, Pizza Hut and McDonald's outlets – which suggest a bubble of wealth. Who's making the money? Pawel explains matter of factly: 'Fifteen years ago, you could import almost anything to Poland and you'd make good cash: chewing gum, cars, whatever. There are a lot of people who got rich quick.'

He has met plenty of western investors himself, acting as their translator. 'Sure people are buying real estate, but it's mainly businesses. We are far away from Warsaw, which is a disadvantage, but we are selling in the EU, to Scandinavia and Germany. The workforce is highly qualified and cheap. The land is cheap. There are large ports and all modes of transport.' Including wonderful Ryanair now, of course.

Szczecin's Old Town is, as the guidebooks described, a mess. A series of buildings in various shades of yellow, aquamarine and ochre have sprung up on a hill beneath the ugly sixteenth-century castle that once belonged to the Pomeranian Princes. Apparently a project began a few years back to rebuild this area, which was left empty after being destroyed in the war, but the backers ran out of cash. Now there are half-finished buildings in a hotchpotch of styles. There is graffiti all over the place, including the word skinheads written next to a Nazi sign on the wall of the castle. With a big road below, down by the river, and a major flyover across the river just a couple of hundred metres away, the whole hillside feels hopeless – or maybe that's just because I'm seeing it on a dull grey day.

'The Allied bombers missed the shipyard and destroyed the

Old Town,' says Pawel, as a couple of people who look like tourists – the first I've seen – walk by. They seem cold and miserable. 'Germans. You get a few on sentimental tours. They were, after all, forced to leave. They just handed their possessions and houses over to us. Some try to visit old family homes – the children, their grandchildren. That is still quite common. "That's my grandma's spoon!" they'll say, and things like that. And a lot of people still have old books and pieces of furniture.'

We drive past signs advertising the Nigel Kennedy Jazz Quintet. Trams zip about. The pavements are busy. Young women, I can't help but notice, are wearing DVT-inducingly tight jeans (I mean really spray-on tight) as they go about their business. Most wear woolly hats, and are wrapped in scarves. Older women seem to like their dogs. But not pathetic Parisian poodles: big dogs like wolfhounds and Alsatians. Men are in heavy coats and there are lots of puffa jackets. People's expressions seem a little long-suffering. But really, if Britain was this cold, we'd probably look like this lot.

Pawel lets slip that he translated for Michael O'Leary, Ryanair's ebullient chief executive, during the Ryanair–Szczecin airport deal. What was that like? 'Well, he was quite an interesting person really,' he says coyly. What do you mean? 'Well, quite a celebrity person. He likes the camera a lot. And he is smart when it comes to promoting Ryanair.' In what way? 'He goes to extremes. For example, he stuck his head out of the captain's window of the plane with a Polish flag in his mouth. He was getting people's attention by doing something different. He took very good care of the media. Two of them had missed the chance of an interview and he asked me to find them.' What were the negotiations like? 'Let's just say they're really smart when it comes to negotiating. Really smart . . . and tough. They say: "We can provide a lot, but perhaps not directly. We will bring business people, tourists and students . . . more people." '

It's a small insight into the low-cost airline model as seen from the other side. How tiny airports like Szczecin, desperate to get on the UK flight map, succumb to the low-cost magic of Ryanair, easyJet and others. A bit of a charm offensive from Mr O'Leary – sticking a Polish flag in his mouth and dangling out of a plane – and on rolls the 1 pence each way revolution, while Szczecin, Poland's second biggest port, suddenly becomes a weekend break destination.

Well, in theory at least.

Pawel drives off, listening to Madonna's 'Material World'. And I turn to the very materialistic Galaxy Centrum mall, where he has left me. It's a monster: a vast complex, four stories high, with a giant atrium, a couple of hundred shops, and huge slow-moving escalators. It looks the business – why are so many Poles coming to live in the UK, if everyone's so well-to-do here? Inside is a gleaming Mercedes SLK, available for a cool £37,000. There are cafés, stalls selling sweets, and lots and lots of people. It's like Oxford Street at Christmas, just in a big building in Poland. High street names include Benetton, H&M, Samsonite, Pierre Cardin, Nike.

There are also Polish-name fashion shops, selling stuff that looks slightly out of date by British fashion standards, I think.

A shop called Ravell selling men's fashion catches my eye. It has lots of what I'd describe as 'pulling shirts': stripy designs in blacks and dark greys. The shop's busy with people browsing. I take a couple of the best 'pullers' to try on. And then I notice something. I'm getting the full, very full, attention of all three members of staff.

I feel a bit uneasy, as though they're thinking: 'We've got one here: he's going to buy something! Oh yes, he is! I think he is. Come on . . . come on!' Like they've been waiting for a long time by the river bank, and finally they've got a biter, and now they're praying he'll stay on the hook. They lead me through to the changing rooms. No one else is there. The shop is packed, but

I'm the only person trying anything on. I'm torn between a purple, satiny number and a more regular black shirt with wide vertical stripes. I go for the latter. Maybe, by some freak movement in fashion trends, it will be 'in' by the time I get home. It costs £8.57.

'Thank you and have a nice day!' says the attendant, who can tell my Polish isn't all that good. I think I hear them high-fiving and whooping behind my back as I leave.

In the mall again, I look at things a bit more closely and it becomes clear. There are an awful lot of people, but very few who have actually *bought* anything. Hardly anyone is carrying shopping bags. Everyone seems to be window shopping, browsing, or meeting their friends. The more I look, the fewer shopping bags I see. Hubert's comment about being able to earn five times as much cash in the UK as he can in Poland springs to mind. You can build a mall, and the shoppers will come. But will they shop?

Maybe not, but they'll eat burgers, fried chicken and pizza. The most profitable part of Galaxy Centrum is clearly the food hall on the top floor. I take the escalators upwards. Soon I'm amid all the usuals: McDonald's, KFC, Pizza Hut. Piped music is playing Phil Collins's 'Another Day in Paradise', while people stuff their faces, just like people stuff their faces everywhere. This really could be the food hall of a retail outlet in the middle of Oklahoma, or a service station on the M1, for that matter. Time to get out of Galaxy Centrum.

One of the best things about visiting out-of-the way places like Szczecin is the welcome you get. Even though Szczecin is a big city, people are as proving to be as friendly and forthcoming as in any tiny town. They're just not used to tourists round here – I've got curiosity value. The hotel manager, whom I met on my way home from the mall, has taken pity on me being in an unpronounceable, gruff, workaday Polish city all on my own, and has arranged for Wojciech, who works in the hotel's sales department, to show me the nightlife.

Wojciech shares the same name as General Wojciech Jaruzelski, the Communist dictator who came to power in Poland in 1981 promising to 'restore social order and defend socialism', but he's a much nicer guy and he doesn't have a penchant for khaki uniforms, dark glasses and torturing political prisoners. Wojciech is twenty-five and wearing a pullover tossed casually over his shoulders – looking a bit like a young multi-millionaire who owns a yacht in St Tropez, but is modest about it. He's on a sofa by the front entrance with two beautiful young women – and they are all ready for a big night out.

He introduces me to his friends: Elvi – who's twenty-one, petite, with brown eyes, brown curly hair and a big smile – and Anna, who's twenty-three, almost 6 foot, slim, with blonde hair and blue eyes. She's wearing knee-high boots and a miniskirt. Both are turning heads. The large Danish chaps who seem to hang around in the lobby bar most of the time are goggle-eyed. They pause amid their usual ribald drinking and joking, and are temporarily speechless; Anna's boots are a particular magnet of attention.

I'm feeling my age, suddenly realising I'm nine years older than any of this lot. I'm very glad I had the sense not to wear the new pulling shirt, because that would definitely have been trying too hard.

'So, Tom. What's it gonna be?' asks Wojciech, who is Mr Enthusiasm, in his perfect English. 'What do you want to do first? We were thinking Café 22. How does that sound?' Great, fantastic, I say, not knowing what Café 22 is at all; probably the average age of its customers.

It turns out to be a café-bar on the twenty-second floor of the tower next to the hotel. Groups of slightly older folk – average age I'd guess about forty (hey, I feel young again) – are up here drinking cocktails and wine, staring out across Szczecin's lit-up city centre. The apartment blocks and docks look better from above at night. It's a circular, but not revolving, bar, going right the way round the tower. Terence Trent d'Arby is playing on the stereo. It's all very mellow.

We sit down on leather chairs and Elvi orders Zubrowka vodkas, explaining: 'It is a type of vodka with a straw in it.' What, you drink it with a straw? 'No, no. It has a straw – like a piece of grass.' Oh. 'And it comes with apple juice, and a bit of cinnamon.' I later discover the 'straw' is bison grass, though I'm still not really sure what I'm drinking.

Never mind: it's delicious. Soon they're telling me about their jobs, studies and plans, and how moving to Britain to get a job is extremely common among their friends. Elvi, who's studying for an economics degree, hasn't made up her mind on what she wants to do yet. Anna is studying for an architecture degree, but is already working part-time at Goleniow Airport, or the place that Ryanair calls Szczecin Airport.

'I've got more friends now in London than I have in Szczecin, that's for sure.' Wojciech tells me. Don't you miss them? 'Sure, of course, but we keep in touch by email, and they come back to visit on Ryanair. I was very worried after the Tube bombings, I emailed them all immediately. Luckily they were all okay.'

I get the feeling that there is enormous pressure to 'get on' by moving west – and that Wojciech, Elvi and Anna will probably give it a try at some point, but that there is an unspoken sadness about flying away on Ryanair to another land. I wonder if it isn't depressing to have his generation split up like this. Apparently, over 80 per cent of the 600,000 'official' post-2004 economic immigrants from New Europe to the UK are aged between eighteen and thirty-four – nobody is sure of the unofficial number, it could be as much as double that.

'Well, you earn the same in pounds as you do in zlotys in most jobs; what would you do?' he asks, looking at me closely.

We don't stick around at Café 22 for long. That's not the way they do it in Szczecin. We catch a taxi – never more than two or three pounds in the city centre – and we're soon at the Can Can Club. It's nothing risqué, set in an old cinema not too far from the Radisson. Now it's time to feel really old. In the queue for the cloakroom I notice everyone looks very young . . . and bright . . . and healthy. Maybe they're just cherry cheeked because they've come in from the cold. But then we go into the club itself, which has the old screen area as a dance-floor, and lots of red leather armchairs with low-level tables spread out where the seats used to be. Eighties hits are being mixed with dance music. There's a sparkly disco ball. And everyone, I'm serious, almost everyone is beautiful.

I feel like I've stepped into a real-life L'Oréal advert. I've never seen anything like it. The women are dressed in glittery retro disco outfits, and the men are smartly dressed, some in suits that wouldn't look out of place in trendy bars in Miami. Everyone is well-behaved but having fun; the dancing is neat, lively, and people are giggling to each other. There's no pushing at the bar. Groups of girls eye groups of guys, but there are couples as well. Nobody's doing shots – as you might have expected in Poland. The drinking is civilised. All in all, it's a million miles from your local Ritzy.

Wojciech has reserved a table near the stage. Elvi and I order more Zubrowkas, while Anna and Wojciech go for vodkas and Redbull.

'To keep us going!' says Anna, who I can sense is out till the very early hours. She's smoking elegant white-tipped Davidoff cigarettes. She says she loves working at the airport. 'I hope the Ryanair will last,' she says a little worriedly, before changing tack. 'People think we have white bears here. People think that we are a small country and we drink lots of vodka. But it's not true . . . Okay, some older people, they drink just the vodkas. But we always have it with something else, not on its own. And not too much.'

A Brazilian percussion band appears, and suddenly everyone forms a civilised crowd to watch them play while capoeira dancers take centre stage. It really is so well-behaved – it feels like we're at some kind of arts show on the South Bank. All we need is Melvyn Bragg to turn up with a film crew.

With the music a bit quieter, Wojciech turns to me. He's clearly feeling reflective, perhaps the Zubrowkas are kicking in. 'I'm so proud of what has happened here. I used to go with my mother at 4 a.m., queuing to buy some meat. Sometimes we got it, sometimes not. Now look at this, just look around here. It's amazing. Do you not think?' I agree. And it is amazing. Watching the L'Oreal people beginning to dance Brazilian-style by the stage, I wonder if I *would* go to London if I was brought up in Szczecin.

Next we go to the Rocker Club – which is in a cellar nearby. People are a bit older, more mid-thirties, letting their hair down and cavorting to live music. We order more drinks. Thee band is playing Rolling Stones, Beatles and Prince covers. Television screens show models walking up and down a catwalk. A man carrying an oversized inflatable football and wearing a crazy blue wig, face-paint and a Manchester United top, comes round claiming to be Ronaldo – he signs an autograph for Elvi. He's not on a stag do, he's part of the entertainment.

Janet, the hotel manager, is nearby with her friends, one of whom is getting married. 'I love this,' she says. 'The Rocker is my favourite!' Looking at the 'football player' she adds, 'For the World Cup, we've already had bookings from the Brazilians and the Portuguese – I guess they think they're going to make the final.' Berlin, where the final is being held, is just a two-hour drive away.

At the City Hall club, where hip-hop is blaring, we have more drinks, but I'm ready for getting back. I catch a cab to the hotel and get to bed by 2 a.m. The others, relieved of their oldie, are up till 5 a.m., according to Wojciech – who was looking as cool, calm and collected as ever the next day.

I'm not. I answer the wake-up call the next morning with a quivering voice that ranges from Michael Jackson to Barry White and back again in one sentence. Not a good start. Then I look in the mirror. Christ. My eyes are like plum tomatoes. This is bad, very bad. It must have been all the smoke. I take a long shower, and have a little lie down to steady myself.

I need it: I'm off to the dentist.

This, Janet assured me last night, is what tourists do in Szczecin: they get their teeth done. So I'm going to get mine done. At the Rocker Club Janet gave me the low down on dental tourism in Szczecin. The Danes are the biggest customers, she said. They come over by ferry for stag and hen weekends and to get their teeth, plus other things, done.

'There are not yet people from Britain. Not tourists. Just businessmen. The Danes and the Germans – they go to the dentist. It's cheap – minimum half of other countries. My friend's husband is a dentist. They have a very good business. Then there is the cosmetic surgery. For the women and for the men. You can have whatever you want done to make you more . . . more . . . whatever. Small things . . .' She paused and cupped her hands to indicate breasts '. . . like breast enlargements. This is normal. People come, and then they go home. They just look different when they do.'

I could do with having my teeth checked, I said in passing. Janet's eyes brightened even more: 'Okay! I will talk to my friend. We will fix it.' And even though I was under the influence of several Zubrowkas and generally quite cheerful, I suddenly went cold. The thought of several large, grim-faced Polish-speaking men in white aprons spattered with blood stains pulling out my molars with Soviet-era pliers flashed into my head.

It's too late now. I jump in a taxi, showing the address for

Dentus II where Janet has booked an appointment. Twenty minutes later, I'm in a waiting room watching what looks like a Venezuelan soap opera dubbed into Polish on a 10-inch television. I'm nervous about dentists. But I'm not nervous for the reasons I think most people are. It's not the pain that bothers me most, or having someone poke about in your mouth for 15 minutes every six months or so. My main concern is financial. Something can go wrong and it can cost thousands, the price of a mid-range car or a fancy holiday somewhere warm in a decent hotel. Even small things seem to cost a lot. And have you ever had a second opinion?

Cezary Turostowski, D.D.S, calls me through; I'm taking it that 'D.D.S.' is the relevant Polish qualification for dentistry. He's a real charmer.

'Hello, Mr Chesshyre. Come here, take a seat.' He's wearing a pale-blue pinafore and white trousers, which match his very white smile, which is set off by his short blond hair and tanned face. The surgery is perfectly clean, about as far from the blood-stained image of Eastern European dentists as could be. We talk for a bit about prices. A consultation is free; normally you need to book at least a week in advance, but because I know Janet, he's fit me in. A filling will cost about £20, a bridge £700, an extraction £30, a crown £200, and an implant £600. Laser whitening, using the latest equipment, will cost about £200, and it takes forty minutes. All these prices are, apparently, as much as a third to half those in the UK.

To stall the inevitable, I ask about British dental tourists. 'They are starting to come. We had one last week, two the week before that, and two the week before that. I'd say it's a trend; it's growing!' Are they coming on Ryanair? 'Oh, yes. Ryanair. Thank God for Ryanair! I hear a composite bridge with a crown can cost £3,000 in the UK. Here it is £700. And in Ireland it is also very expensive.' He has two surgeries, Dentus I and II, and they are link-ed to other established surgeries with English-speaking dentists.

Down to business: poke, poke, poke. He ums and ahs a bit, poking about. 'Mr Chesshyre, you do not have the whitest of teeth.' Gee, thanks a lot, I'm thinking, but am unable to say much while he has his hands in my mouth. 'But they are healthy. They have lots of calcium. They are strong teeth,' he says. 'It is not natural to have sparkling white teeth. Your teeth are right for you. Strong and healthy . . . but here you have a cavity.'

There's always something – and he shows me on a screen (using miniature cameras). It doesn't look pretty: a huge black, horrible crevasse. Great. Twenty minutes of fearful drilling later, the deed is done. I am officially a dental tourist.

Afterwards, we have a chat, and, suddenly turning serious he says, 'I'm very afraid for the future of dentistry and the medical profession in this country. So many people are going to England and Sweden to make money. If people are intelligent, they are taken on abroad. Some cities are having to get people in from the Ukraine to take their place.'

It's a massive trend. The Polish workers contribute, along with visitors from other new EU countries, a vital £2.5 billion a year to the British economy. And as almost everyone says, they tend to be bright, energetic and full of ideas – as Wojciech, Elvi, Anna and Hubert seemed to me. So bright we're sometimes finding it hard to compete. In a recent interview, John Durham, a former Labour minister, asked: 'If you have a choice between hiring someone who has been on incapacity benefit with a mental health problem for five years, or a young, fit Pole, who are you going to go for?'

But the knock-on effects for Poland are perhaps much greater. How will a country cope with being stripped of so much of its young talent? Can it cope? Will Ukrainians have to be shipped in to make up numbers, as Cezary suggests? It's early days now: too early to tell.

Maybe it's better this way, I suggest to Cezary. If we come

over for the cheap prices, and the dentists stay in Poland. Everyone benefits – and Ryanair's planes are full.

'Yes, I think so,' he replies, after a moment's reflection. 'Yes! Please come to Poland! Tell your readers that. Tell them: come and get your teeth done!'

POPRAD, SLOVAKIA

THE LAST OF THE
WASHING MACHINE FACTORIES

If I thought Szczecin had its work cut out for it, I soon changed my mind: it was living on Easy Street compared to my next destination.

Poprad-Zakopane caught my eye as one of the most extravagantly named destinations. I liked the flourish of Poprad and its mysterious relation with Zakopane (which is actually 40 miles northwest from Poprad, across the border in Poland). In fact, Poprad turned out to be a small town in the darkest depths of eastern Slovakia, with a population of 50,000.

The first inhabitant of Poprad I befriend is decidedly down in the dumps. Mirko is the art historian at Tatranska Galeria, a gallery housed in a decrepit red-brick building near the train station. He is twenty-one and, rather bizarrely, has a strong English public school accent. It's not often, I reflect, that you meet someone living in a rundown council estate in the middle of eastern Slovakia who sounds like Michael Howard.

Mirko is not in the best of moods. 'It's so measly here . . . so measly,' he says, in a voice that seems to suggest things in Poprad are really *just not on*. 'After my rent and living costs, I've got 1,500 koruna [about £28] to live on a month. How can I live on this? How? I'm thinking of giving up. I can't go on living like this.'

By 'giving up', Mirko means returning to England, where he went to Sutton Grammar School and the Courtauld Institute of Art. His family is from Slovakia; he was born in Bratislava and lived there till he was ten before his folks moved to the UK. The art historian's job is one of his first since leaving university. He speaks fluent Slovak.

'The student loan people are after me in the UK,' he continues, mournfully. 'They can't understand that I've got a job, but still can't pay them back. It'll take twenty years at this rate. It's hopeless, utterly hopeless.' He looks at me despairingly. 'What am I going to do?'

I'm the only 'customer' at Mirko's gallery. There are three small rooms of watercolours and oil paintings. But we're not looking at the paintings. Mirko wants to talk. He tells me about his apartment in a Soviet-era tower block. 'It was free because the old woman who'd lived there before died. It was terrible. There was one of her gold teeth on a plate on a sideboard, and the washing machine was full of her filthy underwear.' He believes he can hear her ghost at night. A friend has even given him holy water to fight back against apparitions.

Another thing is depressing Mirko: 'Almost everyone in their twenties and thirties with intelligence seems to have gone,' he says. 'Anyone who's interested in culture must work as a teacher – there's little else for them. But the pay is so low. So they go abroad.'

Mirko is finding it tough to meet like-minded people. 'There's no one to speak to. Really. It is not easy.' He gesticulates wildly, to emphasise the point. Then he tells me he finds the pace of life too slow. 'There's little to do at the weekend. All the shops shut at midday on Saturday. I asked one of the shopkeepers: "Why do you close so early? You'd be full if you stayed open later." And he just said: "It is tradition." This place becomes dead at midday on Saturday.' He pauses. I refrain from suggesting that closed shops are probably the best type of shops for a man on his salary.

We walk around the gallery, which is displaying the works of Jozef Bendik, a twentieth-century Slovakian artist who specialised in pictures of countryside scenes and villages. An oil painting of a Gypsy family with a white horse catches my eye.

'It's a sentimentalised view,' says Mirko, sounding particularly Howard-like. 'But it was painted in a different age; so that's fine. People love either to sentimentalise the Gypsies – the romantic Gypsy life – or to ignore them. The Gypsies are a big modern problem in Slovakia. Because they do not know the language, because they are apart and do not get a proper education, they find it terribly difficult to get jobs. It is such a problem. Even the most liberal Slovaks see the Gypsies as being lazy and different in a negative way.'

He hopes one day, possibly through the British Council, 'to bring contemporary Slovak artists together to create something on the Romany problem; so people can confront their prejudices.' There are around 90,000 Romas in Slovakia out of a population of 5.4 million.

He shows me another painting, his favourite, of a Gypsy resting on a haystack, playing a violin for his wife, who is breastfeeding her child while lying in a meadow full of buttercups. 'Doesn't that remind you of Paul Gauguin?' he asks, referring to Gauguin's work in Tahiti. 'When I studied history of art, people always use to joke: "So what are you going to be: an art historian?" And now, I am one.' He pauses, and then says glumly, 'Just not a very well off one.'

Twenty minutes' drive from Poprad, the High Tatras mountains jut up dramatically from pancake flat fields like a row of giant sharks' teeth. They are snow-capped, with sharp ridges of granite exposed in windswept sections. On the other side of the range is Poland. You see the mountains as you come to land at Poprad's tiny airport. They provide a spectacular backdrop for the town, rising to 2,655 metres at their highest point; Poprad itself is at 707 metres. No matter how dreary the living conditions, this is a beautiful setting – especially on a day like today with the sun out and a royal blue sky contrasting with the white peaks.

Mirko, who's munching on a pear, wants to show me Strbske Pleso, one of the main ski resorts in the High Tatras. His mood has lifted and, as we drive past several giant adverts for hypermarkets, he starts talking politics. Mirko has a lot of opinions about politics.

'For most people now, London is the capital of the world. People want capitalism, commercialism, the throw-away have-it-all society immediately. They don't understand that it took many many years for Germany, France and England to get where they are today. They want it all *now*. And they want to do it on their own. Before Czechoslovakia was formed [in 1918] we were the poor relations in the Austro-Hungarian Empire. Then we were abused by the Communists. We are not used to independence. We need to slow down, take advice. Not to rush into things on our own.'

Slovakia and the Czech Republic parted company, ending Czechoslovakia, on New Year's Day 1993, just four years after escaping Communist rule in the Velvet Revolution – so-called because the overthrow of the authorities went so smoothly, without a single shot. The split, which took many by surprise, was tagged the Velvet Divorce, as it also ran without hiccups.

But not everyone, says Mirko, was shocked by the 'quickie divorce'. Those who understood the origins of Czechoslovakia as a marriage of convenience had seen it coming. In 1918, getting together had suited the Czechs, as bringing in the Slovaks meant that German minorities held less sway. It had also suited the Slovaks, who were afraid the Hungarians, who had dominated them for centuries, might gobble them up again. So in 1993, after years of being under the Communist thumb, each country simply decided it was time to go it alone for once.

Mirko believes this history is affecting how some Slovakians regard the EU: 'We have been educated to think that the Slovak people have been used and used for so many years. Now they think they'll be used by the EU. I think we deserve a better approach – to realise that we can run our own country. But there's nothing wrong with foreign investment, of being part of this EU.' He approves of the rapid growth of the car industry around Bratislava, where Kia, Peugeot, Ford, Hyundai and Citroën have already established factories, taking advantage of low wage costs and a skilled workforce – making Slovakia one of the biggest car manufacturers in Europe. The World Bank describes Slovakia as having one of the 'fastest transforming business environments in the world'.

But he disapproves of some people's methods. 'There are a lot of rich, corrupt Slovak people. It's becoming a United States of Bandits. Black BMWs with blacked-out windows. Politicians getting off drink-driving charges for no good reason. There's hardly any middle-class – just this vulgar upper-class and the lower-class doing all the work.' He's slipping into his best Michael Howard voice here. 'I've heard all sorts of things about mafia and heads being found on car bonnets. It's difficult to talk openly about these things.'

At Strbske Pleso, the roads are snow-covered. We pull in by a frozen lake that has a glistening foot of fresh powder on top. The sun is setting. A golden streak of light falls across the lake, and pine trees are silhouetted on the horizon against the deep blue sky. It's wonderfully quiet. These mountains are stunning. Hardly anyone seems to be here, even though the skiing season has begun. Apparently, during the busier months of January and February many Germans come, attracted by the dirt cheap prices of ski hire and lift passes (around £15 a day for both). Now, though, it almost feels like we've got the mountain to ourselves. We walk along a path through the pine trees, leaving the first footprints in the fresh snow.

Not far away there is a wooden chalet with music emanating from inside. We go in for a drink. It's surprisingly busy. A Gypsy band consisting of a violinist, cellist and vocalist is playing a medley of tunes that switch from jolly to mournful from song to song. There is a barbecue in a corner. The chalet is full of smoke and very warm. People are seated along picnic tables eating grilled chicken and drinking frothy beers.

Mirko seems to have cheered up somewhat. 'Isn't this lovely,' he says, looking out of the window at the lake. The sunlight across the frozen surface has turned red and purple as dusk approaches. The landscape is almost eerily empty. 'Sure, there are problems round here. But these mountains are beautiful.'

He pauses. We sip our beers. 'But I've still got to . . .' Mirko says thoughtfully but determinedly. 'I've really just got to get out of this place.'

Not everyone I meet in Poprad is *quite* as downbeat as Mirko. But there's no doubt that there's an undercurrent of 'What are we doing here?' among young people who live in the town.

Poprad has a washing machine factory, a train carriages plant, a lawn mower assembly line, a brewery, and an ice hockey stadium with one of Slovakia's best teams. Lining its suburbs are forests of grey tower blocks of the type Mirko lives in. There's a small precinct with shops selling woolly jumpers, scarves and traditional black hats, and a couple of quiet restaurants including a simple pizzeria. There is an Irish bar. There is a tiny history museum. But in comparison with Szczecin this really is a backwater. Will sleepy places like Poprad in the middle of Eastern Europe ever make their way to the 'throw-away have-it-all society' they so desperately seek?

It's not long before I meet the top dog to find out. The morning after my flight on SkyEurope – £56 return from Stansted – I'm being taken to the mayor's office. Well, if Szczecin could deliver me a President, it didn't surprise me too much that Poprad would wheel me before its leading man.

Anton Danko, Poprad's mayor, looks like the cat that got the cream. We meet in the town hall, a concrete building by a busy road that leads to the washing machine factory. He's wearing a sharp blue suit with a yellow silk tie, and his short, dark hair is slicked back. He smiles indulgently, shaking my hand. Around us, I can't help but notice, five gorgeous secretaries, wearing matching charcoal-grey pinstripe miniskirts, are busy making coffees and offering biscuits.

Danko looks mighty pleased with proceedings. Natalia, my translator, who also works as a DJ at a local English-language radio station, introduces me. He tells me about new 'revolutionary, English-type roundabouts', cycling lanes, and plans to bring pop bands from Ireland for concerts next summer. There should also, he believes, be more flights to London, his favourite city. He has slightly selfish reasons for this. He's a Chelsea season-ticket holder.

Danko is a former ice-hockey player. As a referee, he travelled across the globe to major championships, and knows how he wants to change Poprad. 'The old days of the communist thinking in Poprad have long gone,' he says. 'Some of the people in the older generations may look backwards, but their children don't. In fact, their children are bringing them along; helping them to understand the new way.'

He adds: 'We have plans for a business centre and a five-star hotel.' Who will stay in it? 'People who come for business,' he replies airily. 'We are only at the beginning here, there is a long way to go.' He pauses. 'But we will have a McDonald's. A McDonald's is coming.' I realise Poprad must be just about the only place, outside the Third World, I've visited without a McDonald's. Danko continues, 'Our washing machine factory is one of the last in Europe. All companies are finishing with washing machines in Europe these days: France, everywhere. The labour is too expensive.'

He talks about the 'older generations'. 'There is a problem among some older people, a problem about "success". We have to teach them that success is not weary.' I check with Natalia that 'weary' is right. 'Yes, success should not be seen as something that makes you feel weary. It is a good thing! During communist days people would not forgive success. It was seen as a negative thing. During communism everyone strove to be average. Now it is the time for people to step into the limelight. One day we will be as rich as western countries. I know this! I am confident!'

We discuss football for a while. 'I think we will win, definitely, this season,' he says of Chelsea. 'A good defence, a good midfield, a good attack. Everything is good!' Then he adds, as though he's thinking of how to get to the games: 'Yes, I am happy about the flights on SkyEurope. But I think there should be more! More flights would be excellent. I am looking forward to this day.'

Natalia is smartly dressed and in her twenties, with big brown eyes, brown hair and olive skin. After talking to Danko, we go for a coffee. She explains how she worked at the café we are in for a year before starting at her radio station, Radio Tatras International. Before then she'd been an au pair in Scotland. She took an English degree at Presnov University – Presnov is a city about 50 miles east of Poprad – but gave it up when she thought she had a job in Italy. The job didn't materialise. She didn't complete the degree.

'At university they make me read all these books,' she says, rolling her eyes seemingly independently of each other. 'They give me Shake-es-peare.' She drags out the word deliberately, and rolls her eyes again. 'Oh my God! What did I want with Shake-es-peare.'

We talk about Danko's secretaries. I query why there are so many. 'Let's put it this way,' she says, giving me a look. 'If you were a very important man, would you have five beautiful secretaries?'

Natalia orders me a slice of banana cake. 'Not for me!' she says. 'Or how would I stay so slim!' I eat my cake – which is very good. And then a police patrol car pulls up. An officer in a dark-green uniform with four gold stars on his lapels enters the café. He looks at me and after talking to the café owner points in my direction. He is coming to take me away.

In fact Captain Pavol is coming to take us both away – to visit a Gypsy village. After talking to Mirko yesterday, I'd asked Natalia if she could arrange a visit to meet some Gypsies, as there does not appear to be any living in the centre of Poprad. I'd expected that Natalia and I would go in my hire car and that we'd simply get out and talk to a few people.

Instead, we're with Captain Pavol – 'for protection'. Natalia has contacts with the police through her DJ job. We're whisked away at a rate of knots, heading south, passing snow-covered fields and forests. Soon we arrive at a village called Hranovnica. Captain Pavol tells us about policing the area: 'The problems come when men drink too much and beat the women.' There are also fights when people lend each other things – TVs, stereos – and then don't get them back. 'This is usually because they've been sold to buy alcohol. It's the drink that's to blame. Always the drink.'

In the village, another Pavol awaits. This time it's Sergeant Pavol, the local beat officer, who's been working in Hranovnica for two years. He's got a cheery red face, ginger hair and moustache and a barrel of a belly. We drive to the edge of a dull, downbeat housing estate. It's full of two-storey, grey pebble-dashed, detached houses, on the edge of a sloping snow-covered field.

A little old lady in a black dress with red polka dots, and stripy leg-warmers comes over. She's about 5 feet, probably in her seventies, and is highly amused by our presence. Natalia asks her my questions. 'I don't have any money and I don't live well. My home is not warm enough,' says Dezider. Seven people live in her small house, which has three rooms and a kitchen. 'Me, my son, his wife and four children. All are unemployed.' They live on 15,000 koruna a month – about £275. There's a large black dog tied to a rope in their yard. 'Yes, it's dangerous. We have it to protect our wood from the other Gypsies.'

An even smaller man joins us; he must also be in his seventies, although it's hard to tell. 'We do not have enough money. Simple as that. Food is very expensive,' he mumbles before scuttling off.

Another woman, slightly younger, with a purple, red and white shawl comes up. 'I have two sons and three daughters. They are all unemployed. I have to feed them. I think that politicians think only of themselves. I would be very happy if my children could work. Now they just go to the forest and take the wood. There are no jobs here.'

A man in his thirties says: 'Sure I'd like to have a job. Of course I would. I want the money.' What does he do for fun? This takes him aback. 'Fun?' he pauses and thinks. 'Well, maybe I drive my car,' he says, pointing at a tiny white Lada.

Sergeant Pavol takes us to a dilapidated building that serves as a social services centre. There we meet Maria, a cheery woman in her thirties, wearing large gold-hoop earrings and a white polo neck. 'There are two groups that live here. One that drinks, the other that doesn't. The big problem is getting the children from the group that drinks to school. We now have a system where children who have been absent a certain number of days are taken to school by one of our team. It's the only way to get them to go. People have got to get educations, or they are going nowhere.'

It's all pretty bleak. No-go estates back in the UK feel racy and upbeat by comparison. There's a feeling of hopelessness and resignation, as though the people we've spoken to have given up trying to change their situation. It's utterly depressing. I can't help feeling amazed that there are places like this within the EU. People are foraging in the woods to make ends meet. Meanwhile, not so far away, they're building a McDonald's and inviting pop bands from Ireland for summer concerts.

During my weekend in Poprad, the topic of Gypsies comes up again and again. And it's not an edifying subject. When Mirko said, 'Even the most liberal Slovaks see Gypsies as being lazy and different in a negative way', he was not far wrong. So I began to keep track of what others said about the Gypsies that surprised me. I got the feeling that the Gypsies are a convenient scapegoat for people who want the 'have-it-all' society and want it now.

So here are a few of those comments (not from Mirko or Natalia or anyone else you'll meet in this chapter):

'They're not bad. They're just lazy. They don't work. They steal and they live off the state.'

'They're treated now as whites. It's because of the EU. Maybe they're not ready for this.'

'They steal timber and scrap metal. Anything. Nobody would give them a job.'

'They are dirty. They live in horrible homes. They don't care about the places they live in.'

'When it gets cold, they even burn furniture in the middle of their homes to keep warm.'

'They smell. They really do. They smell.'

I didn't go digging about for this People simply came out and told me. Despite being a cut-off minority, there seems to be little sympathy for Romany living conditions, or their problems with the education system which Maria described to me.

It leaves a nasty taste in your mouth – even when you're just visiting for a weekend.

But it's not all doom and gloom in Poprad. For a start, my hotel is fantastic. It is called AquaCity, and it is connected to an extraordinary geothermal water park. The story behind it is quite unusual. AquaCity was founded by Jan Telensky, who was forced to flee Czechoslovakia – with two death penalties pending – in 1969, aged twenty-one. He took a succession of jobs in the UK, and eventually, aged twenty-nine, became a millionaire.

The Poprad connection came through his wife, a local. On a trip to visit his in-laws in 2002, Telensky was walking along a stream near the ice-hockey stadium, and noticed a rusty pipe on the ground near an old wooden hut. Thinking it looked odd, he reached down to feel it. The pipe was hot. He had stumbled upon Poprad's long overlooked hot water spring. Years before the authorities had drilled in the hope of finding natural gas, but had been sorely disappointed that boring old water, albeit piping hot, was their result.

But Telensky – who believes in renewable energy sources and sells recycled plastic bin-liners from the Czech Republic to Westminster Council – went to the Poprad town council and said 'I want to build a water park please'. And AquaCity came into being.

AquaCity plans to be the biggest geothermal resort in the world. There are fifty rooms, an Olympic pool, outdoor heated pools, hot-tubs galore, steam rooms, saunas, massage rooms, water slides – the lot. There are plans for a further fifty rooms, followed by another two hundred to be completed by 2008, a 'cryotherapy unit' (with really cold treatment rooms reaching minus 121°C), and a tropical garden conservatory.

It is a warren of a place, and incredibly popular with the local population – during my visit it's almost always busy. Walking to the pools from my room, I pass through a heavy plastic curtain into an outdoor pool, where a dozen or so people are sitting around with steam rising into the freezing air. The air temperature is at least minus 3°C. But the water's 36°C and feels great, with just the tiniest hint of a mineral sting. Little red trains slide by on the town's main railway line. The temperature drops a bit. People seem happy to pass the time in silence, just letting the water perform its magic. It gets darker. The temperature drops even further. Somewhere out there in the darkness loom the chilly peaks of the High Tatras mountains. But down here we're still 36°C warm.

This really is very pleasant indeed.

I drag myself out, feeling slightly dizzy. I go to a section called 'Vital World'. This has steam rooms, saunas, solariums, caldariums and whirlpools. I try a room called the 'Hellisch Sauna' –

most of the rooms have zany names, with great little signs explaining how the treatments work. The Hellisch Sauna sign reads, *A steam sauna experience that helps you to strengthen of immunity, it reduces a stress and it hardens the epidermis. It has direct effect on widening of blood vessel, it releases the muscles. Let us to veil the cure cloud of this steam and you outlive your own feeling of perfection.* Nice. It continues. *Effects: An experience and an effective opening of the pores. It helps to secrete a toxical stuffs of blood and fat tissue during the perspiration glands.*

Next is the 'Solar Meadow' solarium. A sign asks: *Do you want to suck in a bit of the summer mood during the whole year?* I do. It is also very nice. Then I come across 'Snow Paradise'. This is not a warm one. *It's snowing in our snow paradise too. This white snow in our snow paradise cools you and never mind that a sunshine is outside. Effect: A beneficial effect of total blood circulation and a congestion of the epidermis by reducing of pulse frequency. Minus 59°F. Two minutes.*

I enter Snow Paradise. Inside, it is indeed snowing. There are two other people in the small room, which has plastic moulds shaped like granite rock faces on its walls. All the heat I stored up in Hellisch Steam comes rushing out. My feet rapidly feel very, very cold indeed. I decide I don't like Snow Paradise, so I get out.

In its antechamber, there is a plunge pool of cold water. What the hell, I might as well do the lot. So I drop straight in off the ladder. It is shockingly cold, like falling off the deck of the *Titanic*. Scrambling out, I read the instructions: *Lower your body slowly. Do not jump in. This can cause complications.*

After almost killing myself in Snow Paradise, I decide I've had enough of this body temperature experiment. I feel like I've been elaborately tortured. I go back to my room to change and then go for a beer. There's a small bar near the entrance to Vital World. It has one other customer. I indicate 'large beer' to the barman with hand signals and pointing. Then, sitting on a high stool, I give myself a toast for doing the cold stuff. What a strange, but rather wonderful hotel this is. Who would have thought you'd find a place like this in a town best known for its washing machine factory?

If the guidebooks were tough on Szczecin, they positively slaughter Poprad. 'It would be difficult to dream up a more unprepossessing town than Poprad . . . with its great swathe of off-white high-rise housing encircling it,' says the *Rough Guide*, adding bluntly: 'It's not a great joy to hang around.' While *Lonely Planet*'s simple slogan is: 'Poprad – not a place to go out of your way for.'

This doesn't seem fair, but at the same time I can hardly spend the whole weekend in Hellisch Saunas or staring at the Soviet tower blocks. I need to explore further out of town. This part of Slovakia is called the Spis region. In years gone by, the Spis region was a wealthy part of the Hungarian empire, when it was colonised by Saxons and known as the Zips region. And about 30 miles to the east of Poprad, I'm surprised to read of a place called Spis Castle – a wonderful looking medieval castle. This castle is, almost unbelievably, according to the *Rough Guide*, the number one attraction in the whole of the Czech Republic and Slovakia. On the road to Spis Castle, there's a medieval walled town called Levoca, which ranks number eight in the same list. Throw in the High Tatras at number twenty-four, and one way or the other I'm going to see three of the top twenty-nine sights.

The temperature is −5°C, says the hire-car display. The windscreen is covered in ice – both inside and out, something I've never come across before. Even the metal on the dashboard has a coating. I turn the heating to full, and head for Spis Castle.

It's easy to find. You can't miss the huge thing. But driving there is far from straightforward. For a start, Slovakians really are, when it comes to overtaking at least, the biggest risk-takers I've ever known. Twice I have to slow down by around 30 miles an hour to avoid head-on collisions. Then I get followed by a police car. I spot it coming and slow to the exact speed limit. It tails me as I nervously stick to the limit. The officers glare at me, the dubious outsider, as they eventually pass. What are you doing here? their look seems to ask. I couldn't possibly be a tourist. No one in their right mind would be a tourist in eastern Slovakia in the middle of the winter.

Spis Castle is breathtaking. It veers up from a rock face that dominates the valley for miles around, looking like a magic castle from a Harry Potter film. You can see it from a long way before you arrive. It was built by Hungarian kings in the thirteenth century, and it has been deserted since a fire in 1780.

There are three other cars in the car park. I climb a twisting path to the top but when I get there I discover the castle is closed for winter. I take a look out of the battlements, which stretch out along the mountain top, reminding me of the Great Wall of China.

Some Slovaks arrive. They walk over to a metal fence where there is an Alsatian barking ferociously and stamping its front paws on the dusty courtyard in frustration at our presence. We take pictures of the beast, which seems to annoy it even more. We chuckle to each other before trudging back down the path to our cars. At the bottom there's a big sign advertising visits to a place called 'Cave Bad Hole', neither the Slovaks or I decide to explore further.

On the way back, I drive through Levoca, which has lots of fine buildings around a central square. In this square, next to the main church, is a centuries-old cage that was once used to 'shame' wives who behaved badly.

On the car radio, as I drive around the pretty narrow streets, there is an English language advert. 'Slovakia has now become the investment property paradise of Europe,' says a confident voice. 'Imagine if you had bought property in Spain twenty years ago, what would it be worth now? You can make a modest investment now in Slovakia and enjoy the boom.'

Nowhere, not even deepest darkest Slovakia, seems safe from property investors these days

Avoiding head-on collisions and an absolute nutcase who somehow manages to overtake me on the *inside* of a corner, I pass the giant washing machine factory, a huge warehouse where the railway carriages are made, and an enormous wedge of Soviet apartments near the mall, jutting upwards starkly from the fields on the edge of town. There are so many of these apartments that internationally renowned photographers have, apparently, come here especially to take pictures of them.

Malcolm and Katja are playing the local property market. Malcolm is from Colchester, and Katja was brought up in Stara Lubovna, 30 miles east of Poprad. He is a statuesque, rugged, fifty-year-old quantity surveyor. She is a pretty, blonde twenty-five-year-old, who used to work as a commercial manager for Regus, an office supply company in west London. They met through work in the UK, where Katja had moved after Slovakia joined the EU and they hit it off immediately, getting married soon afterwards.

'Malcolm was a client, and I remember I wouldn't take any stick from him,' says Katja, sounding spirited.

I meet them at their large detached house in the outskirts of Poprad. Malcolm picks me up in his powder blue Mercedes from AquaCity. The house has four floors and is on the market for £220,000.

'We bought it for £85,000 and have spent £15,000 on doing it up,' says Malcolm, full of Essex swagger. 'It's valued at £220,000 now. People have come to take a look, and we've almost sold it. But the problem is the language. People are terrified – they can't talk to the banks here about finance, because of the language. Anyway, banks here are not used to big loans for property. Then you've got the English banks. They're not keen on Slovakia.

They've got to wise up to the fact that Slovakia is part of the EU. It's frustrating. But it will change.'

They have four properties on the market. Katja takes me round their showcase property. There is under-floor heating, a jacuzzi bathtub, and walk-in wardrobes. There are endless bedrooms with en-suite bathrooms. There is a pool room. A sauna. A laundry room. The place is huge. I ask Kat what look she was going for in the apartment.

'I go for the look that makes money. That is the look I'm going for,' she says.

We start talking about which Eastern European countries are worth investing in. Kat gives me a quick rundown: 'In Poland they are getting a bit cheeky, I think. They have already had their boom in telecommunications. The economy is more advanced. Prices are higher. But you must be very careful. Sometimes when you buy a house, you may also buy the owners' debt. That would not be good.' What about the Czech Republic? 'They are always one step ahead. Everything is twenty per cent more expensive there. Before the split [of Slovakia and the Czech Republic] everything was made here. We are stuck with the factories. So the Czechs are ahead of us.' She is not a fan of Romania.

'Ridiculous prices. Like London prices. Lots of Americans are going to Romania. I don't understand it. Why? I would have thought the prices would be better than here. But they're not. Ridiculous!' The Ukraine is another no-no according to Kat. 'The mafia will rip you off.' Hungary? 'Nice people. Nice wine. But not much work opportunity. I'm really not sure about Hungary.'

Malcolm opens a bottle of Vino Nitra Riesling, pours three enormous glasses and introduces me to a big shaggy black dog. 'It's a Newfoundland-chou cross.' He tells me that tax rates are low in Slovakia. 'The highest level of corporate and personal tax is a flat rate of nineteen per cent.' Then he tells me about the goulash parties he and Kat hold in the summer. 'We invite everyone round. We cook a massive pot of goulash: 30 litres. Then we drink lots of wine in the sunshine and fall over. Then we have a sleep, heat it up again and start all over again. Sober up, and keep going till 4 a.m.'

How are the older generation getting used to the new EU life?

'It is difficult,' says Malcolm. 'People who are aged forty-three and upwards. They are the communist generation. And the mentality is weak. People who work in the factories, they find it hard. During communism they built factories for the sake of building factories. There are big drink problems. People drink to get rid of their boredom.'

'But I liked communism,' Kat interrupts. 'I enjoyed the sports they arranged at school. Everything was given to you: pens and pencils, even books.'

'Yes, I think that maybe it was a bit earlier: the generation before Kat's parents really had it hard. When there was pure communism.'

We drink more wine. The big black dog falls asleep and starts snoring. Kat tells me that property prices are booming in Bratislava, the capital. 'It's got great nightlife. All the pop stars are there. There are loads of brothels though. That is just a fact of life.'

'It couldn't happen round here,' Malcolm says. 'The police would beat them to death.'

'Or put them in a cell.'

Another bottle is opened. Malcolm lets the big black dog, which has woken, out into the garden. It's minus 8°C. But the dog doesn't seem to mind. Kat joins us in the cold as we survey the large landscaped grounds. Looking across them she says: 'My husband came to Slovakia and he made three times his money here. *That's* how good it is. *That's* the investment opportunity. *That's* why it's time to come to Slovakia.'

President Dubya Bush was once asked by a Slovak journalist for his thoughts on Slovakia. He replied: 'The only thing I know about Slovakia is what I learned first-hand from your foreign minister, who came to Texas.' He'd got it mixed up. He'd actually met the leader of Slovenia at his Texas ranch.

Before my trip, I'd known about as much as Dubya. But a weekend in Poprad has opened my eyes to how this small Eastern European country is struggling to raise its game and join the EU fast-set. It's not, as Mirko showed, going to be easy. Mirko ended up moving back to the UK. He told me that more than fifty people had applied for a position as an assistant in his gallery the week before he left. 'There are just not many jobs around,' he'd said.

Compare this with Natalia, who left her DJ job to move to Dublin with her boyfriend, shortly after my visit. After a day she'd had two job offers and her boyfriend had had one. 'I've never been so happy,' she told me on the phone, wanting to share her news. 'I just couldn't believe it. Two jobs! It was amazing!'

Poprad has quite a way to go to reach the have-it-all society. But from talking to the likes of Malcolm, Kat, and the mayor (with all his secretaries) it also seems inevitable that it will get there. Yes, there are people like Mirko, Natalia and Bruno who want to get out, but there are enough who are staying.

The talk about Gypsies is ugly – something I had not been aware of before coming. It's shocking. But isn't travel all about being shocked? And as Mirko, with his finest public school pronunciation, said, 'One day it will go. It may take a long time. But I think we will get there.'

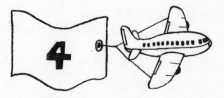

HAUGESUND, NORWAY

'BLOODY HELL, IT'S BEAUTIFUL'

Out in the bay, a scarlet fishing boat is chugging across the calm grey water. The sky is tinted pink and luminous; bright yet seemingly holding back the full strength of the sun, in a way that only seems to happen in far northern countries. Beyond the bay, across a green sloping field, small white houses with red roofs line the craggy coast in the distance.

At the top of the hill, where we've just parked the hire car, stands an imposing cream-coloured stone church. It dates from the thirteenth century, with a mossy slate roof, a copper weather vane and a door shaped like a bishop's hat. On one side, ancient gravestones, some aslant and some with crosses, slope down the peaty landscape towards the water.

This is Avaldsnes on Karmoy, one of the many small islands dotted along Norway's western coast. I'm here with Danny, a university friend, and we're being shown around by Jacob Stensland, the director of the Norwegian History Centre at Avaldnes, who has explained to us that this is a key Viking site that marks the birthplace of modern Norway – a site of incomparable historical importance in the country. The air is fresh and invigorating, and not too cold for February. The scenery is spectacular.

And yet . . . we are *the only people here*. Ours is the only car in the car park.

Jacob is keenly aware of his lack of visitors. He says the Viking ruins at Avaldsnes don't get the recognition they're due. 'If this site was near Oslo, this would be a very, very important place,' he says. 'Everyone who knows about Norway would know about

Avaldsnes. But it's not, so it isn't. People are not so interested in history round here, but if we were fifteen minutes from Bergen or Oslo, things would be very different.'

This may be the birthplace of modern Norway, he explains, but only now is it beginning to attract a trickle of curious weekend breakers who, like us, have caught new Ryanair flights to Haugesund, about ten miles north.

According to Jacob, the 'birth' of Norway was all down to a beautiful, but demanding haughty maid. This spirited young beauty, a Norwegian named Gyda, refused to sleep with the king of Norway, Harald Harfagre (850–933), as she said it would be beneath her to marry a man whose territory was not as large as tiny Denmark's.

'She said she would not marry until Harald conquered the south-west bit of Norway. That was the deal. No south-west bit. No you know what,' says Jacob, putting things plainly. 'So Harald got the south-west bit. And they settled down here on Avaldsnes.' At that moment, Norway's borders took on much the same shape as today.

This story is typical of the days of Viking expansion, which began in the late eighth century. Some say that Vikings were forced to roam abroad because there were not enough women to go around back in Norway. Hence the need to launch raids on Britain, Ireland, France and just about anywhere else they could find – a mixture, if you like, of sex tourism and the very early days of European economic migration (except with the emphasis on pillage rather than plumbers). One Viking warrior called Leifur even crossed the Atlantic around the year 1000, beating Christopher Columbus by a few hundred years.

We descend a stone staircase into an underground visitor centre. Inside, there's a room with a large model of Harald, who has a shock of long blond hair – hence his nickname Fair Hair. He looks a bit like Boris Johnson. Standing next to him is the 'haughty maid', who might pass for a Viking version of Hilary Clinton.

One cabinet contains replicas of the golden neck rings that kings like Harald used to wear to show their standing. 'The real ones are far too valuable to display. Priceless,' says Jacob. 'Much of the history of Norway is like *The Lord of the Rings*. The book is based on Norway . . . on these rings. The men with the rings in those days were the men with power.' The rings are, apparently, a big thing in Norway. Advance ticket sales for the recent *Lord of the Rings* films put them at the top of the Norwegian box office, outselling everything else in cinemas at the time, before they had even been released.

The Vikings had many connections to Britain, Jacob explains. Harald's successor was his youngest son, Erik. Erik killed all his siblings, apart from Hakon, who was safe in England, where he was being raised in the royal court. Eventually Hakon the Good, as he was known, came back to topple the unpopular Erik, who fled to York, where he became known as King Erik Blood-Axe.

'We have some visitors from England who have heard of Erik in York. They come on the Ryanair,' says Jacob, suddenly sounding more upbeat about business.

'What about Stamford Bridge?' asks Danny. He's a Chelsea fan and a regular at the Stamford Bridge ground.

'Well, that was the end of the Vikings,' says Jacob. 'Harald III lost to your Harold at the battle of Stamford Bridge in 1066. It is amazing when you think about it. The Vikings were around for such a short period. Just 250 years. But they are the most famous people in history for northern Europe, not just for Norway.'

Yet another link with Britain, Jacob tells us, was the Viking King Olav Haraldsson, who helped protect London from attack by the Danes by destroying London Bridge. This, we are told, is the origin of the nursery rhyme 'London Bridge is Falling Down'.

We go outside for a walk around the churchyard with Jacob, who seems glad to have some tourists to talk to. It must be bleak on this hilltop without anyone else around.

'For some reason this is the only large church the Germans did not destroy during the Second World War. They flattened the others so the RAF couldn't use them as navigation points. This one they just camouflaged,' Jacob explains. 'But I met one of the RAF pilots once. He said that they could see this church very well. "Turn left at that big thing," they'd say. That's how they planned their attacks.'

I ask about the war. 'Well, our king fled to England, then to the US. The real Norwegian government was in London. The collaborators here had their own government, of course, run by Quisling. When the Nazis arrived, many of the sailors who lived along the coast just went out to sea – they sailed to Scotland or even the US, and didn't come back.'

One of the great things about booking low-cost flights to tucked-away destinations in Europe is the sheer randomness of it all. If it hadn't been for 5 pence fares I'd spotted for Haugesund a couple of weeks ago, I think it's fair to say I would never have met Jacob and learnt the story of Harald and the haughty maid, Hakon the Good or the origin of 'London Bridge is Falling Down'.

The more flights I book, the more I feel that it's the fun of the unexpected, of encounters with people with stories to tell – people I would never have come across were it not for Ryanair or SkyEurope – that makes these weekends work.

And I'm surprised to discover that holidays like this, random and unpredictable, have actually been given a name.

'Experimental tourism' was invented in 1990 by Joel Henry, a Frenchman from Strasbourg. Tired of traditional city breaks and weeks in the Med, Henry, now in his fifties, founded an organisation called the Laboratory of Experimental Tourism. On its website he advocates exactly the sort of roll-the-dice approach to holidays I seem to have been adopting. His A to Z of experimental tourism ranges from literally rolling a dice with destinations assigned to each number; to blindfolding yourself and travelling with a friend around a familiar city centre to experience the place with a sense missing; to Dog-Leg Travel (borrowing a dog and letting it take *you* for a walk).

Other recommended trips include Ero-Travel (going for a weekend away with your partner, but travelling separately and seeing if lover's intuition will bring you together); Nostalgic Travel (using a pre-war *Baedeker* guide to visit a city); or visiting places at the end of train or Tube lines.

The idea seems to be to let impulse and spontaneity lead the way, taking you off the beaten track to see the spots others have neglected – spots like Jacob's Norwegian History Centre.

But where would it take me next in Haugesund? I don't know much about Norway other than that the Vikings came from here, that it's got a lot of North Sea gas, and that beers are £5 a go. You can't fail to know that beers cost £5 as every guidebook and travel article tells you this almost immediately; seemingly to stop people making the mistake of thinking this is cheap stag party territory – which would be a very big mistake indeed. Norway is clearly a well-to-do country: it's got all that gas, it's got high taxes (as much as fifty per cent), and it's got the type of solid public services and social security that we could only dream of back in Britain, precisely because it is so rich and has got such high taxes.

And I'm soon to learn about the source of its wealth close up – albeit in a slightly random way.

Not long after we arrive back at our hotel the phone rings. I'm expecting it to be Danny making noises about going for a beer. But it's Vidar from the local tourist board – I'd contacted them the week before asking them what made Norwegians tick. 'Tom,' says Vidar. 'We are in the reception. We are ready to take you to Gassco!' Right, I say, completely confused, before Vidar explains that Gassco is a gas company, and he's taking me to see the headquarters. This, apparently, is what's making the Norwegians tick these days: gas depots.

I drop by Danny's room to tell him I'm off to see a gas depot. This brightens his mood enormously. He's got his feet up watching the telly, sleepily keeping an eye on the Winter Olympics cross-country skiing. 'Gas depot? Ha, ha, ha. No, I will not join you. Ha, ha, ha.' He finds all this extremely entertaining. 'Tell me everything about the gas depot – or actually, on second thoughts, don't. Ha, ha, ha.' He's buoyant. He asks to borrow the hire-car keys. 'Maybe I'll go for a drive,' he says, as I hand them over.

Vidar and Rita are in reception. Vidar is in his forties with greying hair and the manner of a school teacher who's pretty sure you're Not Quite Taking All This In Are You? Rita seems genuinely suprised to have a journalist in town. The last to pass through was from *Yachting Monthly* 'a couple of years ago'. Not many journalists – or anyone else for that matter – visit Haugesund.

Somewhat surreally, we're soon in the lobby of Gassco, which is state-owned and responsible for shipping gas to Europe from seven pipelines: two to the UK, three to Germany, one to Belgium and one to France. There are about sixty Norwegian oil and gas platforms in the North Sea, I've already learned, courtesy of Vidar. Norway provides fourteen per cent of Europe's gas, and seven per cent of the UK's. Haugesund is at the centre of the biggest network of pipes in the world and has become increasingly important of late, what with Russia's antics switching off its gas supplies to Western Europe to aggravate the government of Ukraine – and causing the West to feel shaky about future supplies.

The lobby is full of modern art, including a pair of models of evil-eyed kangaroos wearing boxing gloves. A large man called Kjell, with an extraordinarily large, friendly face that reminds me of a baseball mitt, and a very British-looking chap in a pinstripe suit called John, who turns out to be from Liverpool, are there to greet me.

We walk past more Guggenheim Museum-style art towards the Control Room, where I'm to be shown how Norway's gas is distributed.

Suddenly I'm getting into the Norwegian oil and gas scene. I'm told that Norway has about fifty years of oil and gas left in its current fields, but expects to find another fifty years' worth of gas in fields to the north of the country in sea close to Russia. Meanwhile, the UK has about 30–40 years left, and recently became a 'net importer'.

'We pipe away 270 million cubic metres a day,' says John.

'A total of thirty-six million cubic metres of these go to Scotland,' Kjell adds. 'Norwegian gas could easily account for a fifth of all UK gas soon. Already it supplies thirty-one per cent of all Germany's gas and 30 per cent of France's.'

'Our Karsto gas pipeline plant [just round the corner from the Gassco offices] is the world's third largest . . . it is BIG, very BIG . . . but it is relatively unknown.' They tell me that oil was what made Norway rich, but gas is what will keep it rich.

The Control Room looks like it could launch a Space Shuttle: giant electronic display panels stretch along the main wall, with flickering lights connected by illuminated lines representing pipes. The others talk me through what all the flickers mean and for a moment or two I get a strange sensation that I'm about to be led to one of the control desks to start my first shift. A couple of doughnuts and a cup of coffee to keep me going and I'd be away, in charge of fourteen per cent of Europe's gas flow, Homer Simpson-style.

I make a joke along these lines. It is not considered funny. 'Our challenge is to keep Europe warm. Every time we have even a minor shutdown we get the financial wires on the line – Bloomsberg, Reuters – saying: don't leave us in the cold!' says John.

How did John end up in Haugesund? I ask. 'Two women drove me out of Birkenhead,' he says. 'Maggie Thatcher and my wife.' John moved in 1983 when he was in his early twenties, after spotting an advert in a paper. 'I had to get out. I was playing in a cricket team at the time, and the whole lot of us was unemployed.' Norway has a shortage of people with engineering skills, and he fit in easily. Then he met his wife. 'If you get past the initial shock of the prices, it's a great place to live. Compared with the UK it is incredibly expensive here. A beer is £5.

'When people travel back to the UK they take an empty suitcase to fill with stuff. Things are that much cheaper. Sometimes, they even buy the suitcase in the UK as well.'

The average wage in Norway is high: about £27,000. In the UK it's about £22,000. But the big difference is the excellent system of state schools, health, pensions and public transport, says Kjell, all of which bring down the cost of living, despite high prices in shops. Plus there are fewer fat cats, he says, looking a little fat cat-ish himself. 'The difference in wages is less here than in other countries. We like wages to be compact around the average: not to have extremely rich or poor people. Yes, beers are £5. But the living here is good: very good.'

Back at the hotel, it turns out that while I've been getting to grips with Norway's gas, Danny has been having adventures of his own. He's looking shaken. It transpires he took the hire car on a drive to the top of a nearby hill, hoping to find a walking path. Before he knew it, he was at the end of a narrow dirt track with a cliff on one side and an enormous drop on the other. He had to do a twenty-eight point turn, right on the edge of the drop, to drive to where the walk was supposed to start. All was going well until the clouds came in, leaving him trapped in a fog and unsure of which way was down. Eventually he had to slide down a steep incline which he was almost afraid was a cliff, but thankfully turned out to be the way back to the car.

Two near death moments and a potential write-off for the hire-car, not bad for a couple of hours' work. To celebrate our cloud walk and gas depot exploits we go to one of the best restaurants in town, Lothes, for dinner. We are about to discover the 'very good living' way of doing things in Norway. Vidar, Rita, a colleague called Tone (Tone is a female Norwegian name) and another colleague called Tormod (male Norwegian name) are taking us to show us the best of Norwegian cuisine.

The restaurant is in an old herring captain's house, dating from the nineteenth century; a clapboard structure with rickety staircases, candles, sepia pictures of old sea dogs, and smiling, smartly dressed, waitresses. It's just round the corner from our hotel. We quaff £50 wines as a succession of fine Norwegian dishes is served: crayfish, asparagus and hot butter sauce, deer, goose, French beans and new potatoes, followed by crème caramel and coffees.

Vidar is full of fascinating Norwegian facts and opinions. So we listen to Vidar and his fascinating facts and opinions, as do Rita, Tone and Tormod, occasionally passing round the bottle (and ordering more when they run out).

'There are no beggars in Haugesund,' says Vidar, confirming Kjell's take on things. 'There is not such a big spread of wealth as you have in the UK. There is not such a big gap between the man who works in the lawyer's office and the secretary.'

He believes Norway is ahead of Sweden when it comes to standards of living. 'The Swedes also have a good social security system. But the difference between us and Sweden is we can afford it! We've got the gas!' He looks pleased about this point. 'I must admit, the Swedes are very systematic. Just look at Sven-Goran Eriksson. But do they have the oil and gas? No!'

Winning the right to North Sea gas was in the 1960s the turning point for Norway's fortunes. 'When Norway gained the right to North Sea oil and gas fields it was one of the biggest political scoops in history!'

Vidar believes there are pros and cons to joining the EU. Norway is not yet a member. 'Our approach to the EU is: what can the EU give us? We have our oil and gas. Already we pay millions every year just to have a part membership of the EU, to be part of the research side of it. And we don't get the benefits. The Scots go to the EU and say "Stop these Norwegians selling salmon". So they do. We get taxed more.' Vidar looks temporarily displeased. But then he says: 'I want to be a member of the EU. The EU helped bring up Portugal and Spain. Now the EU can bring up some of the new Eastern European countries. I would gladly pay for that!'

Rita passes round the wine. We fill our glasses yet again. Yes, Vidar is fascinating, I've decided, but it's hard to get a word in edgeways. All we seem to be able to do is listen . . . and drink. 'We worked very hard to win over Ryanair,' Vidar continues, keeping up his quick fire monologue. 'We had to change our runway from 1,600 metres to 2,000 metres. It cost us £8 million. We think the pilots of Ryanair are chickens. Any Norwegian pilot could have managed!' Vidar chuckles away to himself.

Then he gets reflective: 'God has been very good to us. We have had our herring days. There were 30,000 fishermen in the 1920s and 1940s. But when the herring and canning industry collapsed, then came the oil and the gas!' Vidar looks very pleased once more.

God might have been good to Norway, but we give our own thanks when it's time to go (and escape Vidar's fascinating Norwegian facts).

Our hotel, the Amanda, is a splendid cream and grey structure, all neat and orderly, next to a channel of water with neat and orderly rows of clapboard houses in whites, rusty reds, and orangey-yellows on the other side, connected by a wonderful croquet hoop of a bridge. There's a cobblestone promenade beside the water. Gulls are swooping high above. A pair of swans peddles across the sparkling water. The sun is out this morning; the sky is a delicate blue.

Outside, I'm surprised to come across a bronze statue of
Marilyn Monroe. She's looking haggard, legs akimbo, shoulder
strap of her dress slipping, a high-heeled shoe by her side.
Haugesund, you see, is not only the birthplace of Norway, it's
also a crucial link in the life of the world's favourite dizzy blonde.
Monroe's father came from a village called Skjold, about 15 miles
south of Haugesund. He emigrated from Haugesund to America
in search of the good life. Then he met Marilyn's mother; but the
relationship didn't last long. He soon abandoned his family to go
off in search of another type of life: the wild life. This didn't last
long either. He died in a motorcycle accident before even seeing
his daughter. She was born Norma Jean Mortensen; Mortensen
was his surname.

Out by the waterfront, looking across at the neat rows of
houses, I realise I really quite like Haugesund. Danny agrees. 'It
reminds me of New England: the colours of the houses. Much
better, much better than I thought,' he says. 'This really is very
nice indeed.'

It's a perfect day for what's up next: a fishing trip to a place
called Rovaer island. I've been looking forward to this – it's the
first time in years that I've tried to catch a fish. A phlegmatic
fellow smoking a roll-up has lightened our pockets of £7 for the
return trip. Is this the ferry for Rovaer Island? I ask. He just looks
at me and says: 'If you want.' I take this as a yes. Some locals, you
can't help notice even after a day or two, are just a little
withdrawn about things; maybe it's the 'northern mentality'.

We chug out of town across glassy water. The coast, lined
with Scandinavian houses, looks spectacular. Some houses stand
alone enigmatically, looking like they're waiting for Edward
Hopper to paint them. Small, rocky, uninhabitable islands
emerge and the ferry bisects a series of intricate channels.
Looking out across the calm water, I can't believe that so few
people come here. 'Bloody hell, it's beautiful,' is Danny's verdict.

Helga Rasmussen is waiting for us at the little dock, beside

Rovaer's only shop. She runs a nine-room hotel with a restaurant and offers fishing trips throughout the year.

She tells us all about Rovaer as we walk up a hill past a small whitewashed church and a neat five-a-side football pitch, and cross a narrow bridge to another part of the island. 'Only one hundred people live on Rovaer. There's another hotel down there,' she points to a red building near the ferry dock. 'It takes guests during the summer. Not many people come now.'

An elderly woman in a tiny car drives by. 'We have only two cars on the island. It is because she is old. She does not want to walk.' She tells us there is a small beach with a picnic area that's popular with day-trippers in the summer: 'The water is cold: 11°C or maybe 12°C in the summer. The weather here is getting stranger and stranger. Look, it's sunny today. But it is winter. Sometimes we get the winter in the summer. Snow in June even. You just can't tell.'

We reach a honey-coloured building with a deck overlooking a thin waterway and a small barren island. 'This is our little dream,' says Helga, explaining that this is her hotel, which she runs with her sister and a friend.

A few guests are inside glued to the Winter Olympics on TV. There are rows of tables in a large open room, pillars with nautical rope decorations, and the smell of coffee. But there's no time to stick around – we're going fishing. We get kitted out in heavy blue North Sea fishing outfits, with red lifejackets, and are introduced to Oyvind, Helga's brother, who runs the fishing trips.

'Okay ready for take-off!' he says, and we jump into a tiny red-rimmed chugger of boat which is about 12 feet long. It seems Oyvind can't speak much English beyond that opener, and as we can't exactly speak much Norwegian, we putter out to sea in silence.

This is the type of trip that German tourists apparently take in the summer, to drink beers and fill their buckets with fish. We're beer-less, but the green water in the bay is calm, the air is startlingly fresh, and the sun is beaming, turning the bracken a glorious gold on the small islands. 'I'm not sure we're in the right place,' says Oyvind, switching off the engine and producing our slightly disappointing fishing equipment, which consists of a spindle of nylon cable with a red handle and a series of hooks with brightly coloured lures at the end. I'd been hoping for something a little more *Old Man and the Sea*; at least a rod, for example.

Never mind. Within minutes Danny and I are in hauling in vast numbers of slippery silver-grey coalfish and getting terribly excited indeed. I can't remember the last time I actually caught a fish. And here they are coming up one after the other. Each time we expertly drop our weighted cables and bob the lines up and down like Oyvind showed us, at least two or three coalfish take the bait. Before we know it, we've caught seventeen; about a foot long each (I swear). The bucket's almost full of them flopping about. We're ridiculously pleased with ourselves.

'I can't remember the last time I was this downright, stupidly happy,' says Danny. 'It's bloody brilliant. Brilliant! Ah, I feel like a new man!' I do too. This easy-fishing thing is an out-and-out winner: no skill, plenty of thrills, no hanging about. Fantastic.

Oyvind can't help smiling at our over-enthusiasm. He gets more talkative on the way back – his English is good after all. Fisherman to fisherman, I ask him about the North Sea. 'Well, it is not so good. The fishing now: not so good,' he says, somewhat unbelievably after our experience. They were virtually jumping into the boat, I say. 'Ha, ha, yes, maybe. But a friend of mine is a captain. He says that last year was the worst for cod in forty years. There are just no cod out there.' Oyvind won't say who's to blame. His main gripe is about who is granted licences to fish in which areas. 'It is crazy. Corrupt. How can I make money if I cannot fish where I want to? Crazy!'

Back at the hotel, Helga takes the fish, which Oyvind gutted on the boat. She grills them there and then. We eat them with pepper, some mash and a side salad. It is by far the freshest fish I've ever eaten – and absolutely mouth-watering.

It's great sitting in the warmth of Helga's hotel after the chilly North Sea. We have seconds of coalfish and mash. We drink mugs of coffee. Why don't more people want to live on this island, spend the day out on the water, catch their own fish? I ask Helga about a small house that looked like a museum close to the ferry jetty, thinking this might explain the exodus from Rovaer.

She pauses for a moment, and I wonder if I've asked a wrong question. Then she tells us a harrowing local story, to which the little museum is dedicated. On 13 October 1899, she says, a boat with thirty men and children from Rovaer went down in a terrible storm on the way to Haugesund. They were going to the mainland to attend a funeral. All lives were lost. The bad weather continued, yet while the whole of Norway mourned, the islanders had still not been told of the tragedy, as conditions were too poor to reach Rovaer. The disaster struck on Friday 13th.

'When a boat finally made it back to the island, four days later, the first words to the waiting wives and children were: "Everyone is gone". A book has been written with that title. Almost all the men of working age on the island were gone. My great-grandfather died in the accident.'

Later Helga takes us to the museum, where there are displays showing sepia pictures of the deceased and the ill-fated vessel. Money for the widows was raised across the country. On a sunny day, Rovaer is a magical island, but when the weather turns, as it often does in these parts, there is a very different side to island life.

There aren't many major roads on which to get lost in Norway, mainly as there aren't many places to go. National population: 4.4 million. Geographical size: about the same as the UK. Result: an awful lot of beautiful, empty landscape.

The scenery is breathtaking. As we drive inland in our Citroën, we pass rugged mountains with snow-capped peaks, vast blue-grey fjords and enormous icy fields. The road steadily rises. There is very little traffic. The sky is pastel blue; not a cloud in sight. Tiny villages with small white churches come and go. There is a sense of elemental stillness and a feeling that we are just tiny people moving through a giant, somehow powerful, land. I can't help thinking to myself: if more people knew about this, Haugesund would be full of tourists.

This is Norway's western fjord-land. Most of these fjords, I have learnt, were created over the past 1.5 million years during four periods of glaciation. Fjords were formed when giant glaciers moved into valleys gorging out land, melted when ice ages ended, and were flooded by the sea. For centuries they have been the lifeblood of Norway as they have provided calm waters full of fish.

They are also quite spectacular, worth a 5 pence flight in their own right. We pull up at Etne, a village with a white clapboard church with a grey slate church surrounded by a dry stone wall. A sign reads *Population 4,000*. A magnificent, perfectly still fjord stretches out into the distance. Pine forests run up to snowy peaks. It is cold and it is quiet. Some people travel to the other side of the globe to see scenery like this, all the way out in New Zealand. You don't have to.

We're visiting a hotel called the Fugl Fonix. It caught my eye because it's run by a group of young friends who have made headlines across Norway by converting a rather stuffy old place into an art centre with funky bedrooms and rock concerts at weekends. They have succeeded in reversing a brain-drain of young people from the countryside around Etne; previously most youngsters had been moving to the big smoke in Oslo. Now Etne has become the place to be, with most of the biggest bands that visit Norway coming to play at its small, alternative venue.

So that's why we're in Etne, sitting on small black sofas

underneath a green and blue chandelier, surrounded by tropical plants and splashes of modern art, next to a bookcase with a battered box of Trivial Pursuit, a Fay Weldon novel and Melvyn Bragg's *A Son of War*. Pop music is playing softly in the background. Jan Rafdal and his brother Albert, along with a chap called Audun, have joined us. They are three of the hotel's founders, in their early thirties – and they're keen to tell us all about Etne.

Jan looks like a trendy Van Gogh: blond beard, stylish glasses and a black shirt. 'The hiking in this area is incredible,' he says, sounding evangelical. 'This is an unexplored area. Tourists have been visiting Hardangerfjord [Norway's best known and most spectacular fjord] for two hundred years. No one really knows about Etne. But it's beautiful and it's lovely and quiet. This area is really good for fishing: good for salmon. It is almost over-populated with fish.'

'You get big cod: 20 to 25 kilos. Very big cod,' adds Albert, who as well as being involved with the hotel is a gunsmith. He is dark-haired, wearing a checked shirt, and doesn't say very much.

Audun, the resident artist at the hotel, says, 'It was quite difficult growing up in the countryside. This is a slightly naïve place. It's very slow. The whole atmosphere of these parts is: no stress.'

They opened the hotel six years ago. 'There are twelve of us, aged twenty-six to thirty-six,' says Jan. 'We wanted to create something different. We'd all been travelling, but we'd come back and we didn't want to just rush off to Oslo, like so many people.'

'Now we get the big bands: the Delays, Spiritualised, the Mavericks, Snowball, Al Perkins and Marilyn Manson,' says Audun. 'Marilyn Manson made quite a stir. He "shagged" a model of a cow on stage. People hadn't seen anything quite like that before in Etne.'

Jan tells us there are Viking burial sites in Etne. 'And there are rock carvings, which really should be covered up, we think. This area was the seat of King Magnus Erlingsson, who was crowned when he was just five years old in the twelfth century. He didn't last long – he was killed in battle aged twenty-eight. It was his father who built a chapel that later became the pretty white church.'

The hotel owners invite us to a barbecue in a Finnish wood cabin on the edge of the fjord. Apparently such barbecues are all the rage in Etne. The sun is beginning to set and the sky has turned otherworldly pinks and greys. The water is incredibly calm. Dark mountains are silhouetted on the horizon. I take some pictures, marvelling at the beauty of the fjord.

Inside the cabin there are barbecue coals in a central pit covered by a grill. The cabin is hexagonal and made of pine; it reminds me of a garden shed. There are fluffy reindeer hides on low-level benches fitted to the walls. German-style beer mugs and great big hunting knives hang from hooks. It's very smoky, and there's a strong smell of sausages, which are sizzling on a grill. What an absolutely brilliant invention.

'Oh, yes. We love our Finnish wood cabins,' says Audun. 'We really love them. We think they are – how do you say? – cosy kitsch.'

We're presented with charred sausages and rolls. We smear on mustard and get to work. As soon as we finish one sausage, another is delivered.

'This is the way!' says Jan. 'These are different from British sausages, but they're good sausages!' They are very good. Jan prepares a kind of goulash, which is also very good.

'When we have our barbecues in our Finnish wood cabins we do not do things minimalist . . . we do them maximalist!' Audun says. There's a pause as we slurp the goulash. Outside it is dead quiet. And although we can't see the fjord – the cabin has no windows – I can almost feel its enormous presence. Audun continues, 'A month ago, in January, we could have gone skating on the fjord. It is great when it's frozen over. And in the summer everything is just so green round here. There are sunsets at midnight. It's really nice.'

Albert suddenly pipes up. 'The grouse season is from mid-September till December 23. And fishing in the mountains! It is amazing! Very big trout.'

Somehow, we get on to the subject of the Internet. 'This is a small country and everyone is on the Internet,' says Jan. 'In England I believe some people still have analogue. But here everyone has broadband. It is so easy to keep in touch with people. And it is easy to get your "message" out. There are just four million people, so we can spread the word quickly. We have a good economy and there is a lot of money out there. Soon we want to expand: to move our hotel ideas to other places. To buy up old hotels run by old couples that are not making money. We want to make things happen!'

And I don't doubt they will.

More meat is cooked, smoke billowing up to the roof of the wood cabin. We eat yet more meat – that's the Finnish wood cabin way. Then Danny and I drive through Norway's western fjord-land back to Haugesund.

It's been a great weekened. We experimented with Haugesund. And the experiment paid off.

PADERBORN, GERMANY

CHARLEMAGNE ON THE CHEAP

I'm in Paderborn, in a clothes shop called Mister and Lady Jeans. Trance music is playing on a stereo. And I'm trying to find a squaddie.

Paderborn, you see, is another random destination for me – another metaphorical roll of the travel dice. This time the numbers have landed with Germany facing up, which might sound a little predictable and just plain normal. But, as I soon find, Paderborn has plenty of surprises. And one of the biggest is its *squaddies*. The first thing I've realised about this small cathedral city is that it's home to about 4,500 British troops, with more than 12,000 Britons in total living in the city and its environs.

And I'm looking for a real live specimen.

It doesn't take long to find one. He's wearing a blue tracksuit top with 'Lonsdale' written across it. He looks like a boxer, or a rugby forward or something: wide-shouldered, squat, flattened nose, pale skin, spiky black hair, grey expressionless eyes. Definitely British – he just has to be. He's with a friend, a tall ginger fellow with cargo pants and a pink V-neck jumper of the type that seems to suggest: I'm so hard, I can wear pink. Got something you want to say about that?

Are you lads by any chance in the army, I ask. 'Yeah,' says Lonsdale, who swivels towards me with a 'What have we got here?' look. Pinkie automatically adopts body language that makes me think of one word: Attack! He peers on to see where I'm taking this.

I explain I'm writing about tourism in Paderborn and show

them my card. This seems to relax them. So chaps, I say, trying to take on the manner of a sergeant, what's there to do in these parts? Lonsdale, who's nineteen, says: 'The pubs.' End of comment. Can you elaborate? 'They're quite good.' Then he looks at me again.

Pinkie, who I don't call Pinkie and who's twenty-seven, interjects. 'There's an Argentinian steak house,' he says. 'Yeah, the lads go there about three times a week, like. It's 20 euros for a good feed-up.'

They begin to open up. 'I've been here a year,' says Lonsdale. 'I tell you, life is a lot better than back home. It's cheaper, and people are more friendly. It's clean. You can drink *gluwein*, eat *bratwurst*. I love the food. I'll eat anything.'

Pinkie, who tells me that you can go skiing an hour's drive away, heartily agrees: 'Personally I'm never going back to the UK. Never. You get a lot of respect here. There's very little litter. It's just better.'

Are there any sights they'd recommend, I ask, mentioning the cathedral. Pinkie looks blank. Lonsdale says, 'Yeah, I've been past it, like.' No more information is offered. Have you been to the cathedral? 'The biggest problem is it's not in English,' says Lonsdale, dodging an answer. They look at me for more questions. I decide more questions are probably not worth it. They drift off to look at tops with zips, hoods and slogans.

Paderborn was a bit of a snap decision. Yet again, I'd never heard of it, but it doesn't take long to realise that of all the places I visit this is clearly going to be the most 'British' of the lot. While it seems vast numbers of people in Central and Eastern Europe seem to be coming to our shores – it's quite the opposite in Paderborn.

There's one reason for this: the British military camps that were built here after the Second World War. Having camps on the edge of the Iron Curtain, poised for an attack on the Red

Army, made strategic sense at the time: Paderborn is about one hundred miles from the old German Democratic Republic. Now the Cold War is over, of course, there's a question mark over how useful it is to have thousands of British troops in the country. There is, after all, no Red Army left to attack. A headline recently appeared in *The Times* claiming: 'British Troops In Germany Ready For Mass Withdrawal', explaining that 22,500 troops today will be reduced to 19,600 by 2009 (which doesn't sound like much of a mass withdrawal). This is part of a long-term reduction in troops that has seen numbers fall from a peak of 80,000 in 1945.

The squaddies are why Paderborn has so many flights from the UK with Air Berlin services departing from Stansted, Glasgow, Manchester and Bournemouth. The population of Paderborn is 140,000, which means about one in ten people here are British – which is why it was so easy to track down Lonsdale and Pinkie.

Ralph and Jane, sitting next to me on the plane, had filled me in on the British exodus. Ralph, a Liverpudlian welfare officer, told me he was going to his daughter's wedding. She was marrying a military policeman in the British army. 'You've got quite a few military around Paderborn. From all over the UK. There's a small town, that's really a suburb, that's called Sennelager, where they have the army camps. There are Brits all over the place. You can tell the army lot when you see them – the squaddies – they're the happy people. Generally speaking, they're pretty well-behaved.'

'There are a few bars and clubs, like,' he said. 'You'll see them. They're hard to miss, like. There's this big Argentinian steak restaurant – people normally go there to start off.' The Argentinian steak place is obviously big local news. 'Then it's the pubs afterwards.' There's a place called The Highlander (Scottish), The Limerick (Irish), and another called The Auld Triangle (also Irish). Is there anything else to see and do in Paderborn, I asked. Ralph paused for a moment. He looked at Jane. Jane didn't say anything. Then Ralph said, a little tentatively: 'There's a castle that's supposed to be nice.' But he hasn't been. I begin to wonder what I'm going to do with myself in Paderborn.

It's minus 5°C on my first morning in Paderborn, but never mind about that – I'm off on a tour of the city centre, with Ingrid, my guide, who meets me outside the hotel. 'Ah, you have a proper coat, that is good,' she says enthusiastically. 'The British here. They do not wear enough. That's how you can tell the British. You see mothers with their kids. The kids are hardly wearing anything. They must be British kids. You see people jogging about in shorts. They must be British joggers. They don't seem to feel the cold. It is strange!'

It's not the prettiest of places, but on initial impressions, Paderborn has got a certain charm: the thirteenth-century cathedral, which survived the war relatively unscathed, for a start. This is on a hill at the centre of a spider's web of cobbled streets that spread out in a circle to the edge of a rather ugly ring road.

Passing a baroque church or two, and the sixteenth-century Adam and Eve house (so called because of its picture of Adam and Eve) we arrive at a small river. But it's not just any small river – it is the Pader river, 'the smallest river in Germany', running for four km from five springs that spread out near the base of the cathedral until it meets another river, where it stops being a river in its own right. 'It never freezes,' says Ingrid. 'That's one of the reasons why Paderborn did so well through the years. There was always running water for the mills.' Apparently Paderborn bread is famous throughout Germany and the Netherlands. I had some at breakfast and found it so tough it was impossible to toast.

Ingrid explains how the city was attacked by Allied bombers for three days in February 1945. 'It was a tragedy. Just before the end of the war,' she says. This explains a lot of the ordinary 1950s buildings in the city centre. We walk up a busy pedestrianised street, bustling with Brits and Germans, that runs up the hill to the cathedral. On a square at the top of the hill, market stalls are selling fruit and veg, fish and meat. 'We Germans, we like the sausages!' exclaims Ingrid happily. For many, sausages seem to be the main reason for going to the market. Some stalls heat them up; and outside these, groups of men are dipping giant frankfurters into large dabs of mustard poured onto cardboard cartons – they get mustard all over their moustaches but don't seem to care.

We walk towards the cathedral, passing one of the sources of the Pader, where a few fat ducks look briefly excited as we walk by. On the way, we pop into the local history museum. There are no signs in English, but Ingrid explains a couple of the portraits hanging on the walls: Jerome Bonaparte, Napoleon's younger brother, was ruler here in the eighteenth century. She also points out the portrait of a local who discovered morphine: Friedrich Wilhelm Serturner (1783–1841). 'He tried it himself. In his book he describes how he passed out for twenty-four hours of deep sleep. When he woke, he said he had had sweet dreams, but that he had an aching stomach.'

The cathedral is huge, with a golden double-cross on the spire which, according to Ingrid, means 'we have an archbishop'. Just outside we stop by a space that's about half the size of a croquet pitch, with a crumbling wall surrounding it. This is the most important place in Paderborn. It is where Charlemagne, the mighty eighth-century ruler of these parts, first met Pope Leo III, in 799. 'He was a weak Pope. He had been attacked several times in the streets of Rome. So it was necessary to be protected. And for Charlemagne, it was a good thing to present the Pope to his people. Anyway, they made a deal here, and the result was that Charlemagne was made the first emperor of the Holy Roman Empire the following year.' So the Holy Roman Empire can be traced back to this tiny plot of land in Paderborn. Not a lot of people know that.

The cathedral has huge stone vaults, long rows of pews, racks of orange candles, and a smell of incense. We see a piece of stone work on one window that shows three hares in a circle, each one of them sharing the same pair of ears at the centre of the design. Apparently, this is famous as it was a one of a kind, in Europe at least – China had a similar design 1,500 years earlier.

Paderborn, one way or another, I reflect as we come to the end of the tour, has a lot going for it: Charlemagne and the start of the Holy Roman Empire, morphine, Napoleon's brother, a fantastic cathedral, sausage-munching locals with mustard on their moustaches, a river that never freezes and untoastable bread. What more could you ask for? Well, there's also, of course, its squaddies. To get the full picture of Paderborn, I think I need to infiltrate squaddie land. A night out definitely seems on the cards.

Outside The Highlander pub is a Scottish flag and a glowing yellow and blue Newcastle Brown Ale sign. Inside, after the quiet streets of Paderborn, I'm in for a shock. A football match is on, Arsenal versus Bolton, and about thirty young men with short haircuts, football shirts and tattoos are tightly packed around a large screen. Most are singing a song that goes like this:

'Can you hear Arsenal sing? Nooo-ah. Nooo-ah.
Can you hear Arsenal sing? Nooo-ah. Nooo-ah.
Can you hear Arsenal sing? I can't hear a ******* thing.
Nooo-ah. Nooo-ah. Nooo-ah.

I go to the bar where a few older types – clearly British – are sipping beers. A large bouncer-like fellow stares at me questioningly. Very friendly. To my right is a chap with red-rimmed eyes, and a skinny fellow who looks unsteady on his feet. I order a beer, and I introduce myself to Red-rims, who turns out to be called Mick. I explain I'm researching a 'tourism story', and soon

they're all talking to me – Baldy (whose name is Mac, 'that's M –
A – C', he says watching me write it down), the barman Dave,
and Wobbly Legs (who never gives his name).

Mick is a Germany convert. 'This country is fantastic,' he
says, slurring a bit. 'The general standard. The cleanliness. The
social order.' He's recently retired after twenty-two years in the
army, where he was a technician in the Royal Mechanical
Engineers. 'Paderborn is a beautiful little place,' Mick says. 'It's
the smallest city in Germany. It's got one of the best cathedrals.
It's close to Wewelsburg Castle. We're just an hour from Mohne
– you know, the Dam Busters and all that.'

Mac says his rank is 'Major Catastrophe'. He makes sure I
write this down, too. What does he like about Paderborn?
'Cheap petrol. Cheap cigs. Cheap booze. What more do you
need?' he asks.

'Legalised prostitution. I've heard that it's all above board.
Clean and comfortable. It works,' Mick answers a bit mysteriously.

I ask Dave how business is going. 'Well enough. About eighty-
five per cent of takings is from soldiers. But when they're sent to
Iraq the families and locals come back. It's a real shame but they
don't integrate with locals much. They're young and, how can I
put this . . . quite robust. A bit punchy at times. I'd say it's the
language barrier – that's the main problem.'

I go round the corner to The Auld Triangle Irish Pub. A sign
outside reads *Great new karaoke show with dancing Ian and
crazy Dave*. As I go in, there's a High Noon moment as the
barman checks me out. A waitress takes my order: beer and a
pepperoni pizza. (It was either that or beer and hotdog; the Auld
Triangle does not have a Michelin star.)

Two lads are on the table next to me – Matt from Burgess Hill,
and Paul from New Malden. Both are lance-corporals, and both
are wearing stripy jumpers and jeans. They're about to go out to
Iraq for the second time since 2004. I don't expect you're looking

forward to it, I say. 'It's not like that,' says Paul. 'Sure there's fear, but we're going out to do our bit to help them. It's our role. It'll be good to go out and do some work.' They seem subdued. 'We've been out on exercises a lot recently. We haven't had much spare time,' says Matt, who tells me he's learning German with his wife to try and fit in a bit more.

I get talking to Trevor, the manager, the one who gave me the once-over when I came in. 'I could tell you were British. Straight away. Officer probably,' he says. Do officers mix with the lower ranks? 'No. They tend to keep themselves to themselves. I don't blame them really. They have to spend all week disciplining them. They don't want to hang out with them in their spare time.'

Two guys walk through the door. Trevor takes them in. 'Squaddies. But quiet squaddies.' Then he tells me about a bar he used to run in Frankfurt, which had a big US military base nearby. 'With the Yanks I could even tell if they were army or air force. The army guys would say: "Hey dude, mother ******, give me a beer." The air force lot would say: "Please can I have a beer". Easy really.'

Herbert Hoffman is Mr Paderborn. Whatever there is to know about Paderborn, Herbert Hoffman knows it. He works for the tourist board of 'Paderborner-land', which is to say the area around Paderborn. He is in his forties, with a mop of blond hair, pale chubby face, ten-pence-piece circular glasses, brown slacks and a tweed jacket. He meets me at my hotel the next morning. He's excited that someone has come to write about Paderborn. I can tell that not many people have come to write about Paderborn before. In fact, he tells me as much: 'Before you, *Coach Monthly*. Oh, and *Derbyshire Life And Countryside*. They have been.' That was a couple of years ago.

He tells me about tourism in Paderborner-land. 'The new terminal [at the airport] was built in 1993 for 500,000 passengers a year, but it was extended two years later. Now there are 1.3 million a year. A hotel is being built: 50 euros a night.' Herbert likes his figures. 'Two-thirds of flights are Air Berlin. You can fly to more than forty destinations.'

'We're getting more British tourists,' he adds. 'People see Paderborn as exotic: not explored. We've detected interest because of that. Yes, it's got that exotic – exotic is the right word, I think – appeal.'

Herbert arrived this morning to take me to Wewelsburg Castle, the top attraction of Paderborn and the former head-quarters of the SS. We drive through exotic countryside, covered in snow, out of town. Herbert is extremely talkative. I mention the reunification of East and West Germany. 'Oh, reunification! Oh, it has been an exciting time!' he says. 'Suddenly people started using the motorway to the East. Now it's full of traffic going East–West. We've got express trains to Leipzig. People from the East have come to live and work here. That is quite normal. You can tell them from their accents: very traditional, very strong Saxon accents. Some people from the West like to make fun. But that is not a good thing. It has been a tougher time in the East than it has here, so there is no need for such joking. In the East, in small villages, only the older people have stayed. The younger people have gone. Small local shops close, and older people have to get buses to bigger shops in the cities. In the old GDR, they never used to have any unemployment, now it can be as high as twenty per cent in some places.'

Is there hostility towards people moving to Paderborn from the East? 'No, no, no . . . for years we prayed for the border to open.' The border first 'leaked' when Hungary opened its border with Austria in September 1989, allowing East Germans to travel through Hungary and Austria into West Germany. Then, of course, came the fall of the Berlin Wall in November and the first Germany-wide free elections in December 1990. 'Now it is open, we consider the people from the East to be Germans too. There is no "hostility". Anyway, now it is only the older people who remember those days when the East Germans first came.'

Are people worried about higher taxes? There has been, I've read, huge public spending on updating infrastructure in the East; which has a population of about twenty-two million out of Germany's total eighty-two million. 'Yes, there are people who have trouble with their businesses, who like to blame the East for the high cost of unification. You always get people like that. We have adverts sometimes on TV, reminding us of solidarity – of keeping together. There are terrific places in the East: Dresden, Leipzig. Their history is our history. German history.' Unemployment around Paderborn is ten per cent; low by comparison with many parts of Germany 'We have to be careful – not overly optimistic. But things are definitely better now.'

Herbert seems apologetic about taking me to Wewelsburg. 'I'm sorry that we should start with this. This is not a happy place. This castle belonged to the SS. There was a concentration camp here.' It is, he continues, 'The only castle in Europe in the shape of a triangle.' But then he says again, 'Not a happy place. I'm sorry you should see this first. Really. I am sorry.'

It is indeed shaped like a triangle, a yellow-stone structure with two towers topped by bell-like domes and one wider fortified tower, sitting on a hill overlooking fields spreading towards the airport. There are leaded windows with curtains drawn inside, dark stains spreading across the yellow-stone walls from gutters, thin sprinklings of snow on the northern faces of the bell towers, plus a definite sense of menace. Herbert disappears into the old SS guard house, now a museum, and comes back with Kirsten, who is going to show me around. Kirsten keeps wrapped in her scarf throughout the tour. It is very cold – minus 5°C at least.

We enter the guard house museum, a two-storey building with an aubergine-tiled roof. Inside, school children are being shown round a series of displays explaining the freakish plans Heinrich Himmler, head of the SS, had in mind at Wewelsburg Castle. There's a grainy black and white picture of Himmler taken at the castle, with his pudgy gerbil face, glasses, thin moustache and double chin. 'He wanted to make Wewelsburg the centre of the SS world,' says Kirsten, as we pause by a sturdy medieval-looking chair whose leather back is inscribed with a jagged 'SS'. 'He had a plan for a huge ring of buildings on the slopes above the castle. We don't know exactly what he wanted to do with them. But it appears he wanted to make the north tower of the castle [the one with the fortifications] into an SS shrine of some sort. Where people could remember the SS dead. It would be at the centre of a new SS village. This would be where the Germanic elite group would live. Himmler wanted to create the cult of ideology here.'

The architect's plans are displayed in a glass cabinet on a large yellowing piece of paper. They show the castle's isosceles triangle-shaped foundations, which the architect extended out-wards into a large semi-circular structure that would have curved around the castle like some kind of Roman encampment.

Not shown on the plans is Wewelsburg's concentration camp, on a plot of land just to the east of the castle, where it is believed 1,285 (possibly more) people died. 'There were 3,900 prisoners. There were German and Russian prisoners, some were Jewish,' says Kirsten, in a subdued tone. 'It was a small concentration camp, but there were a lot of dead people. There were very bad conditions. Even worse than at some other camps. The SS did a lot of torture. And prisoners had to work long hours in the quarries.'

Kirsten tells me that the castle was camouflaged during the war, but in 1945 the SS tried to blow it up, to prevent the Allies taking it. Himmler had collected a lot of valuables throughout the occupied territories, which he tried, with some success, to hide. After the war, the camp was turned into temporary accommodation for Germans who had left land reallocated to Poland – conceivably people moved from Szczecin – as well as villagers who had given their land and homes to the SS and got bigger ones in occupied territories, but who returned as refugees. The site of the camp is now an area of normal residential houses. A memorial has only recently been erected – in 2000 – as for many years, Kirsten tells me, villagers felt it was difficult to have a memorial; they wanted to live alone and without any trouble. The old guard house, one of only three stone buildings in the camp, is now a family home and the two eating halls are now social apartments for poor people.

We stop at a cabinet with a copy of an SS 'death head' ring. Apparently, most real ones were taken by American troops and it's easier to find originals in America than it is here. I see an SS belt buckle with the phrase 'My honour is my faith' written on it in German, and a copy of a letter written by Himmler signed off with 'Heil Hitler!' Then we go outside – to take a look at the crypt at the base of the north tower.

It's one spooky place. We walk down a snow-trampled path, open a big metal door, and descend a few steps to a door of iron bars. Kirsten reaches into her pocket, pulls out a bunch of keys and opens the cage-door. We enter a damp circular room, with a central pit and a swastika engraved into the ceiling. We step into the echoing chamber. 'Normally tours can't come into the crypt,' Kirsten says, her voice rebounding around the room. 'We are a little afraid of what might happen.' What do you mean, I ask. 'Well, people from the right scene – neo-Nazis – might come for celebrations or for demonstrations. There are some neo-Nazis who come here – every weekend you get a few. You get four or five each day at the weekend – out of 200 or so visitors.'

How can she tell? 'Some of them have shaved heads – but you can generally spot them. Many ask to go into the crypt – which we will allow if people ask permission in advance. The neo-Nazis that come here see it as a cult place. We will do special guided tours, but before we show them this place, they have to learn about the concentration camps first. They don't cause any trouble. They know that if they did, they would not be able to see these rooms.'

Kirsten gestures for me to step in the middle of the pit, with the swastika directly above me. 'Say something,' she says. And I do. It's very, very strange. It's also extremely disconcerting. It feels as though my voice is being swallowed up by the building, like it's disappearing straight upwards into the small air vents surrounding the swastika. I don't like to think that Himmler and, quite possibly, Hitler once stood here, experiencing the same sensation.

Upstairs is the Hall of the Supreme Leaders – another neo-Nazi haunt. The room is again protected by a cage-door, although entry will be granted if you ask ahead. The SS, apparently, regarded this as the centre of the world – and in the centre of the room, cut in green and black marble on the floor, is a symbol with twelve jagged arms branching off a black circle.

'This symbol is very important to neo-Nazis. It is their symbol. It's called the "black sun" these days. The esoteric groups, they want to see it. This room and the crypt only survived because the man who was told to blow up the castle at the end of the war did not destroy the north tower. He didn't know why he'd been asked to destroy the castle, so he just put dynamite in the other two towers,' says Kirsten, still wrapped in her scarf, peering out of her trendy dark-framed glasses. We stare at the symbol for a while and head out. The tour is over. I thank Kirsten.

That was how a tour should be: no information overload, just stories and straightforward answers . . . about a very un-straightforward past.

Outside, Herbert is raring to go. The sky has a winterish peach-grey haze that seems to magnify the castle's strange feeling of evil. Bells are ringing in the local church, which the SS had considered pulling down, but didn't as they were already unpopular with the local, mainly Roman Catholic, population. Herbert says he used to live in Wewelsburg village. 'My wife and I were here five years. And for five years every morning at 6 a.m. the bells would ring: 178 rings! We moved our bedroom three times to try to find a quieter side. But it was no good, we had to leave.'

We pass the site of the former concentration camp. And the old guard house does indeed look like a normal family home, painted white with a well-tended garden and a child's bike propped against a wall. There's a satellite dish on the roof; as there are on most houses nearby.

Herbert tells me about the local British community. 'They are very important to us,' he says. 'Very important for shopping revenue. There are lots of German–British clubs, and festivities. The British are a part of normal life here. You see the English plates on the cars everywhere. Adverts are in English. They are part of the community.'

Paderborn has a surprising number of museums for a place so small. Herbert wants to take me to them. Well it's not often you get to see a Tractor and Model Car Museum, or the Heinz Nixdorf Museum.

They turn out to be unusual, but bizarrely fun. The Tractor and Car Museum is in a warehouse with an atrium. There are lots and lots of tractors; apparently this is one of the best collections of tractors and model cars in Europe. There's a gleaming allure to all the acrylic navy blues, purples, dark greens, metallic greys; plus a satisfying smell of tyres and oil. We scoot about admiring them and come across the model collection at the back, close to several old Mercedes and a multicoloured Trabant with 'Rolling Memories of German History' written on one side and a picture of Helmut Kohl and Mikhail Gorbachev smiling in a pink heart shape, while Eric Honecker looks on, grimacing.

There are more than 10,000 models including steam machines, tractors, trucks and cars. It's like some kid's obsession grown worryingly big, with endless glass cabinets full of neatly arranged models. We take a look – marvelling at the madness of it all.

The Heinz Nixdorf Museum is also ever so slightly potty. This is in a huge rectangular building covered in gold and black glass. Heinz Nixdorf, a local man (1925–86) who ran a successful computer business, is a Paderborn legend. 'He was like a king in this city,' says Herbert, full of veneration. 'He made things change round here. He would say: "If we do not have a motorway, I will go away."' Paderborn got a motorway. 'He would say: "If we do not have an airport, I will go away."' Paderborn got an airport. 'He died in the eighties, and he found the best way to leave the world. He died at a computer fair. That was where he was happiest – with his computers.'

Klaus Barckow, a computer devotee, is showing us round. 'Most people think computers came from the US. That is wrong,' he says firmly. 'The first computer was built by Konrad Zuse [in the late 1930s] in Berlin. He was a German! It was a German not an American who invented the computer!'

Heinz Nixdorf was born in Paderborn and built up his computer company to become the fourth biggest in Europe. He specialised in scanners for retail outlets and in cashpoint technology. He had always dreamed of building a computer museum, but died before his dreams were realised. But now the Heinz Nixdorf Museum is the biggest computer museum in the world. Klaus informs me it's in the *Guinness Book of World Records*.

The museum's centrepiece is something called the Electronic Numerical Integrator and Computer. 'The Americans say it is the first computer in the world,' says Klaus, warming again to his favourite topic. 'No! It is not!' He watches me, to check I've got the message. 'It was constructed for ballistic reasons. They wanted to send rockets against Germany. It took 80 square metres and had 18,000 vacuum tubes, 70,000 resistors, and weighed about 30 tonnes. It was used from 1946 to 1955. They used it for calculations for weather forecasts and for the hydrogen bomb. The problem was it used a lot of electrical power. The electrical power of a small town.' Klaus explains how space travel forced inventors to make smaller computers: 'If you want to get to the moon you have to have a computer. In the shadow of the earth, you need something taking control of things.' Computer chips came along.

Klaus talks about artificial intelligence being the future for computers: ie, robots. And he shows us some robotic dogs: 'They really act like dogs. If you caress one, its tail will wag. If you poke it with your finger, it will try to bite you.'

The things you discover in Paderborn's museums.

My hotel has a great little pool and sauna on the eighth floor. From here, you can see across the city, which is shrouded in steam coming from central heating units. In the distance, beyond the spires of the grand cathedral, is a giant wind farm on the slopes of a hill. It's very nice indeed, swimming back and forth and looking out across the rooftops.

I go to the sauna room. I'm in my swimming trunks. Others, however, are not. A not-very-shy, naked octogenarian couple is towelling down in the chamber outside the sauna. Another not-very-shy, naked octogenarian woman is lowering herself into a freezing plunge pool in the chamber. There's naked octogenarian flesh everywhere, I suddenly realise. I don't know where to look. So I hang up my towel – my eyes swivelling upwards like Stevie Wonder's, and slip into the sauna.

It's just as bad in there. Two enormous middle-aged men – absolutely starkers – are lying out like beached whales. They're having trouble breathing in the heat. They sound like those things people use to get fires going – or just like rasping, twenty-a-day men. It's lucky the hotel has lifts; I don't think they'd have made it up the building this far otherwise.

Afterwards, feeling clean, I pop into the tourist office, just round the corner from the hotel to pick up a few tourist brochures and maybe some souvenirs before heading to the airport. Paderborn, I discover, has a vast number of brochures. For a place I'd never heard of, it's quite staggering – they seem to cover everything from where to go cycling to where to get your hair cut, to where to take out a book from a library during your visit. I count them: there are thirty-three tourist brochures for Paderborn. I'm still boggling over this statistic, when I get talking to another British chap in the office. Michael is a retired police officer. He's in Paderborn to visit the military camps and talk to soldiers due to leave the army about whether they'd like to join the police.

'I usually have a pretty good success rate. I get about sixty to seventy per cent of people to sign up,' says Michael. What does he think of Germany's smallest city? He's a fan: 'It's a lovely town. It's got a little bit of everything. The old and the new. It's been rebuilt very tastefully.'

He, too, has been to Wewelsburg Castle. 'It's eerie, isn't it? When you think what happened there. That they – the people we're not allowed to mention – wanted to make it the centre of the world.' Then he says, 'Many of the Panzer divisions came from Paderborn. The kids that are still here – they're the descendants.' He clams up and mutters, 'But there are certain things you can talk about, and certain things you can't. We've got to remember we're guests here.'

He's referring to the military being 'guests' in Germany. And the more I thought about it, the odder it seemed to me that so many Brits are living here. They're everywhere. Like Ingrid said, you can't miss them; they stick out like sore thumbs. But what are they doing there, more than half a century after the end of the Second World War, and now the Cold War is consigned to history? Yes, they're training for Iraq, but isn't it about time, you might think, that they left Germany to its own devices?

BRNO, CZECH REPUBLIC

JOSEPH K ALL THE WAY

I T'S not good to dwell on bad experiences, but I guess there's a certain 'sit back and smoke your pipe' amusement factor in hearing about my trip to Brno. That's to say, you didn't have to go through it and I did.

When I look back on Brno, it's almost as though the Czech Republic's second city turned into a case study on 'how a low-cost break to Eastern Europe can go terribly wrong'. So I'll try and keep Brno (pronounced as 'Brrr! No') brief and to the point.

All I'll say in advance is: I couldn't really work out Brno and the people of Brno. They didn't seem to want to let me. I did try. But they just didn't want to play ball. Everything about them just seemed to be difficult. Literally almost everything: even down to finding out what people from Brno like to call themselves, for example. Here is my conversation, by phone in advance, with the tourist board.

Good afternoon. Do you mind telling me what the people of Brno call themselves? . . . You know, London has Londoners, Paris has Parisians. What does Brno have? I ask politely.

'What do you mean?' comes the reply down the line. I explain myself again in almost exactly the same terms, with slight variations in tone. 'In Brno? Ah, I think they call themselves Brnan,' says a sleepy sounding woman. Right, I say, that's great. But I'm cut off in mid-sentence. 'That is what the men are called. The women are called Brnanka.' Err, right, I say, so Brno is a special place and has two collective nouns for its people? There's a pause.

'No, they call themselves Brane,' she says, completely changing tack. This is spelt out. Is this pronounced the same as 'brain', I ask. She pauses. 'No,' she says. 'No, not Brane'. And then she spells out a new variation: Brnane. Is that absolutely right, I ask, more than a little confused now; no 's' at the end, perhaps? 'Yes, it is Brnane,' she says unconvincingly. What about the Brnan and Brnanka theory of thirty seconds ago? She reacts as though I've made this up. I decide to call the people of Brno 'the people of Brno'.

This exchange is par for the course in Brno.

First impressions aren't good, not good at all. Brno is indeed a whole different world from beautiful Haugesund and quirky-but-fun Paderborn: a low grey sky, piles of dirty snow by the road, a large gaudy advert for 'The Only and Real Strip Bar X', crumbling warehouses, disused quarries, factory stacks, single-storey work units that must date from communist days, Orwellian apartment blocks with peeling paint and damp patches that seem to whisper 'misery', a large gloomy 'PetroChem' factory, outskirt estates covered in graffiti, Eros Erotic Videos and Erotic City Sex Shop, a large Tesco, and a strip of dreary bars with fruit machine casinos offering 'beer non-stop'.

That's the view from the airport bus (ticket 31 pence). After I alight, it's a ten-minute walk in the early evening darkness, using a flimsy map from the airport information office, to Hotel Amphone. The receptionist is a small middle-aged blonde woman with a red polo neck and an expression that suggests she's just eaten a lemon. I'd like to check in, I say. 'Humpf,' is the reply. Then, bluntly and accusingly: 'Reservation?' I give my name. She looks doubtfully at me. 'Tom?' she says. Yes, I say. 'Room 117, Breakfast 8am to 10am,' she says robotically. When would you like me to pay? I ask. 'Whenever. Tomorrow,' she suggests, like she really couldn't give a damn.

On my way to the room, I pass a small bar in which a small group of Scottish lads are drinking lagers and cackling loudly, ascend a creaky wooden staircase, pass along a hall that smells of cigarette smoke, and go through a series of fire doors with signs that ask you to 'Shut the Door'. I do my best, but some of the doors are ill-fitting and won't shut properly. My room is tiny, about the size of two double mattresses, with a small en suite shower room emitting sour smells. I lie down on the bed, bumping my back on a hard surface beneath the thin mattress. The room has a noisy mini-bar fridge, a ten-inch TV on a ratchet, beige curtains, a mustard-pot vase with two fake pink roses on a sideboard, and a greasy mark on the paintwork above the headboard.

In the corridor I hear a lad knock on another lad's door and say: 'Come on, time to play! It's 8.30.' There comes a muffled voice from inside a room. 'Come on . . . I'm sure you look beautiful. The night has started!' I take a shower, and dry off on a towel so rough it almost keeps its shape when I bend it.

I go downstairs and take a look in the bar. The Scottish lads are the only customers. They've clearly had one or two too many drinks, one is wiggling his body like a belly dancer and asking the barman about dancing girls. Another starts a long rambling joke about Michael Caine having a party and inviting the Beatles, the Doors and a hooker. The hooker looks after Paul McCartney and Ringo Starr. And the punchline, spoken to the hooker in a complaining Michael Caine *Italian Job* voice, is: 'You were only supposed to blow the bloody Doors off!' It raises a chuckle in me. But his mates are too far gone to know what's happening. They stare into their beers and their empty shot glasses, looking like they're about to pass out. 'Come on, that was the best joke I've heard in years,' says the joke-teller. The others mutter and mumble.

Brno is known on the stag party circuit, hence Club X and the Erotic City shops, and the antics of the Scottish lads. Prague is so full of places like this that the market has spilt over into the Czech Republic's second city, which is cheaper than the capital (where hotel rates can be sky high) and now has the budget flights to bring in the clientele. Looking around on this chilly evening, I can't really see any other reason to visit it. The travel's taken it out of me. All I want is a spot to eat. I cross the street. There's a bar with a pool table and loud music. Too loud to read, and not quite right for how I feel. Not far along is The King's Head with a picture of King Henry XIII outside. There's nowhere else in sight. I feel my feet taking me inside. For some reason, there are Irish pub signs on the walls. Inside there are a few locals dolefully drinking beer. I ask for the menu. It comes in a sticky padded plastic folder and is in English. Roast beef, Yorkshire pudding, American fried potatoes and horseradish are on offer, but instead I go for grilled pork fillet with garlic sausage immediately realising it's going to be a bad choice, but lacking energy to change my order once it's out of my mouth. The barman doesn't speak much English, but asks if I want chips? I hear myself say yes. Music videos are playing on a TV near where I'm sitting. The screen has a graphic that says 'So 80s Hits Music Channel' and the Fat Boys are singing *Let's Do the Twist*.

My meal arrives. It's incredibly greasy. A small dog parts from its owner and begins nuzzling my leg. I ignore it. Then it jumps on the stool next to me and looks like it's going to leap on my meal. Now I like dogs, but not when they're trying to eat my supper. Its owner comes across and pulls it down, not apologising. I finish the greasy meal, nod to the barman for the bill and go back to my lovely hotel.

The room is cold and I can hear a man snoring through the thin walls. The mattress is flimsy and the duvet isn't really big enough to provide cover. When I wake, my first confused thoughts are: I feel very rough indeed. I didn't have a single beer last night. Why do I feel very rough indeed? Hotel Amphone, I've already decided, is one very 'special' place.

The morning receptionist is another woman who also looks

like she's just eaten a lemon. When I ask to use the Internet, she shrugs like she really couldn't care what I do – I could come, I could go; I could use the internet, I could not use the internet; I could be a guest, I might not be a guest; I could disappear before her in a puff of smoke . . . what difference would it make? She points me to a door. The Internet Café consists of one computer in the corner of a small room.

After checking my emails, I go to Lemon Sucker II to pay for the internet. She grimaces and will not accept my 200 koruna note (about £4). 'Pay later!' she snaps, clearly annoyed with me. I go to the breakfast room. There's a small selection of food including pale hotdogs, a few sorry-looking apples and oranges, scrambled egg and some hard-crust rolls. I glance in the kitchen as I walk past and see the chef eating from a spoon used to stir the eggs. I gnaw at a hard-crust roll with some strawberry jam in a dark basement room with tiny windows letting in feeble light. There are a few other miserable-looking guests poking about at their sausages and eggs.

My reading for the weekend is Franz Kafka's *The Trial*. I'm trying to read a good book by a local in each of the places I visit, though this admittedly proved a little difficult in Slovakia. The bookshop assistant in Poprad just laughed and shook her head when I asked for something in English by a Slovak. But there's masses to choose from in the Czech Republic.

Kafka was born in Prague in 1883. *The Trial* is about Joseph K who is arrested for a crime that is never explained to him. He soon becomes ensnared by the complicated processes of the legal system, to the point where he almost forgets that he has done nothing wrong. Early on, he comments bleakly: *It is an essential part of the justice dispensed here that you should be condemned not only in innocence but also in ignorance.*

I read another line or two in the half light. Joseph K is arguing his innocence after being arrested by an inspector at his boarding house.

'I won't say that I regard the whole thing as a joke, for the preparations that have been made seem too elaborate for that. The whole staff of the boarding house would have to be involved, as well as all your people, and that would be past a joke.'

'Quite right,' said the inspector.

'But on the other hand,' K went on, turning to everybody there . . . 'on the other hand, it can't be an affair of any great importance either. I argue this from the fact that though I am accused of something, I cannot recall the slightest offence that might be charged against me.'

That's how I'm beginning to feel at the Hotel Amphone and in Brno in general.

A woman wearing a large fur coat arrives in reception. She's a local estate agent who acts as a part-time city guide, here to show me around. She seems pleasant enough at first, wrapped tightly in her brown fur coat, wearing silver earrings and pink lipstick. She's a little older than me, and wants to know what I want to see. I'll call her X (just in case she was just having a bad day, and isn't, how can I put this, always *quite so challenging*). 'Well, you know, a few of the sights,' I say jovially, and admittedly a bit vaguely.

'Which ones,' she demands, as though checking to see if I've done my homework. I point to a few churches on the map. 'Okay, let's go. It is best if you do not take notes while we walk,' she says, looking at me closely. 'It is better that way. Faster.' Cripes.

Surreptitiously scribbling the occasional thought, I follow her into the city centre. Brno, the capital of the region of Moravia, has a compact centre, with churches and its castle all within walking distance; just a little bigger than Paderborn, despite having a population of 400,000, more than three times as big. It spreads for miles in each direction into suburbs of Soviet-era apartment blocks with nearby factories, many of which produce parts for car production plants across Central Europe. The streets near the pretty churches are narrow and cobbled – there aren't many cars, most roads are pedestrianised. Gothic and medieval architecture looms along labyrinthine passageways with dusty bookshops and small candle-lit bars and cafes in the early March gloom. Buildings seem neglected, but not to the point of crumbling – just a little tired around the edges. There are squares with market stalls selling fruit and vegetables and cheap clothes. There's a crisp chill in the air, with the occasional flurry of snow. There's none of the bustle of Paderborn. It's a sleepy place. And there's a feeling that this is somewhere for a very discreet rendezvous – that nobody would ever track you down to little-known Brno. In the right company, I suppose, it could be very romantic.

I ask X about her estate agent work. 'Construction is booming in the Czech Republic. Oh my God, it is so growing. My question is where is all the money coming from? I suppose it is from mortgages. Mortgages are new to us. Sometimes I cannot sleep I have so much work,' X says, sounding aggrieved by all this work that's hounding her – rather than it being a time of exciting opportunities. 'People want detached houses, which usually cost from about £35,000 to £240,000, depending on how wealthy the person is,' she says, in a tone that suggests: 'Why they want all these detached houses, I haven't a clue.' I try to draw her out, to get her to talk a bit more, but she increases her step, glaring at my notebook.

We pass a functionalist-style café: a one-story whitewashed rectangular block, with large windows and an airy room full of tables, built in 1926. Functionalism is big in Brno, according to the guidebooks. Tomorrow I'm visiting a place called Villa Tugendhat, designed by Ludwig Mies van der Rohe, who was part of the Bauhaus school of design. Can I take a quick look inside? I ask, referring to the café. I can see people moving about, even though it's quite early.

'No it is closed. It is impossible,' says X, striding onwards, leaving me standing.

We stop by an elegant theatre and some well-restored buildings with classical facades, tall windows and iron balconies dating from 1910–20. Then we pass a small ramshackle market selling cheap clothes, suitcases, shoes and bits and pieces. An Asian man is running one stall. 'He is Vietnamese. Most of the stalls are run by the Vietnamese,' says X.

I'm a little surprised to find a Vietnamese community in the middle of Central Europe, and ask X if she would mind translating for me for a moment. I do not expect the barrage that's to come.

'No! I am afraid of such strange people! There are Vietnamese mafia! I'm afraid they can kill you, and they can rob you!' I take a look at the chap in question. He seems a pretty meek fellow, selling umbrellas on this overcast day. He catches my eye in a hopeful, do-you-want-an-umbrella? sort of way. X pays no attention: 'They use drugs, the Vietnamese people. And the Gypsies. There are also Gypsy people. They are doing the black market too. Usually white people do not talk to them. They can kill you, steal your money, or take your ID. Even in the day. The Gypsies they live in a bad area. We call it the Brno Bronx. No I will not take you there!' I asked just to see how she'd respond. I can already tell there's no way X will ever go to the Brno Bronx. 'If such people talk to you on the street, they can observe and follow you.' I look at the umbrella seller. He's shuffling from one foot to another and rubbing his hands to keep warm. 'Usually Czech people do not talk to them,' continues X in an alarming tone of voice, before snapping: 'Please put your notebook away!'

So the Vietnamese and Gypsies are not citizens of the Czech Republic, are they? I'm sure that's news to them. I'm at a loss what to say. It's not often you find yourself with an out and out racist; which X may not be, but is giving a damn good impression of one. Should I just leave at this point? Why is Brno doing this to me? How have I ended up with this person?

X paces onwards, showing me the eleventh-century St Jacob's Church, where she pulls a face when I ask if many people are religious. 'After socialism?' she asks rhetorically, disdainful of my ignorance. 'After socialism, when people were persecuted for being religious? No! Not many people are religious. If people were persecuted for forty years for being religious where you lived, would you be religious?' Well people were persecuted for not being communists, and there are plenty of non-communists around here who appear to be thriving, I feel like saying, but don't. I've decided just to let her say what she's got to say. 'People believe in Darwinism and in yoga and also witchcraft. Black and white magic, that kind of thing.'

At St Jacob's, a wedding ceremony has just come to an end. The bride is dressed in white with a small white fur coat. We leave the church, and enter Liberty Square. Workers are digging up the central paving stones making improvements. The centre-piece of the square is a stone column with a female figure encircled by a halo of golden spikes. This is Brno's plague column, built in the seventeenth-century as a place to pray for deliverance from the deadly disease.

X shows me a small mall on one side of the square with an atrium and three floors. She takes me to the top, where there's a bar with lots of photos of happy young people on nights out on a board.

'Many of these people are models. We have many pretty girls in the Czech Republic. If a girl is stupid and young, she wants to be a model. If they are aged twenty: no problem,' says X, who might have been a model herself once. She has blonde hair and the type of symmetrical face that model agencies might go for. But I don't ask. 'These young girls, they want to go on these reality shows and make fame and make money. For older people, we think this is quite naïve. It is just money and popularity,' she says with disdain.

We go to the Cathedral of St Peter and St Paul, where legend has it that the noon bell was rung an hour early in 1645, thus putting an end to an attack by the Swedish. The Swedes left as they had vowed to give up by noon, and locals had heard of their plan, so managed to trick them into leaving early and save the city.

The Old Town Hall has a stuffed alligator hanging from the ceiling of a walkway and a strange crooked turret at the centre of the decorations on its tower. The alligator is known as the Brno dragon; once believed to have terrorised the city's waterways, but in fact was a seventeenth-century present from a Turkish sultan. The crooked turret is the work of an Austrian architect who was short-changed by Brno councillors in 1510 and exacted his revenge in the centre of his work. An early example of the Brno way of going about things?

It's cold out, and I ask X what her fur coat is made of. 'I am not sure . . . wild dogs,' she says defensively. 'Yes, I think wild dogs,' she says, feeling the arms.

On the way to the castle we pass an underground passageway where there are more Vietnamese stalls – many selling rows of knee-high boots. 'Oh it is horrible in here,' says X, shuddering. I take a picture of one of the stalls selling boots. 'They will steal your camera! Hurry up! They are Vietnamese and Chinese!' I point out that I've been to both countries and come back with camera intact. She glares at me. 'Gypsies steal things round here,' she says, shifting her attack. 'You must be very careful in this area. Near the railway and the bus station. They wait for you at the top of the escalators. And they will steal things.' Have you ever been robbed, I ask. 'No. Not me. But I am very careful.' I bet you are.

By the time we've seen the Mendel Museum and walked around the grounds of the castle, I think it's fair to say we've had more than enough of each other. The Mendel Museum is interesting, although there aren't very many displays, and X is rushing me round. It's set in an Augustinian monastery where Gregor Mendel was a monk in the nineteenth century. In its garden he carried out experiments in cultivating and hybridising peas and bees, which led to the foundation of the science of genetics. The courtyard, which now looks on to apartment block towers, crumbling buildings and factory stacks, has a display explaining his work. There are several large black crows pecking at the grass. 'Russian crows,' says X. 'It is a joke from during socialism: a Russian invasion. We don't like the Russians.'

Or anyone else, it seems.

It's time to release X, who definitely now wants to be elsewhere. We don't exactly exchange email addresses. To complete the day and the tourist sights, I go on alone to a place called Kapucinsku, a vault near the cathedral where dozens of dried and shrivelled bodies discovered in crypts are displayed. It is grim, dismal and grossly voyeuristic: I mean, would you want a bunch of dumb tourists oohhing and ahhing at your dried up corpse?

The hotel bar is closed when I get back. So I go to bed early with Kafka, empathising more and more with Joseph K in *The Trial*, which Brno is definitely turning out to be. I have another bad night's sleep listening to the man snoring in the room next door.

Things get worse. I'd popped into the tourist information centre at the Old Town Hall yesterday for advice on what to do today. They recommended going to Austerlitz to see the chateau where Napoleon signed his peace treaty with the Austrians and Russians after victory against them in 1805, in his last eastern campaign before his demise on the way to Moscow in 1812. It's about twenty miles east of Brno.

The attendant in the tourist office had an American accent,

and had lived in upstate New York for a year. She told me: 'I wish I was back there. People are so friendly in the US. People will say "hey what's up" and talk, but here it's like: "Why do you ask?"'

Even the tourist information people, it seems, don't like living in Brno.

The woman with the American accent instructed me to get number 48 bus at 9.08 a.m. or 10.08 a.m. from the bus station. I get to the bus station just in time for the 9.08 a.m. bus, having had to run a bit to make it in the snow. It began snowing overnight and there's now three inches across the city centre. There's no bus. A large attendant with an enormous cabbage-shaped face, expressionless green eyes and skin the colour of stale milk, who virtually fills the ticket kiosk, hands me a piece of paper with the number eight circled and 10.45 a.m. written on it. She gives me a dead pan look; but deep down I can tell she's enjoying every moment of this. I write the number forty-eight, circle it and show it to her. She dead eyes me again. The look says nothing and everything, with an underlying message that screams: 'Listen tourist, do you really think I remotely care whether you get to your tourist attraction?'

I wander around looking for a taxi. It can't cost that much to go twenty miles in a country with 50 pence beers. I find a taxi rank, and the first nice person I meet in Brno drives me in his battered red Skoda to Austerlitz. Boris manages to tell me that he used to make tractors that were sold to King's Lynn in Norfolk. We have a juddering conversation in which he conveys that his Skoda was built in 1973 and that old people speak Deutsch, young people, English. He even turns on BBC World Service for me so I can listen to something about the Christian Association of Nigeria and hidden agendas in the Islamic nation.

We drive on for about half an hour, and we draw up at an impressive French-looking chateau. It all looks very quiet and I have my suspicions as I approach the gate, which are confirmed when I see the sign. Austerlitz is closed. How could the tourist woman not have known this? Or did she do it on purpose? Okay, she may want to go back to the States, but no need to take it out on all the tourists. Luckily Boris hasn't motored off, or else it might have been a three-hour wait for a bus. It's still snowing. I take a quick walk around the chateau's walls. It has what I suppose you might describe as an elegant French aspect, but I'm too annoyed to notice much else. There's a bubble shaped-dome covering two tennis courts on the far side. I take a look inside and see two doubles matches with guys who look like lorry drivers plonking the ball across to one another. Some are wearing jeans. Nearly all have tattoos and long mullet haircuts that Chris Waddle would have been proud of in his best mullet days.

Despite my Brno-induced mood, I have to concede it's pretty impressive. If even lorry drivers with tattoos and mullets are playing tennis in jeans while it's snowing outside, what hope has Britain with its blame-it-on-the-weather culture ever got of producing a great? No wonder they've come up the likes of Martina Navratilova and Ivan Lendl, and have got plenty of players in the top world rankings now. We can't keep on blaming it on the rain *for ever*. People are playing *in the snow* over here.

I ride back to Brno, with Boris mumbling apologetically about Austerlitz being closed. 'Not good, not good,' when he gets the gist of the tourist info people's role in the trip. To try to make up for it, he even stops at a roadside historical sight and using a pink brush he finds in the boot of the taxi clears the snow from a brass plate showing Napoleon's battle positions. 'See, here Napoleon!' he says, pointing at the brass plate with his pink brush. 'Here and here, the enemy! Boom!' This, I later discover, was Zuran, the key vantage point from which Napoleon planned his campaign.

Nice guy that Boris. Not many of them about in Brno. I trudge through the snow to Villa Tugendhat for my lesson in function-alism – my heart sinking somewhat. Let's be totally frank, 'functionalism' is not what most people want on their holidays. I've booked a 1 p.m. tour; fifteen people are allowed round in guided groups each hour. The villa doesn't look like much from outside: grey metal fence with a locked gate, concrete courtyard, plain white walls with peeling paint and a curved section of opaque windows, all of which cry 'anonymity' and make me wonder how on earth this could be a Unesco World Heritage Site. The previous group leaves and we buy our tickets and follow a bossy middle-aged woman to a terrace at the back with terrific views down a hill across the centre of Brno's spires and snow-covered roofs. From this angle all the factories and estates seem less prominent. The tour guide hands information in English to me and in Japanese to a Japanese guy, and then starts talking in Czech.

As she rabbits away, the Japanese fellow and I read our info sheets. Ludwig Mies van der Rohe (1886–1969) was German. He built Villa Tugendhat for a local family called Tugendhat in 1929–30. The 'radicalism of the main conception and of the technical and the formal' is praised, and the villa is described as 'the most significant European project' by this 'legendary' architect. You're kidding? Looking along the terrace it looks bland and predictably 'futuristic' in a *Clockwork Orange* kind of way.

Christ, what is it with this city: it's just one let down after another.

We troop inside. And I take it all back. If there's one must-see sight in Brno it's Villa Tugendhat. I've never been much of an interiors magazine type of guy, but I've got to take my hat off to Ludwig. Even though it's coming on for a century old now, the interior looks like it could be in any of the latest swish hotels in London or New York. Using big bright windows, dark wood panels, cream linoleum floors, shiny chrome support beams, skylights, a wide open-plan living room, dining room, piano reception and library, an indoor side-garden, shiny onyx partitions, glass coffee tables, a well-placed sculpture or two and leather arm chairs – old Ludwig created a style that clearly still influences everything that's about today, yet still manages to be *classier*. I read my information sheet: 'It is for the first time that, in this type of family villa, the traditional concept of the main "living room" as a system of mutually isolated rooms had been separated by the conception of a continuous place.'

The Japanese architectural-looking chap is taking loads of snaps. It turns out he's a student from Tokyo visiting famous architectural sites in Brno, Dusseldorf, Vienna, Amsterdam and Prague to pick up ideas for his degree. This strikes me as being a pretty intelligent, but bloody expensive, thing to do; can't recall being *quite* that dedicated when I was a student.

'I'm impressed by the materials,' he says, pointing at a stone floor slab in the indoor garden that I would have thought was a rather normal piece of stone. 'Look at the textures. Quite unusual,' he says. And I realise he's right. It is an interesting stone slab. Though it's strange to think I'm discussing stone slabs with a Japanese architecture student in a suburb of a place I don't like in Central Europe.

'Oh, yes. I like the stone,' he says again. I don't think he's got all that much English. An attractive young woman from Linz in Austria overhears our conversational efforts. She flutters her eyelids and starts asking me what I think. Wow, these stone slabs might have something in them after all; maybe *this* is why all these arty interior design-type chaps, with their black polo necks and trendy glasses, are so into all this functionalism stuff. I just love a bit of functionalism! For years, I've been really quite a big functionalist. (I just don't like to talk about it much.)

I discuss texture and how unusual the texture is. She smiles and seems heartened by my take on things. She tells me her name is Katharina. Running out of material, I ask her what *she* likes about the villa. 'Oh I think it's outrageous. Just outrageous!' she says, and I'm wondering if that's 'outrageous' in a good or a bad sort of way. Then she says: 'I'm an architect. I just find it amazing what he managed to realise here. There are things that he has done here people still struggle to do today. If only I could do things like this. But I am not that long in the business.' She's lost me a bit, but she's got lovely hazel eyes and seems very nice indeed. We keep on chatting and then the lady with the pink scarf hurrys us on as another group is coming. Katharina has to run off with her brother and his girlfriend to drive back to Austria.

Well, that's three nice people then: Boris the taxi driver, the Japanese guy and Katharina. Two from out of town, but not so bad, I suppose.

I walk over to the Spilberk Castle, an ugly fortress on a hill just outside the city centre, dating from centries back. Inside there is a museum. It's just after 4 p.m. when I get there and the attendant looks wary when I buy my ticket. It closes at 5 p.m. I say I'll be fine, and start looking around, learning a bit about torture during the Hapsburg Empire and some of the horrors the Nazis dreamt up. Time flies and I find I've got twenty minutes before closing; enough to whiz around the art gallery and take a look at a section on functionalism in Brno. There's more than just Villa Tugendhat in Brno, as I began to notice walking to the castle.

The attendant in the functionalist section has his coat on and his bag tucked under his arm. He's turned off the lights in the display rooms. I point to my watch. He sighs, slams down his bag, and turns on the lights. Then he follows me around turning lights on and off and rudely ushering me past each of the displays. I turn to face him. We have an irate 'discussion', neither of us understanding a word the other is saying, but definitely getting the gist of it. The gist is: You, my friend, are one of the biggest ******** I've ever met . . . No, no. I think you'll find *you* are the bigger ********, mate. And so on and so forth. Muttering to myself, I give up and go.

At the hotel, I go to the café-bar to order tea. It's been a long day and the Englishman in me just wants a nice cup of tea. Not much of a request after a day of traipsing miles in a snow storm to attractions that are closed and having friendly conversations with museum attendants. I'm the only person in the café-bar. The waiter, a cocky-looking bald guy with permanently arched eyebrows and a bit of the James Nesbitt about him, refuses to understand what tea is. He makes no effort to ask me to elaborate. He simply stares at me with the classic 'Listen, tourist. Do you really think I remotely care whether you have your tourist tea?' face. It's as though I'm talking to a tree. He turns without a word, smiles secretively to himself and starts wiping perfectly clean surfaces. I grab the menu and point at 'café'. He takes it from me wordlessly, turns his back, walks to the bar at the pace of a bishop with a solemn task in a cathedral, and starts making a syrupy, over-brewed coffee.

The TV at the far end of the bar is on almost full volume showing a programme that he was glued to when I arrived. When he brings the syrupy over-brewed coffee, I ask him to turn it down a little, gesturing to make the point. He says nothing, turns off the TV, and then switches on the stereo, which starts playing an incredibly annoying song with the main refrain of 'Heidi, heidi ho!' at about the same volume as the TV. I stare at him. He stares back, with his tree-like expression. Rather than have another bad tempered 'conversation', I leave some cash on the table and walk out.

I turn to *The Trial*. It's proving a comfort during Brno, mainly because I can see where Joseph K is coming from: there is a system, we don't understand the system, and the system steadily *works on you*. I'm right at the end; Joseph K has been led away, by guards representing the system, they pass a knife before him and he 'perceived clearly that he was supposed to seize the knife himself, as it travelled from hand to hand above him, and plunge it into his own breast'. I didn't feel quite that down about things, but Brno can sure make you feel awful.

* * *

Rarely have I been so pleased to get to the airport after a 'holiday'. In the departure lounge, I'm filled with relief. No more Brno! No more Lemon Suckers! No more heavy snoring! No more X!

Close to the boarding gate, I meet two young English guys, Dave, aged nineteen, a food and beverage manager at a hotel in Earl's Court, and Pete, aged twenty, a receptionist at a hotel in Canterbury. Both are drinking half-litres of Starobrno, the bubbly yellow local brew, at Brno's small airport bar.

It's nice to have a conversation with some relatively normal people. Somewhat surprisingly (they don't particularly strike me as Alpinists), they've been skiing at a resort called Spindleruv – visiting a mate who works there.

'It was bloody excellent,' says Pete. Did they spend any time in Brno? They look at each other, as though eye-balling one another to get their story straight. 'Well, we were in Bruno [as in Frank, the boxer] for one night at the start. We were in this bar and these four dodgy geezers came up to us. They thought they were mafia, like, but they were just little guys, we weren't afraid,' says Dave.

'They had about twenty whores with them,' said Pete. 'Really nice ladies,' he adds quickly, as though they might hear him and be offended by that description.

'Anyway, before we know it, they're sitting all around us, like.'

'We weren't worried about them.' Pete adds.

'We knew how to handle things . . .' And the story fades out. I look at them searchingly for more. They secretively sip their Starobrnos.

I ask them what they thought of the locals. 'They kept pretending they didn't understand a thing we were trying to say, even when we used sign language and everything,' says Dave. 'It was bloody annoying.'

Pete, who seems even more annoyed than Dave, says: 'I work

at reception at a hotel and I know how to help people who don't have the language. They just didn't give a monkey's.'

Two more satisfied customers returning home from Brno.

In the queue for boarding is Sylvie, a twenty-two-year-old from Olomouc, forty miles north-east of Brno in Northern Moravia. She has green eyes and shiny painted-black fingernails. She's holding a copy of Philip Pullman's *The Amber Spyglass* close to her face. 'It is easy for me to understand, good for my English,' she says. She's another migrant worker, working as a nanny for a couple with fifteen-month-old twins in Burnt Oak in North London for the past half year, going to English classes on the side. 'Everything is easier if you speak English,' she says. 'You can get a better job. Life just becomes easier. It is difficult to learn English properly at university here. You do three hours' lessons a day and then you go home and speak Czech. It's not the same.'

Several of her friends have gone to the UK, some to get full-time jobs. 'In six months they can earn enough to buy a flat in the Czech Republic. It's much better money in the UK. If you are a shop assistant or a teacher in the Czech Republic it is difficult to earn enough to buy a flat – it may never happen.' Even working as a nanny and paying for English school, going out and buying the clothes she wants, Sylvie estimates that she will have saved enough for a flat in two years. 'Friends said I was crazy going to London, that people make you work ten hours a day and pay you just £50 a week, that it would be horrible. But I've been lucky,' she says.

I ask her what her family thinks. I still find it strange that so many young people are moving to the western parts of the EU for jobs, and considering it so normal; such a matter of fact part of growing up in places like the Czech Republic. 'My parents understand. They know I'm doing what's best for me in the long-run.' Can they speak English? 'Nooooo! No way,' she laughs. What does she think of Slovakia? 'Well, I have friends in the east of Slovakia [I'd mentioned Poprad], and they say it is very poor there, almost impossible to get a job.' Compared to Brno, with all its shopping arcades, I found Poprad, just getting its first big shopping malls, far less westernised . . . but far more friendly and open.

We talk about Brno. 'Most people want to go to Prague. Most tourists. I think Brno feels like it is a second-best city.' Which might explain some of the attitude from the people of Brno, I suppose. She glances at Dave and Pete, who look pretty dishevelled and still have beers on the table while they wait for the queue for boarding to go down. 'Men from the UK come on Ryanair to Brno. It is probably cheap for them – the drink and stuff. I don't like it when they talk to you. I just go: "Yeah, yeah, yeah." Just because they have money, they think they are special,' she says.

Those two guys didn't seem like that, I say.

But then I wonder. Here we have Dave and Pete, unshaven, full of beer (they missed their original flight out to Brno after having a few before getting to Stansted), with their stories about dodgy geezers and whores. They also told me in an indignant, can-you-believe-it tone how they'd had to complain about too much head on their beer – 'even though it's really cheap, like' – at their ski resort. Dopey and seemingly harmless, but not exactly the best specimens of British manhood. And here we have Sylvie: neatly dressed, attractive, reading her Pullman, travelling to a scary, fast-moving new country to take on a responsible job and learn a language in her spare time, all the while aware of her future – planning how one day she will be able to afford her own flat.

The contrast is pretty stark, and it's been there on almost every low-cost flight to these unspellable spots. People travelling in one direction for cheap drink and to live it up, people travelling in the other to get on in life and face up to the uncertain world ahead.

Maybe this gulf can go some way towards explaining things in Brno. Maybe that's why almost everyone seemed so unfriendly. If I lived in Brno perhaps I, too, would be sneery towards all these pesky western visitors. Who wants to help someone who's so much better off anyway? Who wants to be a weekend butler to the Ryanair rabble?

Maybe if I lived in Brno I'd have all sorts of opinions I don't now. Maybe I'd be writing off the Brno Bronx, as X so charmingly called the 'Gypsy part of town'? I walked through the Bronx this morning, seeing the type of slum that I didn't think existed anywhere in the EU: rickety apartment blocks with rusting walkways, great piles of litter in courtyards, washing hanging to dry on crumbling walls, graffiti everywhere, bars on street corners offering 30 pence shots of vodka, tacky shops selling £3 jeans, tiny hunched-over women carrying babies wrapped in shawls. Maybe I'd be disgusted and scared of the Vietnamese and the Gypsies. Perhaps, if I lived in Brno, I'd even blame them for my lack of wealth relative to the 'old' EU countries.

But I certainly hope not.

Brno was the most difficult destination to work out yet. *Time Out* describes the city's name as deriving from the Slavonic word for 'mud'. I'd mentioned this to X. 'Nonsense,' she'd said crossly. 'I never heard this! Brno, it means nothing! Nothing!' Whatever you say X, whatever you say. But I leave Brno with an impression of the Czech Republic's second city that's just about as clear as mud.

TAMPERE, FINLAND

LIVING IN A LOWRY

Tampere is Finland's second city, further north than Stockholm, Oslo and Haugesund, it's not that far from the Arctic Circle. It's an inland city on the south-western tip of the drinker's nose of Finland, close to a body of water I'd never heard of before called the Gulf of Bothnia, which separates the country from Sweden. It's also Ryanair's most northerly destination, which gave it a certain allure.

On the Ryanair website, Tampere looked secretive – hidden away on the northernmost edge of Europe; a kind of tourist no-go zone, beyond the wildest dreams of all but the most dedicated, or lost, of travellers. What goes on in such an out of the way place? And do I really want to find out? I hope so, I thought, as I bought my tickets. One thing's for sure: I don't think I can take another Brno.

Guidebooks describe the city as 'Finland's Manchester' – which might well put some people off. Let's face it, going aboard to visit another country's Manchester is not at the top of most peoples' holiday wishlist.

Yet somehow or other – even though it was permanently blizzard conditions and freezing – I had a great time.

It was a Briton who first put Tampere on the map. Finland's first cotton mill, run by a Scot named James Finlayson, opened in Tampere in the 1820s. It soon became the biggest mill in Scandinavia – ahead of anything in Sweden or Norway – employing more than two thousand people. Finlayson chose Tampere because it's perched between two vast lakes with an 18-metre drop between them, connected by a 1,700 metre run of fast-moving water known as the Tammerkoski rapids. These rapids are what powered his mill, as well as several others that set up business nearby. Soon after Finlayson arrived, factory stacks crowded along the Tammerkoski.

It's this industrial past – and present – that makes Tampere special. Walking around on my first afternoon, after dumping my bags at the Holiday Inn, the city quickly grows on me. Along the Tammerkoski rapids, steam is billowing out of giant red-brick stacks. Water is flowing green and fast beneath a grey stone bridge. Figures wrapped in coats and bright scarves are scurrying about their business. A sprinkling of snow begins to fall. The scurrying gets faster. I cross a cobbled street and make my way to the middle of the bridge.

It's mid-March, and very cold. The snow is getting thicker – quite heavy now. I look out across the rapids. And then I realise something. Something I hadn't expected to realise on a weekend break; or at any other time, for that matter.

Squint your eyes a bit in Tampere and suddenly you are transported. You are transported to the 1920s, to Manchester, to the world L. S. Lowry captured on canvas all those years ago after visiting the poorer parts of the city during his job as a rent collector.

It's quite uncanny. Locals are hunched over, exactly as Lowry painted them, heads down in the cold. They look just like his stick people, cutting isolated figures against the snow. Because they are moving along so swiftly in the cold, there is even the feeling that they are flowing from one place to another: precisely the sense you get when looking at a Lowry.

That's when I realise I really quite like Tampere. It's an almost surreal feeling: as though I've hopped on a Ryanair flight and I'm spending the weekend in Manchester during its industrial hey-day. It's all very odd, but it's also strangely exciting.

The city is not, however, down at heel. While guidebooks describe Tampere as Finland's Manchester, many others describe it as being 'Finland's Silicon Valley'. There are also paper and pulp mills – pumping out steam from the stacks – giant engineering plants making parts for machines, a stone-crushing depot, and a big factory making frozen ready-made meals, not far from my hotel.

I pass a McDonald's, a Body Shop, an H&M, a Viking Line ferry agency, a Mr Travel holiday shop, and a restaurant called 'Cow'. It's quiet about. But then, as the snow begins to get very heavy, I reach the central market. It is busy. The stalls have red and white awnings, under which folk are resting for a break from the flurry. Some stalls sell sardines fried in what look like giant upturned dustbin lids. It costs £3.50 for a plate with chips on the side. Fish 'n' chips Finnish-style – they're very good indeed. I wander around, checking out the pancakes and bagels, and a stall selling red-coloured vodka. People are downing sample shots, giggling and sharing jokes.

A Finnish Del Boy tries to sell me a reindeer pelt. 'American? English?' he asks. 'English? All the English are wanting these!' He strokes the fur on the pelt. 'Very good reindeer! When you come to Finland you most definitely must buy the reindeer. Most definitely, or else you might think you are in Copenhagen!'

I say I'm not interested. Anyway, imagine explaining a great fur like that to customs officials at Stansted. No thanks.

'But they are very good in wooden houses; very good on wooden benches. It is unique!' I explain that I live in a brick house. 'That is a pity,' he concedes, losing himself in thought for a moment. 'But the Italians, they love them! The Italians, they are quite crazy!' We discuss the crazy Italians for a while.

I go to the Finlayson centre, this former factory, overlooking the market, has now been turned into a mall. It also houses an intriguing attraction: the Spy Museum. I part with seven euros and take a look around. Finns, it seems, love the subject of spying. This is partly because the country was a buffer zone between the East and the West for so many years. There was a lot of speculation about spies during the Cold War years.

Displays include swords concealed in walking sticks, knives hidden in gear handles of Ladas, flick knives connected to cigarette lighters, an ashtray with an eavesdropping device, parachutes used in daredevil missions, portable radio receivers, and a lie detector box. The latter is annoyingly broken, or I could have tested statements such as: 'I like people from Brno' or 'It's warm in Finland', plus all sorts of other things.

There's quite a crowd around the main displays, where there are sections on Kim Philby (a devote communist . . . suspected of being a triple agent by Stalin), Elizabeth Bentley (an American KGB-agent who had affairs with dozens of powerful men to get secret information), Mathilde 'The Cat' Carre (a triple agent from France described as a ruthless female spy, who always did what was best for her), Elsbeth Schragmuller (who led a German spy school that operated during the First World War and was a determined and unmerciful woman who did not hesitate to sacrifice the lives of her spies), and a chap I've never heard of called Sidney Reilly, born in 1874 in Poland as Salomon Rosenblum, and considered to be Ian Fleming's model for James Bond.

A display describes Reilly as 'a corrupted businessman, collector, freemason, womaniser and political schemer, who tried to have Lenin murdered'. Apparently it was Reilly's idea to carry out the murder attempt on Lenin in August 1918. Fanny Kaplan, a member of a rival socialist party, shot Lenin twice in the chest and he escaped death by a whisker. For Reilly, this was a culmination of years of misdeeds. His first major 'move' was when he came to England in 1895, where he ditched his Jewish background by having a wealthy reverend murdered and marrying his young widow – at the same time taking on a new name given to him by Scotland Yard. He married at least four times (never divorcing), had countless girlfriends, became a millionaire selling armaments during the First World War, and generally (and literally) led the life of Reilly.

Nobody, I learn, quite knows where he ended up. Was he shot in Russia? Did he recruit the Cambridge Five in England? Or become a Mossad agent? All the information about spies is, as the displays explain, a bit cloak and dagger-ish, with varying shades of 'truth'. What does seem certain is that Fleming knew about Reilly – and that parts of him ended up in Bond. A black and white picture shows a suave fellow with dark slicked-back hair and a poker face: Bond to a tee.

Before coming to Tampere (population 201,000), I read a book by Richard D. Lewis entitled *Finland, Cultural Lone Wolf*. Written in an academic style, it is full of quirky facts about the country. Finland, says Lewis, is 'number one in global competitiveness', 'number one in mobile phones', 'regularly voted as the least corrupt country in the world', and 'the world leader in managing water resources'.

The Finnish, he continues, are proportionately the biggest users of libraries in the world – six million visits per annum. He provides plenty of great statistics: there are more saunas in Finland than cars; Finnish radio broadcasts in Latin; Finns spend more per capita on alcohol than any other people; Finns are the world's biggest coffee drinkers; Finns have a high median age: 39.4 years; Santa Claus lives at Korvatunturi, a mountain in Lapland; one of Finland's most popular bands is called the Leningrad Cowboys; and a Finnish couple won the World Tango Dancing Championship in 2000.

Lewis, who seems to be a guru of all things Finnish, goes on to describe Finland as 'the world's best kept secret' and, intriguingly, to proclaim 'the future is Finnish'. Even more intriguing, though, are his sections analysing the Finnish psyche. The Finns, he says, are 'an unusual people of an independent nature, devoted to hard work, yet modest in their aspirations and jealous of their honest reputation', 'quiet . . . poor at blowing their own trumpet', with a 'basic shyness and dislike of exhibitionism lending thickness to an intervening curtain of cultural complexity [and] voluntary withdrawal . . . they feel a sense of separateness from other peoples'. Lewis goes on to describe the Finns as 'taciturn', 'calm' people who 'take talking seriously', with a 'lack of visible jocularity [and] a dislike of gossip' – 'outdoor laughing and smiling are not part of the winter scene. A broad American smile at 15°C below in a Helsinki easterly make's one's front teeth ache.'

Apart from the jolly lot at the market (who'd obviously had a few vodkas), I get the feeling he's right. The people on my plane, mainly Finns, had been terribly quiet and reserved – a pocket of sobriety, thought and lack of exhibitionism among the raucous St Patrick's Day goings on at Stansted airport. The tourist information assistants at the airport had seemed basically shy to the point of embarrassment when I'd asked some simple questions, and my taxi driver from the airport seemed to want to disappear into thin air when I asked him about the city.

How do the Finns unwind? They seem so uptight. I ask the hotel receptionist what Finns do for fun. She pauses for a bit and looks at me like I'm some sort of nutcase. Then she goes into a backroom to discuss my request with a colleague. After a minute or two she returns. She smiles faintly and then says simply: 'They jump in the cold water.' And she gives me the name of a public 'jumping in the cold water' facility.

Which is why I'm now standing in my swimming trunks out in the open, in minus 10°C weather in the middle of Finland.

Cold winds are sweeping across a lake – cold winds that possibly come from the Arctic Circle. I am absolutely frozen. Should I smile? A little English smile, certainly not a broad American one. I'm pretty sure my front teeth would ache quite badly.

Most of the lake is frozen, as it ought to be when it's minus 10°C. But a small corner has been cleared of ice. We are standing, myself and several Finns, in our swimming trunks, shivering and looking at this small corner, contemplating how cold it must be in there.

Then one by one we trundle along a green carpet walkway – like a mini-golf putting surface – and jump in the lake.

I follow a couple, wanting to see how it's done. They leap into the water, shriek a bit, giggle, and lift themselves out. I do the same, thinking back to Poprad's Snow Paradise room at Aqua-City and wondering why Eastern Europeans and people from Nordic lands seem to enjoy freezing themselves so much.

And yes, it is *absolutely* freezing. It is without a doubt the coldest I've ever felt. I can feel my body temperature plunge downwards. I get the sensation that, if I don't get out quickly, I won't have any body temperature left at all. And I think there's a word for that state of being: dead.

I shuffle out of the water and up the green carpet feeling, by comparison, 'warm' in the wind that's whipping off the lake. I am dying to get into the sauna, housed in a small wooden building, but pause outside it with a group of bathers. You're meant to do this after leaving the lake to help your body adjust. I'm feeling a bit self-conscious as I'm wearing a ridiculous pair of borrowed Speedo-style swimming trunks which have the words 'David Collection' written on them.

My body has also turned bright pink; perhaps because I'm not used to this frozen water routine. Other people's bodies are not bright pink and they are staring at me with amusement.

Finally – still bright pink – I get inside the sauna. There's a fifty-fifty mix of men and women. Everyone sits in silence – behaving like true Finns.

The thermometer says 100°C. I close my eyes thinking back to how cold I felt a few moments ago. Now I feel great. But this is completely mad. I take a look around me. Everyone seems a little crazed – a bit manic and happy to be manic, but keeping their manic feelings to themselves. Maybe it's just the water that's done it; the adrenalin rush. Or maybe it's just the Finns in general, I begin to wonder. It's quiet up here near the Arctic Circle. So I guess you just have to make your own fun.

After returning my body to a fairly normal temperature – as normal as it can be when it's minus 10°C outside – I visit the city's Lenin Museum.

I hadn't expected to find a Lenin Museum in Tampere. But with all its nineteenth-century factories, Tampere also has a radical trade unionist past. Russia ruled Finland from 1809 through to the Russian Revolution in 1917 – and in the latter years the city was a hotbed of political discussion, with many workers sympathising with communist plans to overthrow the tsar.

The result was that Tampere had some interesting visitors; the most interesting being a certain Vladimir Lenin and a young gun called Joseph Stalin, who met for the first time at the city's Workers' Hall in December 1905. Quite a famous meeting, for quite a never-heard-of-it place like Tampere, I think.

The Workers' Hall still exists: a five-storey, concrete block next to a shopping mall. And now it houses one of the world's last Lenin museums. As I enter the small, two-room museum, I'm given a leaflet that proudly states: 'Almost all Lenin museums elsewhere in the world have closed down and the few remaining Lenin museums in Russia are only open at certain times.'

Nobody else is about. A young guy with blond boy-band-style streaks in his hair manning the ticket kiosk is almost asleep in his chair. I buy a ticket for a couple of euros. I ask the attendant how many people visit the museum each day. He looks at me sheepishly, and consults a ledger. After a while, he says: 'Ten.' That's it, nothing else, just: 'Ten.'

I ask him if he's a fan of Lenin. He looks sheepish again. 'Umm, yes,' he says, before saying, 'Umm, no.' He's either really shy, doesn't have good English, isn't sure about how he feels about the subject of the museum, or just doesn't like to blow his Finnish trumpet too much. Why are you not a fan? 'Things have changed in some respects,' he says. In what ways? 'The ideology,' he replies, and then pauses. 'I have not really gone into it properly.'

After almost a whole day in Tampere, this is – if you don't count the man trying to sell me a reindeer pelt in the market – my best conversation with a Finn so far.

I pass through the 'Lenin Shop', a cabin-like room with bright red posters screaming communist slogans. Lenin T-shirts are £10, Lenin coffee with a hazelnut flavour £2.40, a red plastic comb with a picture of Lenin on it 60 pence, and a set of three Lenin, Marx and Engels glasses £10. I stoop to look at one shelf. On it is a weird-looking pair of rubber gloves, like the bright-yellow ones you're meant to wear doing washing up, except they've got grey sleeves and bright pink hands. They're called 'A Pair of Gloves for the Hero of Work'. They are, it says, 'suitable for a present to our time's heroes, useful every day: in gardening, changing a tyre, or cleaning a boat': £11.90.

It's a good museum, and the displays have English descriptions accompanying them. I start at a section on the young Lenin, which has black and white pictures and a marble bust of the revolutionary to be. He looks, I decide, quite like an English public school boy, a young Etonian perhaps: confident gaze, wavy foppish hair, a place at Oxbridge coming his way soon.

A panel explains how the death of Lenin's older brother Aleksandra helped fire his revolutionary zeal. In 1887, the twenty-one-year-old Aleksandra was executed for a plot against Tsar Alexander III. An oil painting shows Lenin, who was born in Simbirsk on the Volga in 1870, looking disgruntled while his mother wipes away tears with a handkerchief. His right hand is resting in a fist on a table, his left placed protectively on his mother's shoulder.

Lenin met Stalin when he was in exile. There are pictures of some of the disguises he used while he was on the run, including one with a wig and a hat that makes him look strangely like the Pet Shop Boys' singer Neil Tennant. Lenin and Stalin crossed paths at a conference about workers' rights. Lenin was clearly the more important of the two figures at the time. But this did not stop Stalin later commissioning a propaganda painting that shows him standing purposefully by a table, waving an arm as though making a crucial point, his hair and moustache splendidly bushy, while a bald, squinty-eyed Lenin perches nervously on a nearby chair.

Close by is the highlight of the museum: a battered cherry-wood sofa with a worn olive-green velvet cover. This is, purportedly, where Lenin slept during his stay. It doesn't, I have to say, look particularly comfortable.

The Tampere–Lenin connection wasn't just important for communism, though, but for the future of Finland. While in the city, Lenin 'promised to further Finnish autonomy'. Some believe that it was because Lenin was familiar with the Finnish people from his period in exile, that Finland was later granted independence by Russia, while other nearby states such as Latvia, Lithuania and Estonia were not. Independence was declared on December 6, 1917, shortly after the October Revolution. A copy of the document accepting Finnish autonomy – signed by Lenin, Stalin and Trotsky – is on display.

There is further evidence that Lenin simply quite liked the Finns. He stopped by in Finland on his way to St Petersburg to plan the revolution in April 1917. He later employed Finns as bodyguards, had several Finnish friends, and mentions the Finns or Finland in 340 speeches. It seems he definitely had a soft spot for the country and its people. Was that why the Finns got freedom and, say, the Lithuanians didn't?

I find myself talking to a guide, who has entered the museum with a small group of locals. Sara is very surprised to find an international tourist in March.

I can tell she's a guide because she is wearing a gold badge saying 'Guide' on the lapel of her blue jacket. Having had no one to ask anything – the kiosk chap wasn't exactly flowing with facts – it's a good chance to learn a bit more about Tampere.

One thing has been puzzling me: why is one of Tampere's lakes 18 metres higher than the other? Isn't it odd that one is so much higher? This difference in the lakes' altitude has seemed crucial to Tampere's past: it caused the rapids, which attracted the mill-owners such as Finlayson, and led to the development of the city and its workers' clubs, which helped spark the industrial revolution across Finland, which drew the likes of Lenin and other Russian radicals who were responsible for the independence granted to Finland in 1917.

'Ah, I don't know about this,' says Sara, pausing to consider the point. 'I suppose the landscape is just like that.' But then Sara comes alive. 'I think it has something to do with the ice age, 15,000 years ago,' she says. 'Ice pushed down on Finland, with different pressure on different points. Now the ice has gone, we are rising. The whole of Finland is rising. And it is still rising. Near where I was brought up in Vaasa [on the west coast, overlooking Sweden], even in my lifetime I have seen how things have changed. Now you must go further down the beach to get to the sea. The land has risen! I can actually see this!'

She reels off some stats. Finland is the same size as Britain and Ireland combined and has 17 people per square kilometre versus 383 people per square kilometre in England, 142 in Wales, 125 in Northern Ireland, 65 in Scotland, and – I'm staggered to discover – 4,700 per square kilometre in London.

Sara tells me about the Finnish Civil War. Soon after independence, in 1918, there was a clash between the Reds, who had their base in Tampere and who wanted socialism, and the Whites, made up of troops from the new government. The Whites won, but more than 30,000 people died. 'Tampere was for two months the capital of Red Finland. It was tragic and horrible. Some people have not got over it. The fighting broke up some families – divided them into Red and White for years afterwards. It is so long ago, but some people still think about this.'

I mention my 'conversation' with the man in the kiosk. 'People who live here are very quiet, very serious and sometimes slow,' says Sara, who says she still feels like an out-of-towner, being from Vaasa. 'Especially, they are slow with reactions. If you tell them a joke they won't laugh. Maybe when they get home they will laugh – but only if it's funny.'

After leaving Sara, I have an enlivening meeting with Kalervo Kummola, the managing director of Tampere Hall, a concert venue. He is certainly not shy, but he is quite funny, and holds forth to me on his bitter ice hockey rivalry with 'the bloody Swedes'.

My next appointment is with a local character called Stephen Toms who runs a business called Weigh and Save in a shopping mall in the city centre.

I walk down icy streets lined with nineteenth-century warehouses, enter a rather ordinary mall, descend an escalator and find Weigh and Save, a canary-yellow shop selling a range of two-thousand vegetarian foods. Stephen, who is originally from Plymouth and who met his Finnish wife at a disco in Cambridge, greets me in a canary-yellow Weigh and Save shirt and jeans. He has frameless glasses, a serious side-parting and an intense look that suggests hours of number-crunching in front of a computer.

Like Kalervo, Stephen is a talker. Within minutes, as he walks me around his store, he has told me he has a supplier in Broadstairs in Kent; that he is aged forty, with two children aged eleven and thirteen; how his grandmother's motto – In hard times or in rich times, everyone has to eat – had inspired his business; how he went about wooing his wife and how she fell for him 'because I'd become more handsome'; that he's a church-going Christian; how his Himalayan salt and Costa Rican sugar-cane are selling very well; and that his favourite authors are Jeffrey Archer and John Grisham.

He is much more successful now than he was in the UK. And he admits it feels odd to be an economic migrant (of sorts) moving from Britain to Eastern Europe, when most other people are doing exactly the opposite. But he likes it in Finland, he says. He shows me his Marmite supplies, pick-and-mix nuts, and tins of something called 'Mock Duck: a soya product'.

'The Finns love all this stuff. People have a lot of allergies over here. Half the population has lactose intolerance, you know. That's why I've got so many empty shelves. It's selling faster than I can stock it.' He looks worriedly at a puffed rice shelf.

I ask Stephen about the Finns. This is clearly a favourite subject. 'Oh, the Finnish people are much more private, much more private than us,' he says. 'I might not see my neighbour for a whole winter. Okay, I might see him from a distance, but he'll jump into his car and drive off to work. Even if they drive by, they don't look our way. It takes a while to get used to it.' He pauses. 'We went to a thirtieth birthday party the other day. We thought we must have been the first people there. But then we went to the living room and all these people were sitting around saying nothing.' He pauses, fiddling with his glasses. 'They came out of their shells after a couple of beers mind you . . .'

He grabs my arm and points towards the supermarket across from Weigh and Save. 'See that man there? Look there!' I spot a man wearing a funny hat like the ones golfers used to wear in the days of Jeeves and Wooster. 'He's wearing that so he can pull it down low and hide his eyes when he gets to the till.' He grabs my arm again. 'See that guy there?' I notice someone listening to an iPod. 'He's in his own world. Doesn't have to talk to anyone. You see, you get this everywhere. It's different here. People are just so private. Really, they are. I've had to change my character. I'm not the same person as when I came,' he says. I get the sense that Stephen is *very glad* to have a chance to chat; that he definitely doesn't get the opportunity to shoot the breeze all that often.

I ask Stephen what he likes to see and do in Tampere. He's not brimming with enthusiasm. 'The winter and the summer are two different years,' he says. 'I cannot see what Tampere offers anyone in the winter. It is cold and dark. It has a couple of tiny ski slopes – you're down in a minute. Some people dip into the cold water by the ice on the lakes.' I tell him I have already done this.

He pauses to examine some prunes. 'In the summer, it is so different. Nature is reflected in the lakes,' he continues. 'There are plenty of lakes. There's also a fantastic fun park, rollercoasters, museums, forests, berry picking, mushroom picking. Mid-May to mid-September, that is the time to come. People are different in the winter. Finland can be bleak in the winter: they say it has the highest suicide rate of any country. Bleak. It is a terrible thing.'

I quite like it, I say. He ignores this. 'I could never go back to England though, never. I have a far better time here. Whenever I go back I'm so infuriated by people's ignorance. Where is Finland? Is it part of Russia? People are so opinionated, but they know nothing. People are much better educated here. Yes, we pay higher taxes, but the schools are excellent. The average sixteen-year-old here is more intelligent than a university graduate back in the UK.'

Maybe, but I can't help feeling that Stephen would prefer it if people would swap a bit of intelligence . . . and just talk to each other a little bit more.

One nice thing about visiting somewhere very cold, is taking it easy for a while somewhere warm. During a blizzard, I lie in bed for a while reading a book I picked up at Stansted called *The Giro Playboy*. It is by a twenty-something Londoner called

Michael Smith, who describes his chaotic life working in a string of low-paid bar jobs, dossing in bedsits, taking too many drugs, getting the sack, doing nothing while dreaming of greatness, and not quite getting anywhere.

One passage stands out, making me think of all the Sylvies and the Huberts I've met on low-cost flights of late. Smith is with a friend in a bedsit, imagining becoming a rock star, but suddenly realising how hopeless this is:

> What a pair of losers we felt like . . . at that point neither of us was even allowed bank accounts, that most basic of modern needs . . . the people who couldn't get along in the strongest economy in the world . . . educated young men from decent backgrounds trapped between the dole and the worst jobs in the world, the jobs reserved for people who can't even speak English . . .

People say immigration invigorates an economy – that countries like Britain and America wouldn't be where they are today with immigration – and here is some (anecdotal) proof. Smith becomes embarrassed by his predicament: that people who can't even speak English from Eastern Europe and elsewhere are getting ahead while an educated young man from a decent background like him falls into decline. He drags himself out of his lethargy and starts doing things to 'better himself'.

I haul myself out of bed. Then I do what Finns do – even when it's a blizzard. I'm not sure this will better myself, but I'm about to go long-distance ice-skating.

There is a long-distance skating centre on Nasijarvi, Tampere's northern lake, with a track that runs for about seven kilometres over the frozen surface. I take a look about. Everything is very white indeed; the sky is white. The air is white. The landscape is white. Can you really go skating out there? I ask a cheerful assistant with red hair.

'It is okay, absolutely okay,' she says. 'You know how to skate?' Yes, I do, I say. Just about. 'Fine,' she says. Then she asks for my mobile number and gives me a card for their office, 'Just in case anything goes wrong.' I think she doubts me. 'Don't worry! Everyone, so far, has come back!' I strap on long-bladed skates and disappear into the whiteness.

I wouldn't describe myself as a natural at long-distance ice-skating. I skate about 50 metres very, very slowly. The attendant with red hair sprints up with two Nordic walking poles for stability. 'They are too long, but they should help,' she says. Then she runs off. I go brilliantly for 20 metres and then fall badly. Parents with two small kids pass by. The kids look round and have a good giggle at the English man on the ice.

A jogger on the verge beside the ice track overtakes me, but slows down to ask: 'First time, eh?' Then he says discouragingly, 'not good ice,' and continues on his way. My arms begin to hurt. While shifting my camera behind my back, one of the poles gets simultaneously wedged under my chin and stuck into the ice. It feels like a Tyson uppercut (or how I imagine a Tyson uppercut to be). Another family laughs at me.

I get to a half-way café next to a small lighthouse. I buy a cup of tea and rub my chin. I ask the man selling the tea if he gets many tourists. 'Yes, some tourists,' he says informatively, before lapsing into silence. I've learnt not to expect whole sentences from a Finn.

A man on a snowboard clutching a windsurf sail whizzes up. He says it's called 'kite boarding' and that you can go 100 kilometres an hour. It is his second time trying it. He's already gone 40 kilometres an hour and out-run his dog. He whizzes away. I'm just beginning to get the knack of skating when I get back. The attendant with red hair laughs and says: 'I didn't say it's easy, I just showed you how to do it. But it *is* easy.' Then she adds: 'At the moment it is snowing, so maybe it is more difficult.' She *had* seen me fall. Obviously all these Finnish pastimes take some getting used to: perhaps that's why everyone is so quiet – they're concentrating on getting them right.

I take a well-earned rest at the hotel, until Stephen Toms turns up, raring to go. Snow covers the road. There aren't many cars about. Stephen shocks the life out of me by making a handbrake turn, unannounced, to perform a skidding u-turn and get to a green traffic light in time. 'Neat, huh?' he says, as we drive onwards. 'I drive the same, snow or no snow,' he says, as though handbrake turns are the most natural thing in the world.

We're off for a meal in Stephen's house, but before we get there, we take a detour to visit the fabled town of Nokia. 'There's not much to see, is there?' says Stephen. He's right. Nokia is not likely to win weekend crowds from Paris and Rome. The sky is slate grey. The river is a muddy brown. There's a rubber factory with steam coming out of a stack. There's a dull shopping centre. And not much else. Nokia, the company, does not run any major telecommunications business from Nokia, the town. Oh, well. I take out my Nokia phone and capture a picture of the rubber factory. It's the mobile phone equivalent of rich Americans turning up in Scotland to find their long lost family tartans.

We drive, rapidly, to Stephen's house, a bungalow in a quiet suburb. We open a couple of beers. Arja-Leena, Stephen's cheery Finnish wife, cooks a terrific salmon meal with a mixed berry pudding and freshly baked buns. They chat about how much better the Finnish education system is than the UK's, not to mention house prices. But they also tell me a terrible story, of a lodger they had a few years ago, who committed suicide by shooting himself through the mouth. 'It is a common occurrence in this country. Very common,' Stephen says. 'He was taking hormonal drugs, steroids. He played a lot of computer games – lived a bit of a fantasy life. It was a little scary. Well, actually, it was very scary.'

We change the subject – though I get the feeling that talk about suicides is quite normal in Finland. We eat more buns, drink more beer and discuss the Finns. 'They really can be an odd lot,' he says, peering out of his front windows.

There's not a neighbour in sight.

BOURGAS, BULGARIA

BLACK SEA DREAMS

From the coldest and the furthest north, to the warmest and the furthest east, Bourgas on Bulgaria's Black Sea Coast is a – pleasant – shock to the system after freezing Tampere.

It's early May, almost five months since I went to lovely Szczecin in Poland, and I've packed shorts, T-shirts and swimming trunks. No diving in icy lakes this time, no way. A dip in the sea and a bit of sunbathing could be more the order of the day in Bulgaria.

But not just yet. I'm at Bourgas Airport at 4 a.m. on a Friday morning after a packed Wizz Air flight. I'm feeling very tired indeed. I'm also completely stranded.

A small, bird-like assistant at the Hertz kiosk is staring at me. I'm staring at a small, bird-like assistant at the Hertz kiosk. I've got a voucher for a Hertz rental car; I've put the voucher on the counter, she's glanced at it. Then, somewhat taking me aback, she asks: 'Voucher? Where is your voucher?'

I eyeball the 'invisible' voucher on the counter. A clock clicks on her desk: 4.01 a.m. I'm in the arrivals hall. It's a cavernous place with a row of immigration huts filled with sleepy officials who spent five minutes per person checking documents. A sign on the wall reads, *Passport Control: No Payments Here.* There is a picture of a wallet with a red cross through it.

It seems my car is missing. I've made a mistake with the booking because the departure date was yesterday, there's only one car a day and that has someone else's name on it.

'Other people have rented a car, if they do not turn up, you will have one,' the Hertz receptionist tells me. But they'll probably be here in a second, so I won't have a car, I say. 'This is true,' she says, looking across the hall.

And then they appear, the other Hertz people: Amy and Danny, from Essex. I'd noticed them at Luton. It was hard not to. Danny is wearing a bomber jacket with a flamboyant fur hood, wide-boy jeans with turns-up and flashy trainers. He's got a crew-cut, shifty eyes, a shuffling gait, and earrings in both ears. Amy, his girlfriend, has bright, bleached blonde hair, a peculiar cut-off jacket with a Playboy T-shirt underneath, tight jeans, ankle bracelets and Playboy trainers. They're both in their forties. They look like they went to an Acid House rave twenty years ago and never changed their outfits.

We establish their right to the car. 'It's our car,' says Danny. And then we have a chat while the assistant does the paperwork. 'We bought a place out here two years ago, down by Sunny Beach,' Danny says shiftily. Sunny Beach is the big resort in these parts, fifteen miles north of Bourgas. Lots of Brits have bought places there, he says. What made them think of it? Danny looks even shiftier and mumbles something about getting the idea from a friend he'd met on holiday in the Canaries. 'When he mentioned Bulgaria as a good place to invest, I almost fell off my chair. I mean, Bulgaria? Who goes on holiday in Bulgaria?'

Amy chips in: 'I think it's really lovely here. The people are really lovely.' She pauses, and then says, like she's letting me in on a secret: 'It's *sooo* cheap.' Danny tells me exactly how cheap. 'This one [a one-bed apartment] cost 68,000 euros. We're gonna get another up in Varna: 92,000 euros, like. I've got a philosophy regarding money: if you lose forty-five grand, you lose forty-five grand. There's no point worrying about it.'

Amy starts to tell me about Bulgaria. 'At first I thought "Oh my God, Bulgaria!", but you shouldn't think like that,' she says, twiddling her blonde hair and looking at me with heavily made-up eyes. 'Okay, it's almost a Third World country, but it's not like a communist place at all any more [communism ended in

Bulgaria in 1989]. The potential is great.' She pauses, then adds: 'This country is *going places*. Definitely. I can tell.'

She takes on a bit of a Mother Teresa tone: 'We have built something for them [i.e., their apartment, which they have paid to be built from scratch] and we get something out of it [i.e., a return on the investment].' Then she turns serious: 'We know how things are run by the mafia, like. We're told that by every second person we meet. So it must be true.'

Danny and Amy depart with my car after Danny gives me his email, which is in a completely different name – the idea being for him to see what I write. I am now the last passenger at the airport. The fluorescent strip-lighting is turned off, leaving a few dim low-level lights in the hall. The assistant stares at my voucher once more. At the back of the kiosk a man is lurking smoking Victory cigarettes, the packet rests on the counter. She goes to discuss my plight with this man.

I'm in luck. It's a two-car rental fleet today after all, and I've got the second car – which is on the other side of a large, empty car park. I follow the assistant across. She explains the security system; which involves pressing several buttons on the key to turn off disabling devices. Then I ask her how to get to Bourgas. She hands me a map in Cyrillic script and tells me to 'turn right'. She smiles faintly, tells me I'll be charged for any damage, and says goodbye.

I pass through an airport security barrier, turn right and head into the darkness along a pot-holed road. Did I take the correct right? I have no idea. It was a little confusing back there. Am I going in completely the wrong direction? Possibly. What if I am? Well, then I'm in trouble. If I do find Bourgas, how will I find Hotel Bulgaria? Good question.

Soon I'm amid communist-era housing blocks. Mine is the only car about. Bourgas, I presume? I'm not sure. I take a main road and drive on. I pass through a couple of roundabouts, trying to go in the direction of civilisation. Then, as if by magic, I start seeing small blue signs for Hotel Bulgaria. It's 3.9 kilometres away, says the first. I keep going, weaving along unlikely streets, and there it is: Hotel Bulgaria, an ugly, twenty-storey tower.

How these low-cost airlines make any cash is a mystery to me. It's about 1,500 miles from Luton to Bourgas, a three-hour flight and by far the most easterly of my destinations – draw a line northwards and you cut through Kiev in the Ukraine and Moscow up in Russia. Istanbul and the 'official start' of Asia are just 160 miles south-east (the Turkish border is 50 miles away). For this I paid £20 each way, plus £30 in taxes and a £15 'fuel charge'. Total: £85.65.

I try to work out the pence-per-mile price. If my maths is right, this works out at 1.3 pence a mile on the £20 fare or 2.8 pence with taxes and fuel charge included. Not bad 'value for money', by anyone's standards.

Even so, will it be worth it? On the plane I had my doubts. The *Rough Guide* says: 'Often dismissed as a polluted industrial dump to be passed through quickly on the way to more desirable locations along the coast . . . the Black Sea as a whole is in a sorry state.' Then it goes on to describe the city (population 226,000) as 'surprisingly attractive . . . pleasantly urbane and tourist-friendly.'

Many of my fellow passengers, judging from their conversations, were like Amy and Danny, with their own places out here. The *Wizzit* in-flight magazine even had a *Property Special* supplement. 'How can you resist the allure of the Bulgarian Property Renaissance?' ran an editorial. Prices were incredibly cheap. A company called Balkan Ski Chalets was offering luxury apartments for 29,000 euros. A side-panel asked: 'Why invest in Bulgarian property?' And then it answered: 'Prices rising by forty per cent annually. Full property management and letting service. Nine per cent rental yields in ski resorts, five per cent on coast.'

Another company, Bulgarian Dreams, had an 'exclusive property with a full spa, fitness centre and international restaurant' at the Bansko ski resort for 50,000 euros. A developer called Fort Noks offered luxurious apartments on the Black Sea Coast from 24,000 euros: 'We build your dreams . . . first instalment from ten per cent only.' For 2,400 euros (or £1,639) you could buy your very own 'Bulgarian Black Coast Dream'.

I was interrupted in my property reading by Paul, an accountant from Manchester. 'Are you thinking of buying something?' he asked. I told him I was considering getting a place, and Paul told me about his own Bulgarian Black Coast Dream.

'I took the plunge last September,' he said, between sips of Heineken. 'Unnerving, is the best way to describe it. A leap of faith. You have to believe what everyone tells you.' Last September he bought a 1930s building in a village called Alexandrovo, seven miles inland from Sunny Beach for £24,000. He was flying over to find builders for renovations.

'I'm expecting lots of ups and downs, not a smooth ride by any means. But this is a sunny place. A nice part of the world. It should work out fine from an accounting point of view: it's sound. I'll keep it for ten to fifteen years. It's like a pension plan. I've been quite lucky to be honest. There's nothing absolutely awful that I've found yet. In some places you can push your fist through the plaster, but that's about it. You can easily get duped out here. It's easy to make mistakes. But I had a licensed translator – translators are heavily regulated, so I trusted him. I bought it after two days of transactions.' He said he'd already spent £3,000 on a new roof and expected to spend £65,000 altogether on the three-bed house with a pool. He gave me the number of his agent.

Paul also told me that the Bulgarians are 'quite surly and rude, when you get into villages and that. You're lucky to get served in restaurants at all in some places. Or maybe that's just my experience. I've struggled to find good food. The salads and that are all right, but you get sick of the salads. The rest of the food is just a stodgy mess, though. So it's best to stick to the salads.'

Miglena Penova is not surly and rude. She works for the Sunny Beach office of a company called BH Real Estate. We meet in the lobby of Hotel Bulgaria which has a white-tiled floor, tropical plants in pots, retro seventies-style octagonal shapes decorating the walls, and lots of black leather sofas with men in dark suits smoking and talking in whispers.

Miglena seems far too nice to be an estate agent. She's twenty and she's been an estate agent for two years. She's dark-haired, petite and pretty, and a far cry from the hard-sell south London estate agents I've dealt with in the past. She's going to tell me all about the Bulgarian Black Coast Dream. Is it all it's made out to be? Who are the people buying all these places? And is it right for westerners – i.e., us – to use our economic advantage to make money out of a cash-strapped country struggling to join the western European way?

We walk to a place called Café Nataly's, around the corner from the hotel, with yet more men in suits smoking and talking quietly. 'Pump Up the Jam' is on the stereo. There are several American-style booths, a circular bar and a view through the window across a small park to the red neon lights of a place called Casino Club Vega. Maybe the 's' fell off.

We order coffees. Miglena takes a phone call. And then she apologises and explains that she's got to finish a deal in an hour, so she'll have to shoot off shortly. A couple from Birmingham are buying a place near Sunny Beach. 'We have many clients from Birmingham,' she says. This is partly because of charters from the Midlands. The couple are spending 50,000 euros. 'This is quite normal,' she says, lighting a Virginia Slims cigarette. One-bedroom apartments are 45,000 euros in most places, but double that in Sunny Beach, she says. 'People come for the sunshine and the good nightlife. It is quite amazing round here. In the winter there are just 500 locals living in Sunny Beach. Just 500! But in the summer there are 90,000 apartments full of people.'

What do people do in the winter? 'We go to work at the ski resorts, lots of people are buying places in the ski resorts,' she replies, sounding almost as though the entire population of the Black Sea Coast now consists of itinerant estate agents following British holidaymakers in the hope of selling a Bulgarian Dream. 'About ninety per cent of our business is British or Irish – others come from Russia, Norway, plus some from Finland and Italy. We sell about ten to fifteen places a week. Our record's twenty-one. Interest is very high.'

At ten to fifteen sales a week at an average of 50,000 euros a go, I calculate later, that works out at 26 million euros a year. Pretty good going, even by London estate agent standards.

Miglena blows some smoke and sips her coffee. The music changes to a rap song that has the refrain: 'Shake your keys, shake your house keys; everyone get down!' There's the sound of keys being shaken in the background. I point out the lyrics to Miglena, who hadn't been listening closely. 'Very appropriate!' she says. I ask her if local people feel resentful towards Brits coming over and buying all the best properties. 'No we do not feel that way. We are not jealous about the British,' she says. 'I wanted to live in Britain at one time. Now I don't mind. I don't think like that. The good thing about living round here is that things are not so dynamic: people have time for normal human relationships. It is not like living in a big city here, where everyone is in a big hurry. I went to university in Sofia. People think only of money there, not about life. The same is true in London.'

I'm wondering about all the men in dark suits smoking cigarettes. What about the mafia? I ask. 'Sure there is this thing,' says Miglena, 'but it is not so frightening. Normal people can walk around. There is no instant victim, I suppose. Yes, there are a lot of big guys around. But they are just bodyguards.'

She says all this so nicely that it sounds like it's just a small matter, all these mafia goings on – the fact that people need bodyguards to be safe in this European country. But a columnist in *The Sofia Echo*, the main English-language paper in Bulgaria, a copy of which I found in my room, doesn't think so. Commenting on the job that the country's Prosecutor General has 'tackling small crime, lifting immunity of politicians and locking up the mafia bosses,' he said: 'Of course I wish this man all the success in the world . . . I wish him even more of the personal protection of Jehovah, Allah, Buddha and Krishna.' The underlying message being: good luck my friend, you're going to need it.

There are two main streets, both pedestrianised, in Bourgas. One that runs east from the small square at the base of Hotel Bulgaria towards the seafront, and one that runs north–south. I pass through the small, well-tended park, which connects the two streets and has small rock gardens with herbs, some unusual abstract sculptures and a small rusting sign that says: *Beautiful Bulgaria Project: Executed with the support of the United Nations Development Programme*. The Hotel Bulgaria, built in 1976, sticks out. One side of the tower is covered with large garish adverts for ice creams, banks and petrol stations. It's in the middle of the city's nicest neighbourhood, which has lots of small streets lined with distinguished old buildings.

I walk up the north–south street along rows of sycamores, cafés and lots of fashion shops. As seems to be the case in all these Eastern European countries, everyone is much more healthy, vibrant, and just plain better looking than back home. 'Perfect' couples walk past – guys looking like weightlifters (muscles bulging under T-shirts), women in midriff-exposing tops who look like they could probably make it round a marathon should they ever want to . . . just they're having too much fun in life to bother with all that training. People are smiley and enjoying the sunshine.

There's a definite smart sports-casual look: trainers, jeans, Nike T-shirts, aerobics outfits. The couples look like they've modelled themselves on Posh and Becks on a casual day out. Jeans are ripped just-so to go with the latest trainers. Most people have oversized, insect eye-style sunglasses. And almost everyone seems fit. Ridiculously fit, like they all could be proper sports people – no pimply weeds with bad posture, or fatties stuffing Twix bars as they shuffle along. Just elegant, bronzed Black Sea Bulgarians.

Almost every fashion shop I see is a sports-fashion shop. Beside them are cafés where people sit looking thoughtful or gently discussing some matter of the day in their sports-fashion wear – taking a pause and not rushing about like thoughtless, money-obsessed people from 'dynamic' cities like London and Sofia.

But in between all these sports-fashion shops and cafés, it's hard to ignore another type of shop – one that looks a bit out of place: the Bulgarian Black Sea Dream estate agent. Lots of them. And almost all are pitched at the British market: British Developments Real Estate, Bulgarian Coastal Properties, Garian Property: Bulgarian Property Without the BUL, British Investments Real Estate. I take a look in the window of the latter. At first glance it appears there are amazing bargains: places for 8,000 euros in villages, some for 20,000 euros quite near the beach. But then you look at the pictures closely, and realise a lot of these places need *just a little bit* of work (like new roofs, new walls, new just about everything).

Two British women, in their late sixties I'd guess, join me at the window as I'm reading the ads. I get talking to them. Are they after anything in particular?

'I've already got a place,' says one with curly hair, a tan jacket, three-quarter length trousers and trainers. 'We're looking for one for my friend here. But I'm not sure about these. Oh, no. Not at all sure.' Why? I ask. 'Well, it's quite near a Gypsy village, you know.'

Her friend seems frightened by the prospect. 'I wouldn't want one near a Gypsy village,' she whispers.

The woman with curly hair starts telling me about her Bulgarian home. 'You've got to have run-off for your pool,' she says, clearly considering this a key matter. 'That's a common mistake, not getting run-off for your pool. If there's no run-off, how are you going to clean it twice a year, like it needs to be?' she says. 'There are twenty-five of us in our village. About twenty-five Brits. We've all come in the past two and a half years.'

I tell them I'm a journalist. 'What you ought to put,' she says, pointing at my notebook, 'is that the visas are a right hassle here. That's what you ought to put. Oh, the paperwork! The bureaucracy! Oh, it is dreadful!'

Then she says rather loudly: 'There are a lot of Gypsies in Bulgaria.' She stares at my notebook again. Her friend nervously says, 'You don't want to go into that.' The curly haired woman pauses for a moment, before switching track and telling me why she chose to move to Bulgaria. 'Well, I was pensioned off and I was looking at Spain, but Bulgaria was much cheaper.' Why didn't you want to stay at home? She is from South Wales. 'God, why did I want to move?' she asks rhetorically. 'Because it's all gone to pot, that's why. I listen to the news, Sky and what have you. And let me tell you, because I will tell you. I am a racist. I'll admit that. For a start look at the immigration figures and all of that. I saw a story the other day. A fifteen-year-old child set fire to her best friend. Can you believe that? Out here there is very little violence, no drugs and none of that religious hassle.

'I was a teacher for thirty years,' she continues. 'Parents would come from other countries and I would have to say to them: "Listen you do what we say, you're in our country." The problem with Britain is people can't say these things. Great Britain is too politically correct. People are afraid to speak out. I'm not. I'm just saying what everybody wants to say.' She peers into the estate agent's window. 'Kilroy-Silk had the right idea about a lot of things,' she says determinedly. 'There's a pecking order here, and everyone abides by it. They know their place. First come the Bulgarians, then the Turks, and then the Gypsies.' There are 7.9 million people in Bulgaria of which thirteen per cent are Muslim, many of Turkish background, along with 500,000 Gypsies.

'It's like a caste system,' says her friend.

I suspect they could have gone on in this vein for some time – and that they probably do every evening over gin and tonics back in their Gypsy-less village. They totter away, passing a McDonald's. A Gypsy boy, he must be about nine, dressed in a ragged red top scuttles after them and asks for some spare change. He'll never make that mistake again. The curly haired woman bends down to look him squarely in the face, and the boy momentarily thinks a kind, old lady is about to ruffle his hair and hand him a few lev, the local currency. Instead, having him got him almost face-to-face, she bellows, 'GO AWAY!' The poor kid looks absolutely terrified, leaping back and scampering to his friend, who's standing on the corner by McDonald's clearly glad he kept away from the two of them.

At Hotel Bulgaria, I ask to see the manager. 'My colleague can support you to his office,' says the receptionist. A large man with an anvil-like head wearing a black uniform takes me in the lift to a floor marked 'private'. And soon I'm shaking the hand of another large man with a US marine hair-cut, dark brown eyes and Billy Bunter grin. This is Georgi Mitzov, Hotel Bulgaria's manager. Behind him on a wall is a row of bottles including Johnnie Walker Red Label and Jack Daniels. Next to his desk, beneath several religious icons, there is a shiny silver samurai sword.

Georgi asks what would I like to drink – coffee, juice, or something a little extra? I go for some juice. 'So you are a writer, eh? And you are our first guest to come on Wizz Air! I say: Bravo!

Bravo to our first guest on Wizz Air!' says Georgi, who's the type of chap you can't help but like. What do I think of Bourgas, he asks. I say it's very nice, not mentioning my encounter with the Brits. And it *is* a nice place: peaceful tree-lined streets full of cafés, pleasant people (Brits excluded), and a pretty park on a cliff overlooking a pier onto the Black Sea. The beach may be a bit dirty and not used for bathing by locals – who prefer to use better sands at nearby resorts – but Bourgas feels full of life. And for the first time on these weekends, it is *warm*. It's not quite shorts weather, but it's early May, the sun is out, and the place has a laid-back feel. It's all very relaxing.

Who owns the Hummer outside the hotel? I couldn't help but notice the enormous car parked right by the entrance. 'Oh, that is ours,' Georgi says, suddenly sounding weary. 'It is a stupid car. Very stupid!' Why? 'What can I do with this car? The streets are too small for this car. Everyone looks at me.' Why don't you get rid of it? 'Well, the owners [of the hotel], they provide it, for the VIP guests. We use it as a limo to bring them from the airport.'

At this point Georgi's assistant, Kiril, joins us. Kiril has better English and Georgi disappears to speed up the orange juice while Kiril tells me about the local economy. 'Bourgas is one of the biggest industrial centres in Bulgaria,' he says. It's the second biggest in economic importance after Sofia, although the fourth biggest in terms of population. 'The port here is very important, we also have Lukoil, which runs the oil refinery. We have factories for the electricity. We have factories for the electricity cables. We make wagons for the railways.' Bourgas is, he says, 'quite an industrial type of place really, we don't have many tourists, but those who come here love it, really they do.'

Georgi returns with the orange juice. 'Bourgas is an important city. Many people stay here. We have had Hristo Stoichkov – in 1994 he won the Golden Boot. He played for Barcelona. Now he runs our national team. But we did not qualify for the World Cup. Not good!'

'We also have had Georgi Parvanov!' he adds, looking pleased. He writes this name in my notebook. 'He is president of Bulgaria!'

Parvanov is also a member of the Bulgarian Socialist Party. Politics in Bulgaria have been muddled, to say the least, post-1989. After the collapse of communism, you might have expected the communists to be booted out, as happened just about everywhere else. It didn't quite work that way here. The Bulgarian Communist Party changed its name to the Bulgarian Socialist Party, and many of the old guard remained influential. Disorganisation among pro-democracy parties meant that the socialists stayed in power for much of the 1990s. During this time, there were strikes and much uncertainty about the country's democratic future. The result was that Bulgaria was not included with the likes of Poland, Hungary, Slovakia and the Czech Republic in the countries granted EU membership in 2004.

The former king of Bulgaria, King (or Tsar) Simeon II, was exiled to Madrid aged nine after pressure from the communists. In a bit of a political curveball, he came back as prime minister from 2001–05. This bizarre period of rule by Tsar saw market reforms and a fall in an unemployment rate that had peaked at around twenty per cent. This was when the EU set the wheels in motion to let Bulgaria into the fold. But then the socialists triumphed again in the elections of 2005. And there remains confusion over exactly what direction the country will take. EU officials have expressed particular concern about high-level corruption and organised crime. Klaus Jansen, a high-ranking German police official asked to investigate organised crime in the country in the run-up to EU membership, recently told the BBC, 'The problem was that children in kindergarten know who the big kingpins were in the organised crime area, but the office of combating organised crime did not.'

Which suggests there's a fair way to go yet.

I mention the Tsar, who seems a bit of a mystery figure to me.

Has Simeon II ever stayed in this hotel, I joke. 'Oh, yes,' says Georgi, surprising me. And then he pulls out a photo album which shows him shaking hands with Simeon II and kissing the Tsarina's hand. 'A very nice lady, very nice,' he says fondly.

'One moment!' Georgi suddenly announces, disappearing into another room. 'Here for you,' he says, presenting me with a box. Inside is a bottle of Black Sea Gold thirty-three-year-old brandy. 'They use a special kind of grape, in an oak cask, for thirty-three years,' he says, explaining that it is produced just north of Bourgas in a town called Pomorie.

I thank Georgi. 'It is nothing!' As I leave, clutching my bottle, Georgi repeats: 'From the Wizz Air – our first! Bravo!' He's in an expansive mood. Trying to catch him at his jolliest, I ask: 'What's with the samurai sword? Just for decoration?'

'Well,' he says, suddenly thoughtful. 'What can I say?' He pauses for a moment or two. 'Let's just say, it is "to be good friends."' Then he roars and chuckles to himself. Like the Hummer by the hotel entrance, it seems it helps to make a statement round these parts.

Miglena, the world's sweetest estate agent, takes me for another coffee. She's in no hurry this time. She lights a Virginia Slim. 'Many people are smoking in Bulgaria,' she says. 'We are poor people. But everyone can afford to smoke.' This is despite the government recently more than doubling prices with new taxes; up from 34 pence a pack to 90 pence, she tells me. How much do people earn here? 'If you work for the government you might get 150 lev (£52) a month. The average wage is about 300 lev (£104). A waitress might get 250 lev (£87),' says Miglena, rattling off figures as espressos and two small bottles of mineral water arrive. 'But then again this order is four lev (£1.39). It is difficult to spend ten lev (£3.49) in a day. Really, it is.'

Later, I look up Bulgaria's average per capita earnings. It is £4,329. This makes Bulgaria the poorest country on my travels by a wide margin. The next worse off is Croatia with average per capita earnings of £5,913, just ahead of Poland on £6,335. It contrasts quite sharply with people like Danny and Amy throwing £45,000 at an apartment on Sunny Beach, and not really worrying too much if it all goes wrong. That's eleven years' work for the average person out here.

Miglena says she tries not to think about these things too much. 'Look, our standard of life is actually fine. I don't know if you've noticed, but most people walking down this street are very well dressed. They can afford to go out and go for coffees.' But she can envisage a time when lots of young people like her go to countries like Britain to work; at the time of my visit Bulgaria has not yet joined the EU. Both her older brothers already work in Germany, while her boyfriend recently lived in Britain for two years: 'He worked for a delivery company, delivering things on bikes. He only went for nights out twice in the whole time he was there. He was trying to save money, you see.' She says that she's been to the UK twice on work trips – at real estate shows – and was amazed by the number of foreign people she saw. 'I'd say ninety per cent of the people working in Oxford Street were not English. That is what it seemed like to me. In both the hotels I stayed at there were foreign people working there. It was incredible.'

We go for a walk. In the main square, by a large cleared area where a shopping mall is planned, there is a statue of a soldier with his fist in the air. 'It is a Russian soldier,' says Miglena. I express surprise. Surely the Bulgarians would want few reminders of the period of Soviet influence that has held the country back so much. 'No, it's not like that,' she says. She explains that Bulgaria was ruled by the Turks for five hundred years, as part of the Ottoman Empire, from the late fourteenth century until 1878. In that year, Miglena continues: 'The Russians came and helped us to freedom. This statue was made to say thanks to the Russians. Five hundred years is a long time. I think that it is hard for people from other countries to imagine it – what this five hundred years means to Bulgaria.' This gratitude goes some way to explaining why Bulgaria was one of the most Soviet-compliant of the Eastern European countries following the Second World War, she says. The joke used to go that it was the sixteenth republic of the USSR. It might also explain why socialists are still such a force in politics today.

Miglena has a theory: 'Being under another country's influence [first the Ottoman Empire, then the Soviets] for so long had an effect on us. It affected the way we think – the way Bulgarian people see themselves. Not many Bulgarian people like to be ambitious, to take on responsibility. This is missing in our way of thinking – the creativity. Maybe that is why we are not so wealthy now. If you go almost anywhere else, in Britain for example, you see so many different types of services. But in Bulgaria almost nothing is developed yet. We don't have competitiveness. It doesn't really matter what we do – that is the attitude. No competitiveness.'

We, or rather I, drive to Sunny Beach. 'I am a terrible driver, terrible!' says Miglena. 'I am really bad with things like that. I can't ride a bike. I can't even swim! I am being truthful! I seriously cannot swim. I have tried. Believe me I have tried! But I just can not swim! Impossible!'

Miglena is taking me around one of the hundreds of new construction sites in Bulgaria. This one is the Santa Marina development; a series of four-storey apartment blocks on a hill overlooking the sea. Workers are listening to Madonna. No one wears hard hats. 'Not necessary here,' says Miglena, who adds that workers can expect to earn about £10–£15 a day. A man with an enormous belly and a baseball cap lets us through a mesh gate. Some of the apartments are almost ready. They look good, finished in granite and pine, not the usual unimaginative concrete blocks.

The workers, who are mainly Gypsies according to Miglena,

are rushing about. We walk up a gangplank to take a look inside an apartment. Wires hang out of walls where fittings will be. Dust covers everything. The rooms look small. There is about 70 square metres of floor space, says Miglena, with each square metre going for about £545. This works out at £38,150. There are 160 apartments in total, and the property company promises to provide investors with a seven per cent annual return. This is a 'realistic' return, says Miglena, who doesn't trust places that claim to offer twenty to forty per cent annually. 'Nice view, eh?' she says, looking out to sea. Santa Marina will have a pool, a bar, a restaurant, and a hairdresser, I'm told.

'I always recommend a complex,' says Miglena. 'Because then you have a reception and things like restaurants and pools. There are common territories. You can meet people. The pool is maintained. If it is not a complex, you have nothing. I always recommend a complex.'

I don't buy a place, but Miglena doesn't seem to mind. We part, and I take a walk around Sunny Beach, which might as well be Benidorm. There's the Non-stop Casino, the Go Go Girls Bar, Danceclub Mania, several places selling full English breakfasts and pints of Stella, the James Joyce Bar offering 'Irish Beer, Irish Cuisine, Digital TV and much more', newspaper vendors with *The Sun*, crazy golf and, tattoo parlours.

Outside Elaine's Karaoke, which has a poster that says 'Be a star, babe!', there's a picture of a blonde woman drinking a pint of beer. It offers Thirty Reasons Why A Beer Is Better Than A Woman. The list begins: You can have more than one beer a night and not feel guilty . . . beer doesn't care if you fall asleep after you have it . . . when you say you love beer, you really mean it.' Next to it is a chalkboard advertising a cabaret and, I can hardly believe this, a Children's Drinking Contest. I can just imagine Daddy talking to little Johnny: 'Go on, son! Get it down you! 2.2 seconds for that pint of squash! That's my boy!'

It's all a bit depressing. No way would I want to buy a place here. It's just the Costa del Sol Mark II. Sure, it might be fun for a blow-out Blackpool Beach type break – but who would want a second home here?

Bulgaria has for years been a byword for dodgy wine. I mention this to Georgi, the samurai sword-wielding hotel manager, who is determined to set me straight. He introduces me to his friend Panayot Nikolov, of the Festa Wine Company, which produces Black Sea Gold wines. He's a dynamic twenty-something wearing a flashy pinstripe suit with a pink shirt. He looks a bit like Alexei Sayle.

'We will show you the cellar and the winery!' exclaims Panayot, leading me to a black Mercedes with tinted windows and black leather seats. We get in the back and the driver races away. 'It is an honour to have you. I looked you up on the Internet – you are a very famous person.'

Amazing what a few cuttings on the Internet can do, I'm thinking, as we overtake everything in sight, at breathtaking speed. Panayot fills me in about Bulgarian wine. 'Extreme price–quality ratio. This, I tell you, is the key,' he begins. Bulgarian wine, he explains, was first exported in the late 1970s. Doesn't 'extreme price–quality ratio' just mean 'cheap'? I ask.

Panayot gives me a sideways look. 'It is *not* cheap, it just has an *extreme price–quality ratio*. This is very important.'

Most exports of Black Sea Gold to the UK are to Northern Ireland. 'They like our wine in Northern Ireland, oh yes! But the English market is difficult to crack.' There are too many New World wines, says Panayot. 'We have improved the quality. We want to sell more to the Indian and Chinese markets. This is very big.'

In the 1990s vineyards were privatised, old out-of-date production methods were dropped, and now people like Panayot who work for Black Sea Gold are immensely (and, I soon discover, rightly) proud of their winery. I'm shown around.

The casks are made from Californian oak. 'These barrels take 7,000 litres. They are very huge,' says Panayot, showing me round the cellars. On a wall there is a black and white picture of the first wine men from Pomorie, the local town. They're all smoking cigarettes, grinning inanely and looking slightly mad. 'Yes, I guess they were a funny lot,' Panayot concedes.

As we taste the wine, Panayot starts to wax lyrical about the various vintages. The sauvignon blanc is a 'pale straw colour with the aroma of freshly cut grass and ripe fig'. The chardonnay has 'a vanilla nuance from the oak with an apple fruitiness'. It is like 'a sultry summer afternoon'. I laugh a bit at this one. 'My dictionary surprises you?' asks Panayot.

We try a dry red wine: 'This I call the tannic attack!' It's certainly got a kick. We try another red: 'It is strong. It is concentrated. Yet it hasn't lost its vigour. And it has smoother qualities.' We've had a bit by now. We move on to football, and Panayot takes exception when I describe Stoichkov as 'a very good player'.

'He is a genius, I tell you. A genius!'

Panayot gets philosophical. 'Wine is like a man. If you let a man have everything without trial and effort, he gets lazy and achieves nothing in life.' I'm getting quite hazy now but I think this comment has something to do with the soil and the wind conditions round here, which make wine production tricky.

We try something called Rakia Burgas 63. Rakia is the Bulgarian firewater – and apparently this is the 'gold standard, the ultimate rakia experience!' It's like grappa, with a kick that just makes me think: very bad hangover. We go to see a bottling facility and some vats, plus some brandy, which we try.

'Concentrated sunshine!' exclaims Panayot. 'You are going to be perfumed for the whole evening, be sure of that.' I'm not entirely sure what he means by this, but I nod and raise my glass, and we talk some more about extreme price–quality ratio.

Eventually it's time to leave, and our driver takes us back to

Bourgas in the tinted-window black Mercedes. On the way we pass the enormous housing estates. I ask Panayot if there are any plans to build new housing? Panayot says there aren't. 'These are concrete slabs that are not very pleasing to the eye. But every major world city has this. I went to Osaka in Japan recently, it was very similar there.' A sound bleeps in the Merc – a police radar detector. 'This is a very good device to have here.' We slow down for a while, and then it's back up to top speed again. Bulgaria's Black Sea coast passes by in a silvery blue shimmer.

I'm tired after my Extreme Price–Quality Ratio drinking session, so I take a rest back at Hotel Bulgaria. But then I get a second wind. Miglena recommended Club Budoar when we were in Sunny Beach. 'Don't go before midnight, no one goes before midnight,' she said. 'There are lots of people wearing gold. You'll see,' she added mysteriously.

Club Budoar, is located amid the Soviet-era tower blocks at the airport side of town. There is a giant goon-like security man on the door. I pay 70 pence to the giant goon and enter a long room with dim lighting, extravagant red drapes hanging all over the place, pillars that have been covered in 'cave wall' plastic, gilded mirrors, bars on raised platforms, lots of alcoves and booths, disco music – and some of the most glamorous people in the Balkans. Women with long dark hair (there aren't, for some reason, many blondes) in midriff-exposing tops are with large swarthy men in designer shirts. Many are sitting in American diner-style booths. Occasionally the women, but not the men, stand up and start dancing spontaneously while their friends look on. It's as though they're putting on a private show. The dancefloor is packed. Miglena is right: people are wearing lots of gold jewellery. It's a bustling hive of pretty (and quite posey) people.

I feel conspicuous coming here on my own. But, I figure, a beer will make things better. At the bar, several stools are free. I sit on one and sip my beer. After a couple of minutes, a security man, not the one on the door, comes up and taps me on the shoulder. I can't sit where I'm sitting, for some reason. I go and sit somewhere else. Another goon appears. I can't sit there either.

Sick of being gooned, I go to another club called Galaxy. Within a minute of arriving, a Chief Goon has sidled up to me and pointed at my notebook. He looks like he could be a member of the Bulgarian weightlifting squad. He interrogates me about why I have a notebook, and keeps looking at it as though he's never seen such a strange thing in his life. He gathers that I'm a reporter and everything changes: he tells me his wife sells property and asks if I could I write about her. He gives me his wife's number and he and I are soon good pals.

Bourgas is full of Brits with cheque books and 'property boom' glints in their eyes. They're on the plane, they're queuing outside estate agents, they're buying drinks in 'English' pubs, they're everywhere. Maybe I'm just not getting it, but as I think about it over the weekend, the concept of buying a place abroad has seemed stranger and stranger. I don't see any good reason to limit your travels to one place when there's a whole world out there. Do you really want to spend all your summers for the rest of your life in Bulgaria? Why not save your cash for a series of holidays in wonderful hotels around the globe? Sure, pop by Bulgaria for a break, but don't feel like you've got to settle down here.

There's also – it's impossible to ignore – a darker side. We are buying places and seeing values rise, knowing full well that this process is making it almost impossible for locals to get on the property ladder. Miglena told me that she and her boyfriend were struggling to afford a home of their own. And as we go about flaunting our economic advantages we moan about complications to do with building work and bureaucracy, and live in fear of being ripped off. Locals are treated with suspicion; they are people with whom you've got to be careful. If not, they'll catch you out – as Paul suggested on the plane.

Many of us don't even seem to like the countries to which we flock. We just want to be somewhere *warm*. The woman with the curly hair and the 'I am a racist' views epitomised a (usually hidden) strain of this type of property investor. She seemed in search of an 'ideal' antiseptic existence – away from real life, away from reckless teenagers in South Wales and horrible Bulgarian Gypsies.

I suppose that with her gin and tonic on her balcony, she's achieved her Bulgarian Black Coast Dream. It is warm and it is cheap. But she didn't seem particularly happy to me.

Yet I *can* understand some people's impulse to buy a nice place overseas to retreat to every now and then. And, the worst of the property people aside, Bourgas has a lot going for it. There are some beautiful beaches, with wonderful sands on a par with those in the Caribbean and the Indian Ocean (if you ignore the drinking contests, Irish bars and fake Rolex shops, that is) – all just a short low-cost flight away.

LJUBLJANA, SLOVENIA

HOT HORSE, HOT COUNTRY

I've been in Ljubljana for half an hour and somehow – I'm not quite sure how – I've found myself in a dark, musty, windowless room decorated with umbrellas covered in Christmas tree lights.

This is not a look I've seen anywhere else before.

'Dark industrial' music – as I'm later told it's called – is playing at eardrum-damaging volume. 'I don't give a ****, you don't give a ****, we don't give a ****' screams the lead singer, who sounds in total agony, as though he's been struck by lightning and is in the throes of excruciating aftershocks of pain. It's just about the worst music I've ever heard, lacking any redeeming qualities whatsoever. It shifts to the chorus: '****, ****, ****, ****.' Pause. '****, ****, ****, ****.'

Bottles of booze and roll-up cigarette butts are strewn across the floor. Old car seats are randomly cast about the room, which feels like a converted garage; converted from garage into I'm not sure what. Graffiti-covered oil drums are scattered around, on which small marijuana plants are growing out of white plastic cups. Slouched on the car seats there are three human forms.

Each of these forms is nodding to the music as though lost in a trance. And each seems somewhat alarmed when I tentatively cross to where they're slumped in their car seats with their cans of lager and little white plastic cups of red wine. Above the music, I try to say something along the lines of, 'Hello, I'm a reporter from England. Nice to meet you. My name is Tom.' I feel like some kind of nineteenth-century explorer meeting potentially dangerous natives in the Congo.

My presence appears to have upset them. They suddenly seem gripped by paranoia. They start holding up framed pictures of groups of people who look like them sitting about drinking and smoking, just like they are now. They've got a pile of these on a spare chair. It's almost as though they're pointing religious crosses at an evil spirit, like they do in films. What the hell is going on here? But eventually they begin to get the gist of who I am and what I'm doing. One of them, Panc – seemingly the leader – goes to some DJ-style turntables in a corner, and turns down the music.

'Don't ask so many questions, man,' complains Panc, when he returns. The questions have so far consisted of: 'My name's Tom, what are your names? May I ask you some questions?' All drowned out by the lovely music. We stare at each other for a minute or two, and just as I'm about to give up and leave, Panc pours me a cup of wine, as though he's a university professor offering a drop of something decent to his favourite under-graduate. He asks me to sit down, gesturing to one of the car seats.

This is Panc's thirtieth birthday party. It began three days ago on Thursday evening. It's now noon on Saturday. We're in a building that belongs to nobody, although Panc is the manager. This building is directly behind my digs for the weekend: a youth hostel recommended as 'funky and fun' by various guides, set in a former military prison and called Celica. I'm sharing a 'cell' in Celica with two individuals I've yet to meet; my one and only effort to slum it backpacker-style on my low-cost trips. My cell costs £15 a night on top of a £2.50 each-way flight on Wizz Air from Luton. With taxes and two nights at the hostel, the total cost of flights and accommodation is £77 – the cheapest yet.

And here I am meeting the neighbours. Next to Celica is a *Mad Max* world of buildings covered in graffiti and abstract art: models of aliens hanging from balconies and sculptures of sphinxs with messages like 'FADE TO BLACK', 'MAKE NOISE

NOT MUSIC' and 'BOOT BOYS OI!' Where there is no graffiti, there are fly posters advertising the Anti-Nowhere League, a Vampire Goth Night with DJ Moonchild and VJ Bat, and Rawside: class war punk. Final approach! While reading these and perusing a large picture of a psycho teddy bear with cute red heart-shaped eyes, holding a knife dripping blood, I was accosted by a dreadlocked man called Miha.

Miha was the only person in sight, although there was loud music coming from behind one of the graffiti-covered buildings. It hadn't said anything about all of this in my guidebook, so I asked Miha what was going on.

'This is like total freedom, man,' he'd said, keen to talk. 'That's why I like it here.' I asked him what went on in these parts – what is this place? 'It's like a nowhere land,' he replied. 'No one owns any of this. People used to squat in those buildings, but the security forces threw them out, man. Punks and punkers. Lots of them, man. They weren't causing any trouble. But the city didn't want them. They did not pay electricity or water. They were like rats to the city. So they got them out.'

Now, he continued, the buildings were used for parties. Do people take drugs like marijuana, I asked, having a fair guess at the answer – marijuana-leaf graffiti is all over the walls. 'What? Marijuana?' he'd replied. 'That is not a drug.' He'd paused, searching for the right words. 'Marijuana . . . it is better than tobacco. Not really a drug. Better than tobacco. I don't smoke it though,' he said. I was about to say, 'That's probably best. It can be very bad for you,' or something like that, when he continued:

'I eat it. I eat it with cookies and milk. I really like it here. It's, like, total freedom, man.'

I asked Miha about himself. He was twenty-seven and made parquet floors and roofs. Then he said, 'Go in there, man,' pointing to one of the buildings. 'They've been there since

Thursday. It's open still. It's the largest birthday party in history. Go! You will see.'

This is how I've come to be with Panc, an artist, Tomo, a programme manager, and Sasha, who works in her mother's office. We're sipping quite a nice cabernet sauvignon from our plastic cups and staring at one another. It's as if I'm in the study of some heavy metal professor, with a couple of other students. It's still difficult to understand a word anyone's saying because the 'music' is so loud. But I can make out a few snippets of Panc's earnest mutterings.

'This is the culture. This is the pure culture,' he says, waving an arm around the darkened room with its upturned umbrellas and its Christmas tree lights. 'Nobody pays you for this culture. Not this culture. No. It is not for money.'

Sasha, who seems to be Panc's girlfriend, says, 'If Panc was not here, nobody would be here.'

'Oh, thank you.' He says fondly, seeming pleased. He shows me the framed pictures they'd been holding up earlier. 'This is Satan,' he says almost proudly, pointing. 'He is my brother.' I look at the photo, which shows a mad-looking guy with a huge ginger afro, clasping a beer can.

I ask what it's like to live in Ljubljana. 'This is a tricky question. So many questions,' says Panc, ruffling his brow, and pulling a small bottle of Finlandia vodka from somewhere in his car seat. He seems perfectly sober despite his three-day binge.

'It's a small city. Small enough. Not a big city,' The population of Ljubljana, Slovenia's capital, is about 300,000 – the entire Slovenian population is two million. 'It's like a big village. Most people know each other.'

'It is much better than where I am from.' Tomo cuts in. 'I come from an artificial place. Constructed by Tito – on the border with Italy.' He writes down the name: Nova Gorica. 'It is like a Las Vegas now. There is a big casino. The biggest company in town is a casino. Here in Ljubljana, there is culture,' he says. And we pause for a minute to soak in the culture. The lyrics are now screaming: '**** the system . . . **** the system.'

'We don't like hip hop. We like good music.' So you prefer this heavy metal music? 'No, no. It is not *heavy metal*, it is *dark industrial*,' corrects Tomo. Sasha nods her bleached-blonde bird's nest energetically.

'In the old days, there used to be respect for Yugoslavia around the world.' Panc says. 'People would see a Yugoslav passport and nod you through. Then came the trouble. But now we are in the EU. We have standards. Things are more materialistic.' I ask if he likes this. 'Of course I don't. I'm a socialist,' he says.

And Sasha, sounding a bit offended (whether by me or Panc I'm not sure), says, 'But it is better than before.' And then Panc turns up the music again – it's come to a 'good' bit. They start nodding, dark industrial-style. I look at them for a while, sipping my cabernet sauvignon every now and then. It's all quite surreal. A few hours ago I was having a coffee at Pret a Manger at Luton Airport. Now I'm at a dark industrial party drinking red wine. They appear as though they'd be happier nodding alone. So I get up to say goodbye. We shake hands like we've just had a business meeting and I step out into the startling sunshine – leaving them in the dark industrial gloom of their umbrella light.

Well, well, well – welcome to Ljubljana. Whatever next? I certainly hadn't been expecting a dark industrial scene in Slovenia's capital. Ljubljana is almost always referred to as lovely Ljubljana in the tourist brochures. It is pitched as a pretty student town, with romantic cafés and elegant old buildings and churches along a small twisting river. *Lonely Planet*'s description is: 'A little Prague without the crowds (or the hype) or a more intimate Budapest.' After visiting some of the *really* lesser known places, I've been looking forward to Ljubljana as a kind of treat – a place I'd expected to be full of young couples in love and arty types hanging out in all those cafés; not quite like Panc and his pals.

Though the name may look like a terrible typo, Ljubljana (pronounced *lub-ly-ana*) is the biggest, as in the most famous, of the places I've been to so far: the first capital city – and the capital of perhaps the most thriving of all the new entry EU countries. On the Internet, *The Slovenia Times*, a local English-language newspaper, quotes Slovenia's prime minister, Janez Jansa, describing Slovenia as 'the undisputed front-runner among new member states'. The editorial continued:

When, in 2004, Slovenia joined the EU, people saw it as a realisation of a goal that had dated back to the early nineties. Slovenia was the best-prepared candidate country and the gap between Slovenia and the other nine new-comers is still evident today. On 1 January 2007 it will become the first of the newcomers to introduce the euro, a year later it will also be the first of them to preside over the EU.

In other words, it's doing rather well – and it's not afraid of saying so.

The UK papers wax lyrical about Ljubljana – for once there was actually the odd newspaper cutting. People had (annoyingly) been here before me, and not just *Coach* and *Yacht Monthlies*. The *Observer* described it as 'a little gem of a city . . . the perfect city break'. *The Times* opted for 'it's a Balkan gem [travel sections love their "gems"]'. The *Sunday Telegraph* reporter described it simply as 'the most engaging small city I've visited'. *Time Out* said it has 'all the fairytale charm of other Eastern European favourites, minus the stag parties . . . the perfect city break.' Even *Rough Guide* and *Lonely Planet* were on my side – which was a first on my travels so far. It was like hitting the weekend-break jackpot.

So this is how I find myself in the Celica hostel, next door to the Dark Industrialists. I'm sitting in a bright airy conservatory with Massive Attack playing on the stereo and a lesbian couple on the table behind me holding hands and discussing the Arab–Israeli conflict. They're English – I saw them on the plane earlier.

They start picking a day trip for tomorrow. It's either going to be 'the caves' or a place called 'Lake Bled'.

Nearby a tall, scraggly elderly fellow dressed in an LA Lakers outfit is making a commotion about filling up a huge water bottle. His possessions are in a funny-looking granny shopper's trolley. He looks like a tramp, not a traveller, though there is often, I suppose, a fine line. Another American with a guitar in a black plastic cover is by the reception asking loudly about trains to Sofia. 'Ya'll know the train times? No? You just go there? To the station? Gee, okay.'

Further along, a group of guys, whose voices I can't quite make out, are trying to encourage a mate who has a third of a beer left. He looks like he'd fall asleep for a few hours if they'd let him put his head down on the table. Close to the lesbians, a Scandinavian chap with a *Lonely Planet: Europe on a Shoestring* on the table is desperately persuading two young women to go clubbing with him tonight.

As a non-backpacker, I'm looking forward to observing these backpackers this weekend. I secretly hope they'll start behaving atrociously later on. It could be so much fun.

It's time to explore. Leaving the hostel and the graffiti zone behind, I head down a small street, passing a basketball court and a park with chestnut trees in bloom. I find myself on a cute passageway full of funky cafés, avant-garde art galleries and fashion shops selling trendy trainers and combat trousers. Posey people are walking by with posey little dogs. Bike bells ring as cyclists peddle past. Youngsters are hanging out smoking cigarettes at cafés, looking thoughtful and occasionally animated (I've read that Ljubljana has 56,000 students). On-line skaters whiz along. Well-to-do couples walk past on their way to a row of smart restaurants by the Ljubljanica river. The sun is shining. There are no Dark Industrialists. This is more like it! I follow the street down to a lovely art nouveau bridge across the small green river. At each end of the bridge, there are two fearsome copper dragons, looking like creatures out of a horror film – almost comically OTT. On the other side, I pass through a fruit and veg market where elderly women with ruddy faces are selling grapes, tomatoes, oranges, strawberries, pineapples, onions, potatoes, cabbages, sweet peppers and asparagus from baskets, as though this Ljubljana is some kind of land of plenty. There are elegant churches and freshly painted pink, yellow and cream gothic and art nouveau buildings all around.

The feeling hits me immediately – the way this kind of feeling does: this is definitely the prettiest of the cities yet. Poor old Szczecin and its Solidarity docks struggles a bit against this one.

I'm hungry. From a distance, I'd seen a decent-looking burger bar over the Dragon Bridge, so I head back that way. But, as I soon find out, it's not your average burger bar. I guess the name – Hot Horse – should have given that away.

Hot Horse, which has a chain of three shops in Ljubljana, serves horse burgers. I'd read in one of the guidebooks that people ate horse in these parts, but I hadn't realised quite how openly. Two groups of local guys are sitting outside at Hot Horse tables under a yellow Hot Horse awning, munching large horse burgers. They look extremely contented. I go inside to order.

An elderly man with a yellow apron and a yellow baseball cap, asks me in Slovenian what I'd like. I say 'horse burger' in English. 'Excellent!' he says, as though I've chosen wisely (though it's just about all Hot Horse serves). 'Toppings?' he asks, pointing at a selection. 'Everything,' I reply. 'Excellent!' he repeats, most pleased with me – and giving me a look that suggests: 'Now here is a man who knows how to enjoy a good horse burger!' He piles on the toppings: onions, tomatoes, lettuce, ketchup, mustard, mayonnaise, jalapeños, hot sauce and gherkins. He wraps this in a silver wrapper. With a bottle of water, this comes to £2.57. I ask him if it really is horse as he hands over the package. He looks upset that I might question the quality of his horse. 'Yes, really.' He confirms. Then I go outside to sit at one of the tables under the yellow awnings.

I pull open the silver wrapper. An enormous burger – just about the biggest I've ever seen – stares back at me. The bun is a good five inches across and it's about three inches high thanks to all those toppings. It's a monster. It's a Hot Horse monster. I open the top bun to take a peek inside. The burger bit of the burger is actually quite thin. It's chestnut coloured, not as grey-brown as your usual beef burger. I imagine a lovely chestnut filly leaping over fences at Kempton Park on a sunny Boxing Day. I almost always go to Kempton Park on Boxing Day – and almost always lose when a chestnut filly, or some other beast, falls at the last. Here's to all you final hurdle flops! If only you could see me now! I chomp into the burger. Hot Horse sauces slop onto the tray as I munch away. It really is, I must admit, a very fine burger. The bun is soft, the toppings a fast food connoisseur's dream, the meat tender and tasty. Simply delightful.

Tourists walk by, some grimacing and staring. My fellow Hot Horse customers and I stare back defiantly, eating our burgers. For a few seconds it feels like we're sharing moments of almost blissful Hot Horse happiness. Who cares what the world thinks. We are horse eaters and we don't care who knows it. We finish the lot – disappointing a row of pigeons observing us from a nearby fence. That was very good indeed.

I highly recommend Hot Horse.

An unshaven man with tired-looking grey eyes peering out from under a black Fred Perry cap is at the hostel. This is my guide for my architectural tour – and he is, he says, going to explain why people should come to Ljubljana, not Prague, if they want to get the best Central European experience.

'Forget Prague! Why do people go to Prague?' he says daringly. But he doesn't want me to use his name. 'I am too political, it gets me in trouble,' he says. Instead I must make up a name. 'Try a common Slovenian name,' he suggests. Like what? 'How about Janez, Peter, Tone or Maks?' Okay, I'll call you Maks. 'Great,' he replies, delighted with this. Then he confides something: 'I am very hungover. Tired. Last night we went out. Oh, yes, we had a few. It was very jolly.'

And we head off into graffiti-land on the way to see the glories of Ljubljana.

Maks turns out to be an amusing, unconventional fellow. Just as he predicted, he turns to politics remarkably soon. 'The right-wingers want to knock this place down,' he tells me, pointing towards the garage area where Panc, Tomo and Sasha are probably still happily listening to dark industrial and polishing off the cabernet sauvignon. 'There has been a shift to the right in politics recently,' Maks explains. 'But these right-wingers make me laugh. These are the people who were quite passive in the late 1980s. They were the ones letting things go on as they were. It was the artists who were the anti-communists. It was these people who were pushing for changes. They were the activists.' In other words: exactly the type of people who hang out around graffiti-land, which Maks tells me is called Metelkova.

Apparently, since the 1970s, punk bands such as Pankrti (The Bastards) had been at the forefront of a movement called *Neve Slowenische Kunst*, New Slovene Art, which provided a counter-culture in favour of democracy during Yugoslav days. Many, but not all, people now in Metelkova were at the heart of that movement. 'Now these right-wingers present themselves as the liberators from communism, when in fact they were not so. And they call anyone who is left-wing, communist. Personally, I am from a family of non-communists going way back. But I am also left-wing.' He finds the way the right-wing has twisted politics extremely frustrating.

Sounds like he's got a point.

We pass some dire concrete housing blocks, next to some smart yuppy-ish flats, on our way to the main sights. 'There you see,' he says with a flourish. 'We have the rich, the working class and the middle class living side by side in Ljubljana. So we don't have what I call the vicious circle of the slums. It is not like the UK. We do not have our Sheffields or our East Londons. We don't have slums. This is a pretty balanced city really – just like this is a pretty balanced country. There are far fewer differences between life in the capital and life in the countryside in Slovenia than you get in parts of Eastern Europe like Bulgaria and Slovakia. We have, and I believe this is the right phrase, *polycentric development*. Yes, *polycentric*.'

It's impossible not to find Ljubljana's architecture stunning. Walking about on my Hot Horse sortie, I'd been struck by the buildings, which I could just about recognise as Art Nouveau or Gothic or perhaps Art Deco. But let's face it, I didn't really know what I was talking about.

Maks, though, knows his architecture back to front. We walk down a street called Miklosiceva. Maks explains that a big earthquake in 1895 meant that much of the centre of Ljubljana was rebuilt in the Art Nouveau style. He points out Art Nouveau buildings with decorative stucco swirls and fancy ironwork balconies. We pass an amazingly colourful pink building with red, white, yellow and blue patterns in traditional Slovenian style round the windows, built in 1922. Next come some Art Deco buildings with exteriors that look like 1930s cruise ships. Then there is the 'Renaissance Revival' Palace of Justice, which Maks finds too austere. Farther along is the Grand Hotel Union, a great white building with Art Nouveau influences: stucco strips of flowers, lion heads and spooky visages of Statue of Liberty-like women.

These two buildings – the Palace of Justice and the Grand Hotel Union – explain something of the politics of Slovenia in the run-up to the First World War, says Maks. The Grand Hotel represents Slovenia's desire to express its national identity, to show its individuality and its extravagant side, while the Palace of Justice shows how the Austro-Hungarian rulers wanted to stamp their sense of authority: 'They were the ruling political class, they wanted to give expression to the state through their buildings. So they did. The Slavics then were the underdogs.'

But many of the greatest buildings in Ljubljana came later, after the Austro-Hungarian influence ended. They were created by one man: Joze Plecnik, one of Slovenia's national heroes, depicted on the pink 500 tolar note.

Plecnik was born in Ljubljana in 1872, studied architecture in Graz, and moved to Prague where he worked on Prague Castle, before returning to Ljubljana to create several masterpieces as he attempted to make his name in the city. As Plecnik came from Slovenia, says Maks, many locals joke that Prague is the 'New Ljubljana' – turning round the usual 'new Prague' description of almost any city 'discovered' by tourists in Central or Eastern Europe. Which is quite a nice way of looking at it. The result of Plecnik's creative burst is an amazing array of buildings that Maks believes were 'way ahead of their time . . . post-modernism, before post-modernism existed.' While other architects were moving into modernism and functionalism (good old functionalism; very useful with cute women from Linz), Plecnik went back to classical buildings, putting his own spin on Greek and Roman designs.

Triple Bridge, at the end of Miklosiceva street, is a good example. 'You see here,' says Maks. 'Plecnik used a classical style, but in his very, very own way.' I look at the bridge, which has three parts: a central road with two pedestrian mini-bridges on each side. There are steps down to the riverbank on each of the mini-bridges, Art Nouveau-style lamps, bulbous concrete decorations – it's just a bridge, but there is so much going on and so many little touches that the overall effect is mesmerising. Maks says: 'You see the way the bridge opens up into the new city, moving away from the old. That is deliberate. He could have just created a much larger bridge, but then that might have looked like a big square over the river. So he did something different. That is his genius!' Maks points to a colonnaded area near the fruit and veg market I went to earlier – which gives the river front a quirkily classical look. 'All Plecnik!'

'I really don't like these names though,' says Maks, peering intently from under his Fred Perry cap. 'I mean there are so many expressions: modernism and post-modernism and all of this. I just like architecture full-stop. It affects things – the way we look at places – much more than we realise. . . if you really think about it.' I take a look around. I understand what you mean, I say, both to keep Maks happy and because Ljubljana is definitely a place where architecture is important. Because its architecture is positive and creative, with a touch of flamboyance, this seems to rub off on the people who live here. Arty people are rushing about in combat trousers and trendy sunglasses. There are lots of young people, and they all seem happy. There is, Maks says, hardly any emigration from Slovenia as people are enjoying life here.

Filled with new-found architectural zeal, I point at a building with a zig-zag pattern on it. 'Art Deco!' I say. Maks gazes at me through half-opened eyes, as though I'm a hopeless cause. 'That is just something someone painted on that building. A decoration. Probably from the 1980s,' he says. 'Oh,' I say.

We walk along the river and pass into the Old City, at the foot of a hill on top of which sits Ljubljana Castle, almost hidden amid trees, with a tower flying the red, white and green Slovenian flag. Several shops in the Old City look like they have recently closed, and I ask Maks why. He explains that, strangely enough, Ljubljana's shops were thriving under communism in the former Yugoslavia.

'Well, by 1991, when we gained independence, there were already many, many shops here. Even though there was communism, it was a normal city. We had a lot of freedom in the 1980s, much more than people realise,' says Maks. It was in 1991 that Slovenia declared independence from Yugoslavia, turning back the Serb-dominated Yugoslav army after a ten-day war. This also marked the end of communism and the beginning of rule by democratic, market-orientated parties. 'But since then we have seen big developments. Malls in the suburbs have taken shops away. People here are not making so much profit. But then again, there are *some* shops here, and the malls are very good.'

What does he think about what has happened in other parts of the Balkans since 1991? 'We were very very lucky. We had a short war. Others didn't,' says Maks, before examining my question in his mind and exclaiming: 'But we are not in the Balkans!' I thought you were, I say. 'Well, we were tied to Vienna for years. Do you consider us part of the Austrian region?' He glares at me from under his Fred Perry cap, his eyes still looking red from last night. 'We were taken by Germany in the Second World War. Germany stretched as far north as the Baltics. Are we part of the Baltics?' Another glare. 'I don't think so. What is the Balkans anyway?' I don't answer this. 'We are not the most developed country in the Balkans, as people like to say. We are the most developed country in the former Yugoslavia! That is the way to look at it!'

Okay, I get it: don't mention the Balkans. Later, I check exactly how much more developed Slovenia is than other parts of the former Yugoslavia. GDP per capita figures make stark reading: Slovenia £10,544, Croatia £6,025, Macedonia £3,819, Bosnia & Herzegovina £3,496, and Serbia and Montenegro £1,291 – which gives a pretty strong indication of how far advanced Slovenia is. To put things in perspective, as I wrote this, the GDP per capita for Portugal was £9,629, meaning Slovenia is now ahead of a country that hosted the 2004

European Championship in football and whose capital city was recently a European Capital of Culture.

My Celica cell is tiny. I'm sharing it with two 'cell-mates'. Their backpacks are on the floor, leaving me just enough room to stand and survey things. No sign of the backpack owners – well, you wouldn't want to hang around in here. Original prison bars have been left on the door and on the windows. There's enough room for two single mattresses on the floor in front of me. Above, a bunk provides the third berth. I'm left with one of the lower beds. A starchy sheet, a pillow cover, a duvet cover and a towel are piled on this – I feel like I've just arrived for a long stretch.

I make my bed, wondering whether I should just go and find somewhere a *little bit* better than this. A prison-like sign on the wall says: 'Respect other guests and treat them like you would like them to treat you.' I shut the inner cage door to leave. It rattles, echoing down the hall. The title sequence to *Porridge* flashes before me: 'Norman Stanley Fletcher [Thomas Doyle Chesshyre]. You have pleaded guilty to the charges brought by this court [that you're a complete cheapskate] and it is now my duty to pass sentence [and show you this room]. You are a habitual criminal [long-standing tight wad] who accepts arrest [poor digs] as an occupational hazard [all part of my travels] and presumably accepts imprisonment in the same casual manner [in an old Slovenian cell]. We therefore feel constrained to commit you to the maximum term allowed for these offences. You will go to prison for five years [two nights].' *Cer-chunk*.

Downstairs, people are smoking hookah pipes in a Moroccan-themed room with low level tables. They all look very young. Some of them have pink hair. I log on at one of the free Internet terminals. *Montenegrins Look Set To Choose Independence From Serbia To Advance Their EU Memberships Hopes* runs the headline on the BBC – a big story for these parts. I eat a bowl of beef goulash, with hunks of bread and two pints of lager, down at a café by the river. This seems suitably prison-like food, if you take away the beer. It comes to £8.86 – its lovely and cheap in Slovenia. I wander around for a while. It's a balmy evening and lots of people are out and about; there's a buzz on the streets.

And there's excitement back at Celica too, where people are glued to the Eurovision Song Contest in the bar. It's amusing to watch the Finns run away with it – they have fielded a heavy metal group called Lordi, with all its members dressed in mutant monster outfits. Great Britain is miles off the lead. Slovenia isn't even in it. I have a pint and try to discuss the score with the lesbians, who have materialised and also ordered pints. They don't really want to talk to me.

At 11.30 p.m. I stumble to my cell. More or less simultaneously the other two occupants arrive. There's a British man called Clive, who's just been to watch *La Boheme* at the opera house, and a guy from America who enters and loudly announces, 'Hi! I'm Randy!' Clive and I exchange glances: he's from America and he's Randy. We mutter a few words, like old prison lags; I'm sleeping next to Clive, not Randy. And we crash out to the sound of dark industrial music pounding through our bars – Panc, Tomo and Sasha must be back at it again.

Clive is gone in the morning. He had said something about leaving early to go to Serbia. But Randy's still around. Randy Sharp, thirty-seven, a herbal tea mixer from Boulder, Colorado, turns out to be an all-round American nice guy. He's in Slovenia to see a woman he first met in a hostel in San Francisco. She's a professional flautist in Ljubljana. He's on a month's tour of Europe. We have breakfast in the conservatory and Randy tells me about herbal teas. 'We have forty-two different kinds. We sell tonnes of "Sleepy Time", which has valerian root in it.' I never knew that, I say. 'It's our biggest seller. Then comes camomile. Lipton is our biggest competition. Our company is called Celestial Seasonings. But I haven't seen any over here,' he says, scratching his goatee, as though he can't understand European indifference to Sleepy Time. I tell him about Hot Horse; everyone I talk to in Ljubljana seems to love to hear about Hot Horse. 'I can't believe you ate a horse! In Boulder we have a lot of what we call "crystal hunters". I don't think the crystal hunters would like that too much.'

I leave Randy to his own adventures and set off to see the Modern History Museum in Tivoli park. There's an olive-green tank outside the big, bright pink museum building. Inside a couple of Americans are being shown round by a guide. They're the only other people there. I follow the group round, at a polite distance, listening to their guide. She tells them about the events of the early 1990s.

'In 1990 we had a referendum. There was a ninety-three per cent turnout and eighty-nine per cent voted for independence. On 26 June 1991 we celebrated independence. A big celebration. The next morning they [the Serbs] attacked. It was over in ten days. The EU said it would recognise Slovenia if we made changes to our constitution. So we made them. We were recognised in January 1992.'

The Americans depart. I start chatting to Mojca Baus, the guide, who's in her twenties and a studious type. She's got a chair with a couple of books on it resting on the museum's balcony. Did she remember the ten-day war? 'Oh, yes. I lived in Ljubljana but my family decided to send me to my grandparents in the country in case there was any trouble. When I woke up that morning [the morning of the start of the conflict] I looked out of my grandparents' window. It looked like the whole forest was moving. But when I looked closer, I could see it was people in camouflage: our army! They told us to take the dog inside because it was barking. We heard shooting so we went in the basement. My grandparents had lived through the Second World War, they thought the basement was safest. We stayed there a while. It was over soon. We feel very lucky to be the first ones to get out of Yugoslavia. We feel lucky we only had a ten-day war. For others in this region the wars lasted ten years,' she says, sounding upbeat and optimistic. 'We are very proud that we live here. For the first time in our history we are independent. Before 1991 – never. Always other rulers.'

Just like what's happening in Bulgaria: freedom from rulers after hundreds of years. Just different rulers: Austrians, Hungarians and Tito in Slovenia, and Turks and Soviet influence in Bulgaria. This part of the world is going through an incredible period of change. Being in Central and Eastern Europe now as the EU expands and brings prosperity that was unimaginable twenty years ago is – and you just can't help feeling it – *exciting*.

In the breakfast room, I'd seen the two women I met the night before, looking at pictures of a mystical castle overlooking a beautiful lake. This turns out to be Lake Bled, top of Slovenia's list of sights. It's an hour and a quarter drive by bus, past lush, green landscape, neatly ploughed fields with shiny red tractors, mountains shrouded in thick grey cloud, and little villages with churches with ornate, almost eastern-looking, spires. According to government figures, seventy per cent of Slovenians are Roman Catholic, one per cent Muslim, one per cent Lutheran, four per cent atheist and twenty-three per cent 'other'.

Bled is beautiful. Even though it's cloudy, the church on the small island and the castle on the cliff-top are spectacular. The water is like a sheet of glass. Occasional boats crossing to the island ruffle the surface. I try to walk to the castle. I follow signs and soon find myself hiking up a path without a soul in sight. There had been crowds down below. Have I somehow managed to climb the wrong hill? The trees make it impossible to see the top, so I persevere, cursing Slovene signs and wondering how on earth I've managed to come all this way to visit a major tourist attraction and been stupid enough to miss the attraction. But eventually, ramparts emerge, and yes: it *is* the right hill. It's just most people don't climb it – they take little golf-buggy trains instead.

I take a few snaps from the castle walls. I didn't realise fairytale lakes with castles like this really existed. The clouds form a mist over the mountains. The lake is dead calm, with shapes of the clouds reflected in its surface. It's almost eerily quiet. The little white church with the pointy steeple on the small island emerges out of the misty distance. I'm standing next to a couple who ask me to take their picture. They're Ian and Jill from Sydney, and they're travelling through Croatia and Slovenia.

Ian starts raving about Slovenia. 'There's been no fanfare about it. They've just got on and done it,' he says. 'They've pulled themselves out of the Yugoslav years. When we drove through Croatia into Slovenia you could notice the difference almost immediately. Things smartened up. Farm land looked better maintained. The roads were better.'

'We can't get over it really. Slovenia is just so nice.' Jill adds.

I'm shattered after my Art Deco and Lake Bled escapades. A quiet evening in low-cost land is in order. But it's not to be. I've just bought a beer at the bar when Randy bounds up to me. 'We're having a party upstairs. Come and join us!' he says enthusiastically. He orders a vast number of beers and balances them precariously on a tray. We've got new digs this evening, in a five-bunk room in the loft. Randy excitedly tells me that two tall, beautiful sisters from Vancouver will be sharing our room. They're out. But in the communal area for the loft rooms, various people in various states of stages of inebriation – ranging from drunk to very drunk to truly appallingly drunk – are drinking beer and having a mini (very messy) salami, cheese and bread picnic.

Everyone is talking at the same time, and occasionally demanding salami and cheese between slurps of beer. There are three British lads in their twenties and thirties 'on a jolly' (Stuart, Chris and Andy), an Austrian chap called Rainer, a slightly surly young woman from Australia called Crystal who tells me 'I fix stuff in computers, okay?' when asked what she does, and two amusing fellows from Iceland called Adalsteinn and Smari.

The Icelanders are possibly the most drunk. Adalsteinn, who has just qualified as a registered nurse and is very large and dressed head to toe in black, starts to tell me the history of the Westman Islands, where he's from. 'We eat puffins!' he exclaims at one point. 'They're smaller than guinea fowl. They've got a really rich, salty taste. They taste like . . .' He pauses. 'Puffins!'

His friend Smari sidles up to me and says, 'If anyone asks, I'm a mathematician and I'm drunk!' Then he goes in search of the cheese.

The Brits are also very drunk. Stuart, a short bald guy wearing a Tottenham Hotspurs T-shirt and shorts, stands up and starts saying 'Love it, love it, love it, love it' and stamping his feet when a bit of music he likes come on. Nobody bats an eyelid. 'This is definitely the best hostel I've ever stayed in!' Stuart adds.

'Slovenia is not like France, Belgium or Spain,' his mate Chris informatively tells me.

Smari wants to know what I'm up to. I explain my low-cost adventures and that I've even got a name for the challenge I'm setting myself: How low can you go? On hearing this, he roars with laughter and says with great comic timing, 'You, my friend . . .' he belches again. 'I believe, my friend, you can safely say that now you have reached [belch] the very bottom!'

I say he's probably right and he roars and belches some more. They disappear, looking wobbly, in search of the Cutty Sark pub. Randy departs, randily, in search of the Vancouver sisters.

I knew the backpackers wouldn't let me down.

Ljubljana has got so much going for it: prosperity, lovely architecture, artistic people (I'll give the Dark Industrialists the benefit of the doubt), mountains and mystical lakes close at hand, beaches on the Adriatic not far away, and an exciting feeling that people are enjoying their newfound freedom. It feels, as Mojca said, lucky – like things are definitely going right in Slovenia.

I don't buy the T-shirt that says, 'The country of natural beauty – Slovenia – Europe's hidden pearl' at the airport. For a start, I've run out of tolars.

But I definitely know where it's coming from.

TALLINN, ESTONIA

PHWOAR BLIMEY

I'm sitting at Gate One at Stansted, waiting for my 6.45 a.m. easyJet flight to Tallinn, the capital of Estonia, glancing (I dare not stare) at The Gimp.

I know he's The Gimp because hanging from his neck is a sign attached to a piece of pink ribbon that says so. The Gimp is wearing a skin-tight red and black rubber outfit with cut-off arms and tiny shorts. To accompany this look, he has large, almost knee-high motorcycle boots. His hair has been gelled back in Gordon 'greed is good' Gekko style. He has had his fingernails painted scarlet. Occasionally, as though he's not used to having his fingernails painted scarlet (which I dare say he's not), he examines his scarlet fingernails. He seems impressed by their finish.

Surrounding The Gimp is a crew of about a dozen guys – the Gimpettes. Fortunately they are not wearing gimp costumes. Instead, they are all dressed for a game of tennis – a game played in the 1980s. They have towel-effect headbands and wristbands, Fila shirts, old-fashioned tennis shorts, Sergio Tacchini shell-suit tops and aviator sunglasses. Everything is in white; the All England Lawn Tennis Club would surely approve. One chap twiddles an old cat-gut Slazenger racket as though waiting to return a Bjorn Borg serve. Another takes it and pretends to play the guitar. The Gimp appears amused.

A man in a floral one-piece women's swimming costume and high heel shoes walks by followed by a group of lads who all look a bit worse for wear. It's 5.30 a.m., but I'd seen quite a few of them drinking lagers in the bar earlier. The swimming suit fellow looks acutely embarrassed. I suppose you would.

A cluster of women in bright pink T-shirts saying 'Pussycat Girls On Tour' arrives. They look upset. They slump on seats close by and start talking agitatedly. They've just missed their easyJet flight to Ibiza. The plane is (mockingly) still outside, about to move away. 'We were held up by the footballers. It was the footballers!' pleads a woman, who looks a clubber-type with curly brown hair and three-quarter length turn-up jeans. She's talking to an easyJet rep. The Pussycat Girls say they were held up by security checks for football hooligans by the X-ray machine – today is the morning of the start of the World Cup and there is a team of officers asking questions.

'Where are you flying to?' one had asked me. 'Tallinn,' I replied. He'd scratched his chin as though he wasn't really sure where this Tallinn place was. 'In Estonia,' I'd added. He'd looked blank. 'Go on, go on then,' he'd said, seemingly satisfied that, as this funny place was not holding the World Cup, I was unlikely to be a hooligan. He'd also handed me a small red card (which seemed a bit unfair) with 'World Cup 2006 Ports Police Operation: you have been spoken to by police officers as part of the national World Cup 2006 Ports Policing Operation.' On the back it explained that all this was to do with section 21 of the Football Spectators Act. I had not been identified as a 'risk supporter'. I was going to non-risky Estonia. Non-risky, generally good people go to Estonia, even if the officers aren't that sure where Estonia is. I wonder, though, what they made of The Gimp.

The bride-to-be starts crying. The easyJet rep won't buy her excuse and is about to lead them back to check-in. 'If you're late, we won't wait! It does say that at check-in,' says the rep strictly. The bride-to-be sobs some more. 'But I don't want to spend all day at Stansted airport,' she cries. 'I want to be in Ibiza! I want to see the sun set over the sea!'

*   *   *

Although I've come across the odd stag and hen group in Szczecin, Ljubljana and Brno, the very nature of these trips means I've not yet visited any of the major party destinations. Yet when I've mentioned these trips to friends, some have asked: 'Aren't you sick of all the stag parties on the planes? Isn't it the same everywhere you go: just one big stag party after another?' Well, no, I say. The places I'm going to are so far off the beaten track most stag groups don't even know they exist. Stag parties go to Prague (not Brno), Warsaw (not Szczecin), Bratislava (not Poprad). Best men and bridesmaids don't want to risk getting it wrong, so they go for the big name cities: why go to Brno when you've got all the bars and clubs in Prague?

Tallinn, despite being pretty much unheard of by most people, is a different kettle of fish. Tallinn is very much known by Britain's stag parties. It's got all the right ingredients: low-cost flights (obviously), cheap beer (again, obviously), very pretty local women (obviously, obviously, obviously), and a proliferation of websites with names like stagweb.co.uk, big-weekends.com, lastnightoffreedom.co.uk and – the biggie – tallinnpissup.com.

When I searched for Tallinn on Google UK, this was the order of the sites that came up:

1) A BBC *Holiday* programme report on the city
2) tallinnpissup.com
3) The British Embassy in Tallinn website
4) easyjet.com
5) The *Time Out* guidebook site.

In other words, as far as British internet users are concerned, the second most interesting aspect of Tallinn is its ability to provide a venue for cheap beer and a good old-fashioned pissup. First check where the place actually is using BBC (useful to know roughly where you're going), then check how cheap the beer is on tallinnpissup.com, then check there is embassy support (in case you lose your wallet while sleeping in the gutter, perhaps), then and only then – seeing as the beer is definitely cheap enough – book your low-cost flight on easyJet.

The homepage of Tallinn Pissup showed a cartoon picture of a bloke with red eyes and stars encircling his head. Beneath this was the headline: Let's Hear It For The Beer and *The Sun* rating a Tallinn stag as five out of five, and a quote from *The New York Times*: 'Party capital of the year'. A series of Mutt's Nuts Activities on offer included Dr Death's Shooting Academy in which 'Dr Death will train you in military guns, pump action shotguns . . .', Demolition Derby in which participants 'ram, roll and even blow-up old Soviet wrecks', and a Medieval lesbian strip show, which was billed as 'a slap up banquet and one-hour lap-dancing medieval festival.'

Mark Robertson, thirty-five, from Newhaven in Sussex, is the founder of Tallinn Pissup, along with Budapest Pissup, Bratislava Pissup and Prague Pissup – the first of his Pissup brands and the most successful, responsible for 15,000 British men going on stag trips to the Czech capital each year. About 5,000 a year go to Tallinn (where Brits are believed to be sixty per cent of the stag and hen market), 7,000 to Budapest and 4,000 to Bratislava. Robertson set up his business in 2000. He'd been working as a purchaser for an international supermarket chain in Prague and had found himself continually arranging weekends for friends visiting from the UK.

'It was becoming a bit of a burden,' he told me when I called him before my visit. 'And I thought, well, no one else is doing this.' So he quit his job and began to offer packages pitched at the stag market – people buy their own flights, but are provided with airport transports and guides, almost always a twenty-something local woman. 'What we offer is cheap beer and good-looking girls: no sex and no drugs,' he said. 'A guy can come out here and feel a bit of a lad. There are all these fantastic Swedish-looking girls, foreign girls, you know. We get doctors, lawyers, brick-layers – everyone. Normally the highlight is a steak and chips meal and a striptease. The girl comes in and embarrasses the groom.' He chuckles a bit – embarrassing the groom, as The Gimp proved, is at the very heart of the stag experience.

'I knew it was going to be big as soon as the cheap flights started,' he continued. 'It just made sense. People like doing it through us because we look after them. It takes the heat off the best man. We can tell them about local customs and horror stories about the police [this is to keep people well-behaved, or at least *better behaved*]. We have pub tours, but we never go to a pub at the same time as other stag groups, and we take them to good places. It's 50 pence a beer normally. Sometimes you see groups that have done their own thing, and they're just in the boring Irish bar, looking a bit disillusioned. Many of them get ripped off. There are a lot of people out here trying to make a fast buck off whoever they can who's western. That's the Eastern European mentality.'

Robertson, who has married a Czech woman, told me about guys who get so drunk they wander around for three or four hours and can't even find their hotels, and how his guides will co-ordinate matters with embassies when people lose passports, which is apparently – and not unsurprisingly – common. Hen groups are a 'tiny minority', less than one per cent of business. Activities cost about £25 per night per person. Click on parts of the website and burp sounds (and worse) ring out. The Medieval lesbian strip show – burp! – which comes with three 'free' beers, has, it says, been 'a tradition in Tallinn since sixteen hundred and phwoar!'

I think I've done my time in quirky, totally unknown destinations. It's time to investigate Tallinn.

The Radisson SAS has twenty-four floors and it's a damn sight more comfortable than my prison back in Ljubljana. Okay, the room is £80 a night. But that would be £40 each between two, not bad after a return easyJet ticket of £44.98. Anyway, I deserve it after sticking it out with Clive and Randy, listening to the dark industrialists.

My eleventh-floor room overlooks what appears to be Tallin's Old Town, a hill about half a mile away with an eye-catching Russian Orthodox church at its summit – lots of onion-shaped spires silhouetted against the dark-blue sky – plus several medieval-looking towers. Down a wide street there seem to be more malls, plus another multi-storey hotel standing up starkly on the far side of town called Sokos. Tallinn looks generally well-to-do: lots of well-preserved turn of the nineteenth-century buildings with terracotta tile roofs, small parks and neat apartment blocks. Past a clutch of yellow cranes and a red-and-white telecommunications pylon, there's the hazy-blue expanse of the Baltic Sea.

I've expected to see stags everywhere but, apart from at the airport, I haven't spotted a single one yet. The town looks prosperous and quiet; seemingly too at ease with itself to need a mob of beered up Brits to sustain the economy. I wonder what the locals make of the city's infamous stag groups (wherever they're hiding now). There must be lots of tensions – people reacting against the exuberant behaviour. But surely having a guaranteed stream of high-spending visitors can only be a good thing? I arrange to meet Kersti Vaino, the sales director of the hotel, to see what she makes of it all. Kersti, who's young and dark-haired, meets me in the hotel lobby. She's pleasant and friendly, but I can feel her assessing me as I start rambling about stag parties.

'Actually, we do not welcome them,' she says, cutting me short. 'If they say they are an all-male group wanting single occupancy, we say no. We don't work with *this segment*. Tallinn sincerely hopes it is getting rid of this image,' she continues. 'Riga is taking over in this area. This is what we hope. We have better restaurants than nightclubs anyway. Tallinn is a small city with 400,000 inhabitants [Estonia's population is 1.4 million]. The balance here is quite delicate.'

This all sounds hopeful rather than likely – after all, as long as there are easyJet flights it seems stag groups will come to Tallin. But perhaps it is realistic. Tallinn, if all the cuttings I've read are to be believed, is on the up as far as its economy goes. The *Guardian* described it as a 'Baltic tiger . . . the Hong Kong of Eastern Europe' with strong financial services and IT companies: ninety per cent of people own mobiles, while about the same percentage have Internet access, and ninety-five per cent do their banking online. Economic growth in the last year was more than a quarter. the *Independent on Sunday* referred to the country, which was recognised by the United Nations in 1991 after breaking free from the Soviet Union, as 'E-Stonia'. It said that Estonia has 'coped admirably' with stag groups and 'prospered' on the back of them since easyJet began flights in November 2004. Meanwhile, the *Sun*, skipping the economics stuff and recommending the local elk roast, described it as 'a delightful fairytale town. . . . Estonia is justly proud of its supermodels – the most famous is Carmen Kass.'

'We don't go to the bank at all,' says Kersti, who, like almost all people in Tallinn, enjoys telling you this. 'All our banking, honestly, we do it on the Internet. We pay bills – electricity, phone, gas, water everything – over the Internet.' Very impressive, I say – and it *is* very impressive especially when you think how far behind the 'advanced' UK is with all these things. Then Kersti tells me the other thing that everyone in Tallinn likes to tell you. 'We pay for parking using mobile phones.' She explains how people can send a text to a central number to buy a parking spot; you never have to bother with change for a metre.

Kersti could talk for a long time about e-banking and mobile phone advances. It's clear this is what interests her, *not* British stag parties. She's not in the slightest bit interested in the world of Tallin Pissup. And who could blame her? She does, however, give

me a few tips as to where I might find a few stag groups later on; a
few tips that I'm hoping the next person I meet might add to. I'm
about to visit a man who has British stag groups on his mind an
awful lot these days (since the advent of easyJet), perhaps more
than he would care to – the British ambassador to Estonia.

The walk to the embassy is pleasant. Tallinn is a pretty place,
especially on a sunny day in June, with narrow cobbled streets,
avocado-green and salmon-pink buildings with terracotta roofs.
In the Old Town on the hilltop it's busy, but far from crowded –
just about the right amount of bustle. There are beech trees, tubs
of purple and white flowers, and hazy views across the city from
old ramparts. Birdsong fills the air. Tallinn Pissup or not, this
city is – like Ljubljana – a nice place for a weekend break.

It doesn't take long to find Her Majesty's embassy, a cream
building with a glass facade overlooking a park with chestnut
trees. There's a big metal fence and a security hut, where a guard
takes my mobile phone – not quite in the Tallinn new technology
spirit, I can't help thinking. I'm shown in and a young man in a
pale-grey pinstripe suit and a neat side-parting rushes up,
introduces himself as Raimo Poom, and gives me the bad news:
'The ambassador is unavailable. The ambassador is ill.'

I try not to look disappointed: I'd been looking forward to
stories of drunken Brits abroad and lost passports. Instead I'm
taken to a room with a couple of dried-out tropical plants and a
bookcase filled with tomes with titles like *Inside the House of
Lords*. Here I am to talk to Marti Rillo, head of the embassy's
Trade and Investment Section, and Raimo, the embassy press
officer. Just like Kersti, they don't want to discuss stag parties.
Instead, we have a chat that I might as well call: Estonia and
Tallinn in general according to Marti and Raimo, the embassy
chaps.

Marti and Raimo tell me early on that ninety-five per cent of
Estonians do their banking online. This fact appears to be very

close to the hearts of Estonians. Marti, who's in his late twenties, adds: 'Most of us have never even seen a cheque. "What is this cheque book thing," is what most people would probably say, if you gave them one.'

Raimo, also in his twenties, asks: 'Did you know eighty-five per cent of people do their tax returns online in Estonia these days – eighty-five per cent! Five days later they get their money back, the returns are completed. It is all so integrated. Doing your returns takes just five minutes.' I nod in a way that suggests that five minutes is very impressive.

'During the local elections last year,' Raimo continues, 'people with ID cards could vote online from home. About 10,000 people did.' This, I can't help thinking, *would* be convenient – no trudging to the local church hall in the rain. But then again – no striding into the polling booth and that split-second feeling, as you grab the pencil tied to a grubby piece of string, that your vote *really* makes a difference (not that it usually does of course).

Everything seems to be very techy in Estonia – I can understand the 'E-Stonia' nickname. Marti is very enthused about Skype, a company which offers free phone calls over the Internet. It was set up in 2003 by a 'Swedish guy, a Danish guy and some local guys': i.e., by a whole bunch of Scandi-Baltic guys.

Unsurprisingly Skype has proved immensely popular – in the way free things usually do. The Swede, Niklas Zennstrom, and the Dane, Janus Riis, the key founders, both billed by some as the new Bill Gates, are already multi-millionaires. Skype now has more than one hundred million users, including me. It's great. Skype people can contact each other wherever they are in the world using the Internet. I signed up just before going to Szczecin. Being free, it had a certain budget-traveller appeal. It's also proved handy for keeping in touch with the various people I've met so far on my weekends (especially Natalia, my translator from Poprad, who has been telling me about her plans to move to the UK or Ireland to find a job). According to an article in *Vanity Fair*, Skype is 'transforming the way the world communicates'. Some even say it's the biggest innovation in telecommunications since Alexander Graham Bell made the first phone call in 1876. Pretty impressive. 'And it is here in Tallinn!' exclaims Marti proudly.

Marti says that rather than be depressed about the legacy of the Soviet Union, the first post-1990 governments jumped into the liberal economy. As though to prove this, he tells me about the mobile phone parking payments. 'We have mobile parking! We have e-government! We have paperless government!' he says, getting a bit excited. Many other countries, he says, are looking at what happens in Estonia, which is able to introduce all these high-tech systems partly because the small population makes changes manageable. Estonia has, apparently, become an international guinea pig for Internet innovation.

Marti and Raimo have another theory about why Estonians like to use the Internet so much. The net cuts down on unnecessary chat. Text messaging, rather than making phone calls, is also very popular for the same reason. This appeals to Estonians because, according to Marti, 'Estonians are maybe even more reserved than the Finns.' After my experiences of Tampere I find that hard to believe. 'No, no, it is true. If an Estonian taps his finger on his knee,' he taps his finger slowly on his jeans 'that means he is outraged, truly outraged! Estonians are emotional, but reserved. They speak very little, but when they do they mean it.'

That should make for interesting nightlife, I think, as we say our goodbyes. Silent Estonians and drunken Brits over here on easyJet flights – what a wonderful combination of evening companions.

Estonians may be reserved, but drivers seem in a terrible hurry in Tallinn – lots of speedy bursts and overtaking. I walk down a small hill past a large picture of Thierry Henry and Ronaldinho advertising the World Cup. Next to Henry is the word 'Honor'.

And next to Ronaldinho it says 'Joy'. At the bottom of the hill, close to the hotel, is a shopping mall called the Viru Centre. In the middle of the ground floor a dozen gleaming grand pianos are displayed, which makes a nice change from the usual Mercedes four-wheel drives with tinted windows. There are lots of designer and brand name shops – Diesel, Zara, Nike, Sergio Tacchini. Some of these are completely empty. Despite Estonia being on the up, its annual income per head is just £7,728. This compares to £6,215 in Latvia and £6,755 in Lithuania, which at least makes Estonia the wealthiest of the ex-Soviet Baltic states. Just like in Szczecin, shop assistants seem to sense I'm easy prey and stare almost plaintively at me. There's not exactly a frenzy of buying going on. So how does this city make its money? I'm about to meet Anet from Tallinn Pissup at the hotel – and I get the feeling she may just have some answers.

Anet is one of the ten reps who works for Mike, taking British men around town and showing them a good – and legal – time. She's waiting for me in the lobby when I get back from the embassy. She's charming: big smile, short brown hair, nice blue eyes. She's wearing a black and white dress like she's ready to go out for the night. She is also – I think this is the polite and PC description – buxom. And she doesn't care who knows it. Her fingernails are painted bright scarlet.

We take the lift to Lounge 24 on the twenty-fourth floor, which has brilliant views across to the Old Town and the Baltic Sea. Anet orders Evian for us both as if to prove it's not all pissup at Tallinn Pissup. She fills me in on her job and her ten colleagues. 'They are always female. They are always aged twenty to twenty-five. And they are always single,' she explains. Why is this? I ask – a little naïvely. 'That is just the way it is,' she says. She pauses. 'Some of them are looking for boyfriends.' Ah, right I say. Have there been any rep–client romances? She ducks this, saying, 'I have a better story.'

Apparently, Anet had a groom not so long ago on one of her

trips, a very quiet and reserved guy who seemed quite awkward when the stripper appeared. She was shocked to see him arrive back in Tallinn recently, having cancelled the wedding and declared he'd fallen in love with the stripper. 'I was like: "No! Go back! Get married!" His voice was quivering. He said: "But I love her!" He started crying. I couldn't believe it. He was the quietest guy.' She says she hasn't heard the latest on this saga, which is currently doing the Tallinn rounds. She pauses for a second. 'It's weird though. I call her "the stripper", like I call all the strippers. I just can't remember all their names. To me, they are just "the strippers".'

What does she think of what the strippers do, I ask. Do local people look down on them? 'I was talking to my friend about this the other day,' she says, taking a sip of Evian. 'I think it is not a bad thing that they do. They actually enjoy what they do. But I think stripping is changing.' Well, you could put it like that. 'Before, strippers used to have more fun. They would mess around. They would crawl like dogs with very little clothes on, or they would ride on the stag.

'Now, they are trying to be more exotic, to be sexier. Sometimes they feel ashamed of this, I think. Sometimes they ask the reps to go to the other room while they strip. I think they feel "lower" if we are there.' Most of the strippers, Anet adds, are Russians. 'But there is not a sex industry like there is in Prague. In Prague it's almost impossible to walk anywhere after 10 p.m. They say "Come to our club, come to our club." They try to drag you in. They give you vouchers. Here there are just ads in magazines for the sex industry.' Tallin Pissup, she says, has nothing to do with this side of things. But there's no doubt, from the sound of it, that there's quite a lot of 'stuff' going on.

Anet finds that groups that come on the early morning easyJet flights are almost always drunk, so their first night is ruined. After that, on the Saturday, they either go paint-balling, demolition derby driving, or shooting guns in the forest with Dr Death's

Shooting Academy. This of course is followed by a night out, which is when Anet mainly works.

Do you ever get embarrassed going about with so many loud drunken British men? Do you worry what people think? 'Actually people don't say anything, but I know what they are thinking,' Anet says, not at all shyly. 'I overhear them in the restrooms. I hear them say: "There's that girl again tonight with a different bunch of guys." That's just the way it is.' What about hen parties? 'To be honest we get very, very few – just five or six a year really.'

I ask about bad groups. 'Well of course some do stupid things. But if you do this job, you have to be tolerant. You have to be nice even if they say something bad. I say to them: "Don't! It's offensive!" But we don't really want arguments.' What do locals think of the stag groups? 'For Estonian females, they are interesting. They are *British men* – many are interesting.' Hard to believe, I suppose, but evidently true. 'But for the Estonian males it is different. They see the Estonian women talking to the British men in the nightclubs and they get jealous. They say: "Why aren't you at home ironing and doing the cooking."'

Sounds like *that* may be why Estonian women are into the British men – even drunken British stag party men.

Anet shows me a neat computer print-out listing ten groups visiting this weekend. I hadn't been sure if she'd play ball, but suddenly she's telling me I can join a couple of groups to observe their antics up close. I'm going to join one, with a groom called Marcus, to go shooting with Dr Death. Then I'm joining another group to attend a medieval lesbian banquet. 'It is just a medieval meal, then a strip show after.' Anet shrugs. 'It is nothing much, really.'

All in the line of duty, I say.

It's time to join the stags. I'm in a taxi with Crystal, a rather tired-looking twenty-something woman with auburn hair, shiny pink nails and a fake tan.

We are going to shoot some guns.

Crystal is one of Anet's colleagues. Unlike Anet, she does both day and night shifts, and she's just had five hours' sleep. She tells me she was out last night with 'a very nice group of lads . . . sometimes you get some real arseholes who really don't know how to behave, these guys were really nice.' Flicking her long, perfectly straight hair, Crystal says, 'I'm so thirsty.' Heavy night? 'Yes. I'm allowed to drink on the job and I do. But it's surprising. I have no hangover. It's probably because of the dancing. I was dancing most of the night.'

We arrive at a grey concrete, no-stars hotel, in a dreary suburb. A group of haggard, hungover chaps wearing 'traditional' Estonian hats emerges. They're in their twenties and thirties. The groom is wearing a plastic mask depicting Craig David, the pop star, as portrayed by the comedian Avid Merrion. He can do the Craig David voice perfectly and he's saying 'Oh ah, Bobby Brown!' The lads find this immensely amusing. We pile into a bus and soon are on the road out of town, heading towards Dr Death's Shooting Academy.

The lads have had a good night and seem pretty happy with the trip so far. Marcus, the groom, works for the Home Office, and he seems to have a pretty well-behaved bunch of mates. Willie, who's wearing a Ramones T-shirt, describes his highlights so far: 'Yesterday we went on a microbrewery tour. We ate pigs' ears for breakfast. Then we went to a club called Hollywood. Now I'm a clubber and I go clubbing a lot, but the women there were just stunning. Better than anywhere else I've been. There must have been 400 of them. We were stunned. Now we are shooting guns. Girls! Guns! Food! Beer! Traditional Estonian hats! What more could you possibly want?' Indeed. Look no further: Tallinn has it all.

The best man, Simon, also thinks the women here are stunning. He says: 'I've travelled a lot around the world. The women here are attractive without trying to be attractive. They are slim.

There seems to be no "fat slag" mentality.' He doesn't seem embarrassed to use this phrase. 'Well, it's true! It was like a supermodel convention. It was like: "I'm in love with you." But then another supermodel would come past, and then it was like: "No, I'm in love with *you*." And then another would walk past and it would be: "No, no. I'm in love with *you*." ' He's obviously a big fan of Estonian women.

We turn off the main road into a small forest. After a minute the bus stops near a sandy clearing filled with piles of lorry tyres and surrounded with small sandbanks – Dr Death's Shooting Academy.

Dr Death is a genial Estonian named Martin, who's wearing camouflage trousers and a beige fishing jacket. He's got two gold bullet shells stuck in his ears to keep out gun noise. 'Nice hats!' Martin says, admiring the lads' outfits. Then he gives us a safety spiel. 'We are shooting real guns today. The most important rule is to point the gun in the direction of the target. Bullets go at 500 miles per second. Unless you can run that fast, you must lie down if a bullet hits you. So don't wipe your hair with the gun in your hand. Don't go: "Where is the bullet?" ' He looks down the barrel of the gun. 'That would not be a healthy thing to do.' He hands out a waiver form. 'Don't worry it just says: "All your assets will be transferred to us." Remember print clearly, so we can put it on your stone. Grave digging is okay now. In the winter it is difficult. The ground is frozen.'

Dr Death issues us with our guns. Boxes with cardboard cartons of ammunition are nearby. About ten metres away, between pine trees, are two white cardboard cut-outs in the shape of human torsos. Willie puts his Ramones T-shirt over one of the targets and Marcus, gets a five-dollar bill and pins it to the other target. We're given red ear-muffs. And then we start to shoot guns, two at a time – first pistols, then Magnums, then pump-action shot guns, and finally AK-47s.

Call me a gun-crazed loon, but there's no denying that this is a whole lot of fun. We start off a little shakily. 'Is any one else really scared or is it just me?' asks Willie as he lines up among the first to shoot. Soon there is the smell of cordite in the air and we're beginning to aim shots close to Abraham Lincoln on the five-dollar bill. 'I shot Lincoln!' says a tall guy with a crew-cut. 'Now I'm a man!' yells Marcus after letting off a round from an AK-47.

Afterwards, Martin's Dr Death partner, Thomas, tells me, 'We have quite liberal gun laws for Estonians. You have to go to the police station and apply for a gun permit. If you have no police record, then you can get a gun. You can carry it, but it must be concealed.' Do you carry your gun? 'Yes, always. Under my coat. Always.'

Worth bearing in mind in the event of any squabbles with Estonians this weekend. The lads are off to have a few beers in readiness for the England versus Paraguay World Cup match later. One of them, James, is telling me how much cash he's spent so far.

'Must be £300 so far. I've brought £800. I don't think it'll be enough.' He says this uncomplainingly. I'm amazed. If the estimated 8,500 stag men who visit Tallinn each year spend £800 each on their weekends, then that would come to almost £7 million a year: quite an industry. And that's just the spare cash, not covering hotels and flights.

I take a look about.

Tallinn, it seems, has always been popular with visitors and invaders. The city's name comes from a period of Danish rule in the thirteenth century; Tallinn means 'Danish city' in Estonian. It was dominated for many years by German merchants. Then there were the periods of Swedish and Russian rule. In the eighteenth century, when many of the prettiest old buildings were built, Tallinn was the ice-free port of Peter the Great's empire; he even built a palace, Kadriorg Palace, two miles east of the city centre. Then, of course, there were the German and Russian occupations of the twentieth century.

One remnant of the Russian empire is the Alexander Nevsky Cathedral. It's easily the most spectacular building in the Old Town. It was completed in 1900 partly as a show of power in Estonia at a time when Tsarist influence was waning – only for everything to go slightly wrong seventeen years later with the Russian Revolution. But the Estonians haven't knocked it down – as it's too nice a structure to destroy. Fancy white stucco windows frames dazzle in the sunlight and rusty red brickwork leads up to onion-shaped domes with gold crosses at the top. The interior is intriguing. Elderly women in red shawls are mopping the floors. There's a smell of candle wax from racks of thin orange candles. Almost everything is golden: golden icons, golden picture frames, golden wood-work, even a golden painted collection box for our 'gold'. There is a 'Keep Silence' sign and people are obeying. It's a very peaceful place (especially after the morning I've just spent with Dr Death).

Outside, a hunched-over woman in a red shawl is begging with an empty yoghurt pot. I give her a few Estonian kroons and she cackles a bit. Then I walk down a slope to the Occupation Museum. Tallinn has quite a few museums, but this is one of the most peculiar. A sign at the beginning, referring to Soviet control from 1944–91, says: 'For Estonia this was a divided and schizo-phrenic half-century in all aspects of our existence.' Then there are seemingly random displays showing hairdressers' chairs, a telephone booth, a selection of suitcases and an old car. The brunette woman at the ticket desk gives me a piece of laminated paper that comically and simply lists the various items on display. I study these hairdresser chairs, telephone booths and old suitcases trying to absorb whatever it is I'm supposed to absorb.

There's a good section on the 'singing revolution', the phrase used to described a series of late-night 'patriotic song fests' which began in the summer of 1988 – 300,000 turned up for one (about a quarter of the population). Thus began a series of steps leading to full independence in 1991, including an enormous human-chain of hand-holding protesting Estonians, Latvians and Lithuanians that stretched from Tallinn to Vilnius, Lithuania's capital, in August 1989.

The Kumu Art Museum is quite different. It's a wonderful new art gallery close to the elegant pink buildings of Peter the Great's Kadriorg Palace, which is described as a 'mini Versailles' in my guidebook and is also the residence of the president of Estonia. Kumu looks like a giant, lemon slice made from glass and grey stone, jutting up out of grass banks, four storeys high. Inside, it consists of a series of large exhibition rooms connected by long sloping walkways surrounding a vast curving atrium. It was designed by a Finn called Pekka Vapaavuori, the small brochure tells me. It strikes me that any city would be proud to have a building like this. I wander about taking in the impressionist art, portraits, and surrealist twentieth-century works.

What a great place. By the gift shop in the lobby, I talk to Tiina Randviir of the Estonian Institute, who I've arranged to meet. 'The Latvians don't have anything like this,' she says provocatively. 'Okay, it was a Finnish architect, but we don't mind about that.' She points across to the presidential palace. 'It is very unusual. You can just go up and ring the doorbell. Where else can you just go up and ring a president's doorbell?' Isn't there any security? 'I think there is a guard, but that doesn't make much difference. I think they're going to build a fence some time soon – that is what I've heard.'

The Estonian Institute is like the British Council in that it promotes the country's interests overseas. There was, says Tiina, a recent conference in Glasgow; Glasgow University has a Baltic studies department. Estonian is a Finno-Ugrian language – only spoken in parts of Scandinavia, Hungary and the former Soviet Union – as opposed to Indo-European, a language group that covers most of the other main languages including English. Tiina tells me that it is one of the most difficult languages to learn in the world. An English friend of Tiina's who could speak French, German and Chinese had tried to learn Estonian. 'After a while, he just said: "Forget it!" He said that compared to learning Estonian, Chinese was a piece of cake.' We talk about stag groups. 'I don't see them much but I don't go where they go.' Yet another Estonian who seems oblivious to the stag parties taking place in their town.

Enough of art, museums and Estonian Institutes . . . the medieval lesbians are waiting.

I'm about to attend my first ever medieval lesbian banquet and strip show. I've joined another stag group at a bar on a cobbled street in the city centre. They're a bit rougher round the edges than the last lot. They've clearly had a lot to drink. And they're (very) suspicious about my motives.

'No names!' says a scary fellow, who turns out to be the groom. As he says this he points two fingers at me as though he might poke my eyes out. 'What goes on tour stays on tour!' he says. And he definitely means it.

I begin to wonder if this is all a dreadful mistake.

'We're very cultured, very philosophical, like Jean Paul Sartre,' says a dishevelled chap who adds that he had his first beer in the morning at Luton airport. He burps a bit. I think his Sartre comment was ironic.

'Prague's had its day. Tallinn is the new Jerusalem: cheap, cheap, cheap. Lots of models. Good drink,' says a guy with a shaved head.

We enter a bar and go to a basement vault where the medieval lesbian strip show is held. 'You owe me!' says the scary groom, pointing his fingers at me again.

'Is this going to end up as four pages in Monday's *Guardian*? I bet it is!' says the best man. 'No names!'

'Okay!' I say. I've got the message.

Beer is drunk. Sausages and soup appear. My new companions do not like the soup. 'The gruel is off . . . there's no apparent taste . . . a dog would not eat this . . . please sir, don't give us any more . . . Oliver Twist would have walked out,' they tell me in the style of haughty restaurant critics.

Our rep, a pretty blonde woman working for Tallinn Pissup who looks terrified by the lads, goes into a sideroom. Two gorgeous, scantily clad women arrive. The groom is put on a chair in the middle of the room. *Justify My Love* by Madonna comes on the stereo. The slow funky beat fills our basement vault. This room must have seen quite a few gorgeous scantily clad women in its time, I'm thinking to myself, as they twist and turn to the music. Not long after thinking this, the two gorgeous women are no longer scantily clad. The groom refuses to take off his trousers. The women emplore him to take off his trousers. But he won't budge. The women wiggle about, swishing undergarments about provocatively. My neighbour says: 'The brunette's got a boil on her butt.' So she does, I reply. The two gorgeous women swish about some more. Then they gather their undergarments. They kiss the groom, say something sweet sounding in Estonian, and depart. End of medieval lesbian strip show.

Next stop is the Hollywood nightclub, via a couple of bars. There is a fight in the street by a taxi rank. Nothing to do with our group, but quite close by. We enter Hollywood, which is in a large building that looks like an old cinema. The nightclub is very busy. It consists of a vast room with walkways running off all over the place to different levels. It's totally packed with people squeezing past to get to the dancefloor. It's smoky and noisy. Dance music is playing – the type you might expect to hear in Ibiza. It's hard to hear what we're saying to each other. Not that we're likely to be missing much great conversation after all the beers we've had waiting for the medieval lesbians. I meet Anet and the other stag group, and make my escape – with Anet – into a VIP bit where it's quieter and she orders shots of green vodka.

We talk for quite a while about this and that, and Anet suddenly says, 'You're very reserved.' Which no one, I reflect, has ever told me after I've had six pints of lager and several funny green vodkas before.

We polish off more shots, looking down from a balcony at the dancing hordes below. It really is raucous, hectic and packed. There are plenty of lovely Estonian women – absolutely loads of them. 'There are lots of lovely Estonian women,' says Anet, seemingly reading my mind. Everyone is clearly having a lot of fun. There are men dressed as super heroes – Superman, Spiderman – cavorting with beautiful blondes. There are 'supermodel' girls in tiny miniskirts dancing alone like pop star divas. There is a vast scrum of people by the bar, everyone trying to get served.

This is clearly the epicentre of the Tallinn stag experience – Hollywood is *the* club for stag groups to visit. I wonder to myself: is this really so bad? Everyone loves to criticise stag weekends, but is this really such a terrible thing? Yes, people have had a few – *I've* had a few. But they don't seem to be doing any harm. They just seem to be having a blast – *I'm* having a blast. From what I've seen of the Tallinn stag groups today, they've kept themselves to themselves, going to bars and clubs that have clearly been designed precisely with them in mind. Sure, it does mean that there is a street or two in Tallinn that has been rather taken over by the Brits. But there are plenty of parts of London that have been overrun by tourists – that's just the way things go these days. Tourism is a big money earner. It's part of the way of life of almost any city (even ones you haven't heard of in Eastern Europe).

As I ponder this, obviously going through a reflective stage brought on by green vodka, Anet orders yet more shots. We drink yet more shots.

It's a great night – medieval lesbians and all, Tallinn is a fantastic place for a stag do.

In the morning, I don't feel so hot. In fact, I feel distinctly the worse for wear. I look in the mirror: plum tomato eyes again. But before I can slink away back on easyJet to Stansted, I have a quick meeting with Andrus Purde, the media marketing manager at Skype. We meet at a café, not far from Hollywood – the scene of last night's revelry.

Andrus is twenty-seven and wearing a Hawaiian shirt, jeans and shades. He has almost annoyingly handsome film star looks. He is also almost annoyingly upbeat and *positive*, perhaps too positive for me this (hungover) morning. He tells me that more than 250,000 people a day are signing up to Skype. So how far can Skype go?

'Well, there are seven billion people on the planet and about one billion computers. At the moment one billion computers is the limit – there's a lot to do yet!'

He explains how the development of wi-fi will make using mobile-phone-sized devices in wi-fi areas increasingly popular in future – the only difference being that phone calls are free, of course. There is only payment for calls to landlines which are usually 1.7 euro cents a minute or 1.5 euro cents to mobiles. The way Andrus describes it, it all sounds so simple: we'll all be doing this soon. Should phone companies be worried? 'Absolutely.' He tells me he *believes* in what he's doing: 'This is the good thing about Skype,' he says fervently, 'it's doing something mean-ingful. It's helping people communicate. That makes me feel good.'

Reminding me of the guys from the Embassy, he continues: 'Estonia had nothing fifteen years ago. Because we had nothing, we had to do something and some of these things have worked. The online and technology thing has happened for us because we had nothing to start with. In the UK you had a banking system going back hundreds of years. Here we started from scratch. So we tried online banking and it worked.' Online banking – yet again. 'Maybe it also helped that we have a northern mentality. It's easier to talk to each other when we are apart from each other, if you like. We are reserved people. The Internet suits us.'

We talk about British stag groups. Andrus is not a fan – and it is interesting, after last night, to hear his perspective. 'I wish the air tickets doubled in price,' he says. 'They're noisy and they expect everyone to find them amusing. I would probably enjoy it a lot if I was with them. But I'm not. Some of the groups are okay, but some are rude, harassing the girls. If I am on a date, they might hassle the girl I am walking with. It is not good.'

I'd not seen this side of things with my group, but I put Andrus's point of view to Nigel Haywood, Her Majesty's Ambassador to Estonia, who has recovered and kindly agreed to meet me before I leave. He's exactly how I'd imagined an ambassador would look: crisp white shirt, blue suit, grey hair in neat side-parting, Oxford brogues, plummy self-assured voice, a picture of the Queen behind his desk.

'The reputation of Tallinn is strong as a night venue,' he says diplomatically. 'Quite often the media like to make a meal of it and look for things that are going wrong. But very little does. Yes, most groups are boisterous – but they are boisterous rather than damaging . . . I was talking to a senior director at the foreign ministry the other day. He said: "We regard them affectionately. We laugh at them rather than feel threatened".' Haywood said that ten passports were lost last year and there was only one arrest – for possession of drugs.

So I guess stag groups are *not* a problem on one level at least: the ambassador says so (it must be true).

Then he tells me Tallinn is a wonderful place to be, that he likes fishing for trout in Estonia's many rivers, that he doesn't use the mobile phone parking system ('I've got my own driver'), that Estonia could 'do with a Nokia' (i.e., a really big international company like Nokia), and that 'just because the beer's cheaper, doesn't make it any weaker'.

All sensible British Ambassador stuff.

At the airport a few of the guys I met over the weekend are sampling their final cheap beers. We chat a bit and the best man, supping a 50 pence beer, says in complete honesty: 'It was great, but we thought it would be *seedier*.' The medieval lesbians had not been dirty enough, he complains.

Well, you can't have everything. Tallinn, like Ljubljana, is definitely a fun place for a cheap weekend break. I'm in two minds about whether stag groups deserve the bad press they usually get. There's no doubt that a big night out in Tallinn is a blast. But Andrus had a fair point. And it's clear that the 'girls, guns and beer' mentality is not exactly one to make you proud of being British. I also wonder whether many 'staggers' take in their surroundings. I didn't see any British men dressed as superheroes at the cathedral or the art gallery. Do these weekends just turn into a big blur? Is cheap beer and pretty women all they care about?

Or is the answer to that just a little bit obvious?

I suppose the best thing to say is: go and make up your own mind . . . just don't forget your traditional Estonian drinking hat.

In any case, I'm already boarding the easyJet plane, looking ahead to my next destination. It may be very different – but it's more than likely to be just as thought-provoking.

CAMDEN, LONDON

'THERE WOULD BE WAR'

This journey cost £2 on the Tube – even less than Szczecin with all those taxes on top of the 1 pence fare to Poland. Latino bongo music and hip hop is blaring from street stalls – the sounds clashing as crowds swirl about in the June sunshine. There are rastas, punks, Goths, traders with suitcases full of watches, groups of lads who look Eastern European and like they're taking a break from work on a construction site, and guys who could pass for New York pimps. A rack of T-shirts with slogans catches my eye. The T-shirts say: 'Barbie is a slut', 'Feed me Chocolate' and 'Psycho Bitch'. An Asian man in a hooded top hisses 'Skunk, man, you want skunk?' I move on, passing a large woman with a bright pink Mohican and an impressive collection of nose studs. I am in Camden, north London.

What the hell am I doing here? Why aren't I off in Lithuania or Latvia or somewhere like that?

I'm in Camden among the Goths and the Mohicans for a very specific reason: to see where low-cost airlines in the UK all began – to visit the grassroots of budget flying, if you like – at the headquarters of the man who started the country's biggest no frills airline by far: Stelios's easyJet.

I'm wondering what his secret is, and what he makes of all the upheavals I've been noticing on my travels. It seems to me that the budget airlines have changed the face of Europe completely. Brits are travelling and even moving abroad ever more frequently, and are just as likely to have a second home in Bourgas, Bulgaria as in Cornwall. Meanwhile people from the new EU countries – the Sylvies and Natalias – are coming over here in return, to make a new life. Will the low-cost flight boom keep on shuttling them and us back and forth?

There's another question. As I've been merrily hopping on one low-cost flight after another, a debate has been raging – impossible to ignore – about whether we all need to cut down the number of flights we take. Latest Government statistics show that flying now accounts for 5.5 per cent of carbon emissions in the UK but this figure is likely to grow to a quarter by 2050, while almost all other areas of emissions are predicted to decrease. Low-cost planes, and no one doubts this, are helping to increase emissions at precisely the moment the world needs to cut back or else face the inevitable climate change consequences that scientists foretell. Suddenly, it seems, taking a low-cost flight has become a political and moral decision (of sorts). Jumping on a 1 pence plane to Szczecin has taken on a dimension that most of us could not have guessed at when low-cost planes first came into being about a decade ago.

Can we just keep on flying? Or should we all cut back? It will be interesting to meet the man behind Britain's biggest low-cost fleet, and ask him what he thinks.

Stelios Haji-Ioannou is no longer chairman of easyJet, nor involved in the day-to-day running of the airline. He stood down as chairman in 2002 to pursue his many other entrepreneurial ideas, including easyPizza and easyCinema. The latter idea recently failed, mainly because big Hollywood suppliers refused to provide films and allow him to undercut long-standing cinema outlets. But he invented low-cost flights in Britain, and is still a major shareholder and an important symbolic figure at the airline. As far as budget flights go, Stelios, as he prefers to be known, is *the* man in the UK.

In 1995, when his first flights began taking passengers from Luton to Glasgow for £29 each way – 'the price of a pair of jeans' – people mocked him. How could flights be so cheap? Were the planes safe? But the son of a billionaire Greek shipping magnate persevered, and became known for his publicity stunts like dressing up in an 'easyJet orange' boiler suit and boarding the first flight offered by BA's now-defunct low-cost airline, Go.

The public began to get the idea of his planes: they may be shockingly orange, with giant telephone numbers painted down their sides, and Stelios may be a gentle giant, but they were, absolutely no doubt about it, *cheap*. You couldn't argue with £29 flights. The British public could understand £29 flights. Stelios had tapped into a core British quality: the love of a good deal.

Back in the mid-1990s, Luton Airport was best known for one thing: a very funny advert for Campari in which an upper-class fellow in a white suit and tie is trying to woo the actress Lorraine Chase, playing a cockney girl on holiday. Romantic piano music tinkles in the background as he pours her a Campari. She demands it with lemonade, causing him to raise an eyebrow. He ploughs on, after adding the lemonade. 'Were you truly wafted here from paradise?' he asks, gazing into her eyes. Chase, common as muck, replies, 'Nooo, Luton Airport.'

Despite the Luton Airport jokes, Stelios's cheap-flight ploy worked. It didn't matter that Luton was a bit Campari-with-lemonade, or that it was quite a long way from London, or that calling it 'London Luton' was stretching things somewhat, or that the planes were bright orange. All this didn't matter in the slightest. The main thing was: it was cheap, cheap, cheap.

But why was easyJet so cheap? Several things worked in Stelios's favour. As Luton wasn't one of the London's main airports, its landing charges were much less than Heathrow's or Gatwick's. Combine this with his decision to cut all extras such as free meals and drinks, and to cancel allocated seats, and fares could be kept to rock-bottom. Fast turnarounds allowed more plane rotations each day – and brought in greater profits, just as they had for Southwest Airlines, the pioneer of budget flights in the United States, on which Stelios based much of his business model. Travel agents were dropped. Who needs a middle man? They just make things more expensive. Call the big number on the side of the plane.

Ryanair, the Irish carrier that had already been working on low-cost plans, was spurred into action, introducing its own budget flights. Soon easyJet and Ryanair were winning over the public in their hundreds of thousands – now in their millions (about eighty million between them in 2005). Safety was not compromised; it was treated just the same way as it was on any other airline. British Airways and other national carriers across Europe were forced, reluctantly, to respond. They slashed jobs, cut unprofitable routes, scaled back in-flight service and, eventually, reduced prices. After years of being subsidised and protected by governments across Europe, the 'BAs of this world' – as Michael O'Leary, Ryanair's motor-mouth chief executive, describes traditional national carriers, almost spitting out the phrase – were forced to shape up or ship out.

Then something else came along: the Internet. Initially, Stelios considered the Internet to be for nerds. But after a while he realised it would soon have a wider audience and that if people booked online, fewer telephone operators would be needed. Costs would fall. Prices could fall even further. They did. The low-cost airline boom, still in its early days, boomed like never before. People started flying for £1 each way all over Europe. They loved it. It was *even cheaper*. New low-cost carriers came and went (it's a cut throat business). And soon some of us – me included – were flying to places we'd never heard of before. We were even buying places abroad. Why not? Property is much cheaper than in the UK, flights don't cost much any more. Pour a nice Campari and lemonade . . . watch the sun set.

EasyGroup's HQ is an interesting choice of office location – a former piano factory in a round building, called The Rotunda, just a minute's walk from all the hustle and bustle of Camden

High Street. No gleaming office in a Canary Wharf tower for Stelios. That's not the Easy way of doing things. Instead it's the ground floor of a funny old factory in a decidedly dodgy neighbourhood – about as far from the shiny image of the 'BAs of this world' as you could imagine.

I press a buzzer connected to a speaker, feeling as if I'm trying to get into a student party. I'm buzzed through and find myself in a tiny reception leading to an open-plan office. On the walls are cuttings with headlines saying 'Easy Squeeze' (about Stelios's £20-a-night easyHotel venture), 'Here Comes Stelios . . . Just When You Thought It Was Safe To Go To The Riviera' (a piece poking fun at the orange cabins on easyCruise, another of his operations). Beneath these, a plastic container displays an array of orange easyWatches. There's a model of an easyJet plane with 'Low-cost Hero' written on the side of it. I later learn this is a present from Richard Branson, Britain's other famous airline entrepreneur, on the occasion of easyJet's tenth anniversary.

Stelios is sitting at a swivel chair at a round table in the centre of the round building. There must be about fifty people working in the office, each at computers at banks of desks that are positioned like spokes around the centre.

'Ah, Tom!' he booms, smiling a chubby smile and setting his brown 'serial entrepreneur' eyes on me (Stelios likes to be referred to as a 'serial entrepreneur'). 'Right on time!' He's wearing what he always seems to wear: a blue blazer, blue-and-white striped shirt, tan chinos and one of his orange easy-Watches.

Stelios leads the way to his boardroom, a tiny room down a corridor with a sign that says 'Board'. Inside is a cheap wood table that would, at a squeeze, seat about eight. There's a painting of *easyCruiseOne*, his first cruise ship, behind him; a flat-screen television at one end of the table; a paper board with 'Web sale' written in green felt-tip; and a pile of the type of rubbish you'd keep in the back of a garage – bits of plastic that look like they once formed a go-kart, an old monitor, wires, piles of paper.

We get talking about the role low-cost flights have played in economic migration in New Europe.

'There was an editorial a while ago,' says Stelios, leaning forward, looking the very picture of the entrepreneur – at thirty-eight, with an estimated fortune of £727 million that makes him one of the one hundred wealthiest people in Britain – 'It was in *The Economist*. It said something like: "O'Leary and Stelios have done more for European integration than all the politicians in Brussels put together". It even suggested there should be a square or something.' A square? 'In Brussels. A square in Brussels – named after us.' He laughs, a bit of a naughty schoolkid laugh. 'Really, in front of the European Commission,' he says in a tone that suggests he wouldn't dream of thinking himself that important.

He turns serious. Low-cost flights are bringing integration, he says, 'at many levels, in all echelons of society, and every socio-economic level.' He continues: 'I think the most profound effect the low-cost airlines have had is the concept of the second home in the sense that it is now feasible, it's not just the preserve of the good and wealthy, to share your life between two places, apart a thousand miles. The benefit, of course, of living in two places that are that far apart, or up to that far apart, is you basically work in a main city where the weather might not be as good and you have a place in the sun or a place on the mountains for skiing or whatever.'

He quotes another magazine. '*Newsweek* had a piece about the new jet-set a couple of weeks ago and it said something like fourteen per cent of all homes now are second homes.' Really, in the whole of Europe? Stelios scratches his head. 'I don't know. But it's that sort of profound impact.'

I check later and the report said that 'by some estimates fifteen per cent of properties in Western Europe are now second homes.' Quite amazing when you think about it – are we all that well off?

Second homes are bringing Europeans closer together, he continues. 'What it means is there are French people who live in London, there are British people who live in the south of France, there are French people who live in the south of Spain . . . I think we're now discovering that constantly being rooted in one place is out of date. Anachronistic. The by-product of having a second home in another place is you get to understand that place a lot better. You tend to be more open-minded, to understand other cultures, to understand that not everybody's the same, that not everybody can speak the same language. Sometimes when I struggle with French or Spanish, I feel and I remember how it must feel when people are struggling with English in London. What's the difference? There is no difference. They are the same. And I am the same. I'm just struggling with a different language.'

Does he think the whole of Europe will speak English eventually, I ask. 'Yes. I think English will prevail. The French are already getting upset about it so they must think it too,' he says. 'We're better off all speaking English. A Greek going to Spain is more likely to be understood if he gets by speaking English.'

EasyJet has a slightly different approach to Ryanair. While Ryanair loves all the Szczecins and Poznams in obscure parts of Poland, easyJet has mainly stuck to bigger cities. In Central and Eastern Europe it covers Tallinn, Riga (the capital of Latvia), Warsaw and Krakow in Poland, Budapest, Prague, lovely Ljubljana, and Split and Rijeka in Croatia. I ask him what he likes most about these cities. Does he have a favourite?

He looks at me a little blankly. 'I haven't been to these places myself,' says Stelios, 'I don't travel like that. Ever since I started easyJet, two things have become habit, which are to go back to Greece once a month and to go to the south of France every other weekend. I'm the commuter to these places. Outside these two places. I go to a few other European cities, mostly on business.'

Have you ever been to Ljubljana? 'I've never been to Ljublja-na,' he replies. What about Tallinn? 'No.' Prague? 'Yes, I have been.' He says, not elaborating. Been to Bratislava? 'No. I'm a bit thin on Eastern Europe, I have to admit.'

How about Rijeka? He looks blankly at me again. The place that easyJet are about to start flying to in Croatia, I prompt him. I'm going on the inaugural flight later this month. 'No,' he says. Hungary? Been to Budapest? 'No,' he replies. 'It's embarrassing, given how much I travel, how few places I have been to yet. For the record there are 264 routes on easyJet and I could not have possibly flown on all of them,' he says, in defence of his south of France–Athens existence. 'I think I'm going to have to travel a little more.'

I tell him it's lovely in Ljubljana. 'You should go there,' I say, telling him a bit about Plecnik. He says: 'Yes, I should.'

Does easyJet have an archetypal customer? 'Different people at different times and you need all of them,' he replies. 'The second home owner. The cost-conscious business traveller be-cause he's the one that's going to get up at 4 a.m. in the morning to get the 6 a.m. departure. You need the casual traveller, the person who goes for short breaks here and there. You need the traditional family holiday, going away for one or two weeks or whatever. Because it is very strong demand that makes all the profits in the summer. You need the ethnic communities. Ethnic communities are very good for low-cost airlines. For every expatriate, you're likely to get – and I'm guessing now – you're likely to get up to ten trips a year. It's not only the expatriate himself or herself going back, it's the likelihood of them having relatives come over to visit them. So the Polish plumber sooner or later will either fly his wife or his girlfriend or will go back to see them or eventually the mother and father may come and see London one day.'

We talk some more about economic migration. Stelios takes an angle: 'I think another very interesting by-product of this phenomenon is how cosmopolitan London has become. I think London must be the most cosmopolitan city on Earth now. In the sense that New York is cosmopolitan, but less so because a lot of New Yorkers actually come from the rest of America, so they're more culturally integrated when they arrive. Whilst if you count nationalities I think London must be way more cosmopolitan.'

I mention my walk from the Tube station. 'Yes, yes,' says Stelios. 'Especially round here.' He continues: 'None of the other capital cities comes close [to London]. There are not enough foreigners in Shanghai or any of these places. Did I see somewhere that forty per cent of people in inner London were born in the UK? Track your everyday life. I mean I bought a Diet Coke when I got off the bus earlier today – the lady was Polish. It's languages and it's accents as well. Even if they're integrated, they've still got accents, like me. So you know they were not born here. Wasn't there an ancient version of this, it was called Babel, wasn't it?'

What countries are next for low-cost flights? Is it only a matter of time before the whole of 'New Europe' is completely covered? 'I think it's going to go beyond the traditional definition of European Union,' says Stelios, sounding thoughtful. 'I think Morocco is going to become pretty much integrated. Not just the easyJet flights. Ryanair announced twenty different routes to Morocco. So it shows you that a country with a similar climate to the southern bit of Spain, that was considered just a little bit more exotic, if you like, and therefore difficult to get to, is all of a sudden very close and very accessible. I think it will become the next property boom in Morocco now. It doesn't matter about the European Union. Join the open skies! It's called the "open skies". There is the political definition of the European Union and then there's the Aviation Club definition, if you like. The open skies! So you can join the open skies, without actually being a member of the Union. Turkey's opening up as well.'

With Tallinn still fresh in my mind, I ask about stag parties. Stelios is defensive: 'Stag parties? I think it's part of the culture in the sense that people who are about to get married want to do that thing. I don't think it's up to airlines to prevent it. In any event it's impossible to detect it in the sense that you don't believe in advance what people tell you they are going to do; people just book their seats and they turn up. We can't even stop them going on easyCruise. I'm seeing it at the easyCruise level. Suddenly five cabins get booked. It's ten guys turning up on a stag party. What are you going to do, refuse entry? It's perfectly within their rights, so provided they behave I don't have a problem with it. The difference is that twenty years ago it was at most a night out in London, now it is about going away for a weekend. That's what has changed. Because it's so cheap to go away for a weekend that's what people do.'

But how do you feel when papers say a town is 'ruined'? 'I think it's about behaving or misbehaving,' he says. 'It's not about who got them there that matters. There are plenty of legitimate uses of flying that I think you can't possibly argue that flying is bad just because some people might actually misbehave when they get there. It's a bit like the telephone or the Internet. Yes, there are ways you can abuse those media, but on the whole they're so positive they're worth having. So I would argue the same about flying.'

We move on to the Big Question: what about the damage flying causes the atmosphere? Can we keep on flying as much as we do now? What does Stelios think about the harm these new low-cost flights are causing in terms of increasing carbon emissions?

In response, Stelios holds up a small piece of paper in front of me. It's a bus ticket. 'I came down on an easyBus from Luton, instead of having my private minicab Mercedes. I actually went on a Mercedes minibus instead,' he says.

'I didn't make this up,' he continues. 'I just reached in my pocket and show you [the ticket].' I ask him how much it cost. '£8,' he says proudly. 'I shared my trip with eight other people. Instead of having one car going down the motorway with me in it and a driver, I shared it with eight other people. The point I'm trying to make is I think the environment needs to be protected and we need to constantly think about how we behave and how we can behave more environmentally responsibly.'

That doesn't quite answer my question, I say. Stelios shifts his argument. 'Now, aviation is not the biggest culprit [regarding carbon emissions],' he says. 'The biggest culprit is actually cars collectively in terms of emissions. Motor vehicles count for about a third of emissions. Aviation is actually under five per cent [of emissions].' This is true if you look at the global rather than the UK figures; in the UK flying is responsible for about 5.5 per cent, as said earlier, while globally the figure is more like three per cent. 'Now, that's not an excuse not to do anything about it, but I think you have to accept a couple of facts. First of all, there is no greener substitute to flying over a couple of hours. Some people, some greens, believe that trains are actually greener. I'm yet to be convinced. But even if you accept it as true, it's not a viable option over seven hundred miles. So if there isn't a greener alternative it becomes a question of: which airline do I fly? And I would argue that flying low-cost is environmentally more re-sponsible than flying high-cost.'

This is because there are more seats on low-cost planes than high-cost planes, because their fleets are in almost all cases younger and more fuel efficient than traditional airlines, and because low-cost planes fly less distance than high-cost planes, he says.

What would happen if people got rid of flights altogether, I ask – as some people seem to want this. 'If you get rid of flights you might even create wars again,' says Stelios, deadly earnest. How? 'Well, you remove the cultural understanding and the friendship and people go back to fighting with each other. I mean why do you think Muslims misunderstand the cartoons made in Denmark? Because there are not enough flights between Denmark and Afghanistan.'

That's one way of looking at it I suppose, I say. Stelios expands on the subject: 'No matter how much you hate the French as an English person, with one and a half million English people living in France you're not going to start a war. It's bringing people together. It's good for business. It's good for peace. It's good for stability. It's good for cultural understanding. And there isn't a greener option. If you told me you could go in a new sort of contraption that could get you there in about the same time and half the fuel, I'd do it. You have the option, for example, not to drive the Range Rover. You can drive a small car. Or you can go on the bus.'

He pauses to catch his breath. 'I drive a Smart car,' he says. And I try to imagine Stelios's big frame squeezed into one of those tiny toy-like cars – it must be quite a sight. 'I drive a Smart car not because of the environmental impact as such, it's because it's a more modest car. It fits my belief about conspicuous consumption. I can see environmentalists making arguments when you actually have an option – [for example] what car you drive. When there is no substitute that is clearly greener you're just talking about restricting freedom and taking people backwards.'

It's rather a stark contrast he's presenting. Weekend breaks or war – which side are you on?

Stelios warms to his theme: 'I think [travel] is a force for peace. It's a force for cultural and mutual understanding. It also creates jobs by the way. Let's not underestimate that travel and tourism is the largest single employer as an industry in the world. In the past they used to make cars to create jobs. That's not how you create jobs any more. You set up a tourism business. Working in travel and tourism now represents about ten per cent of the worldwide labour force.'

I say I've heard that oil and narcotics are bigger earners. 'In revenue you might be right,' he replies. 'But in terms of jobs, it's travel and tourism. Why do you think all these smaller countries have very strong ministries of tourism? It's because they figured out the only way to get people employed is to create a tourism industry. It creates jobs at every level. For bus drivers, ice-cream vendors, for waitresses. It's an equal opportunities employer: men and women of all educational levels. You need hotel managers, you need interpreters.'

Does he really think low-cost flights are so positive? It seems he does. 'The great thing about capitalism is that, acting in their individual self interest, [people can] actually contribute to the common good,' he says. 'We all act in our own best interests and yet the whole thing works. We make flights affordable. We make flights affordable and accessible because it's profitable. At the risk of offending trade unionists here, one of the benefits of the phenomena of integration is that you get some sort of wage stability as well. You don't allow wages in one country to go up when people are starving in another. I'm an economist by trade. Supply and demand is my instinct. So if there is a shortage of employees here and a shortage of jobs there what you do is take people from one place to the other. In centrally planned economies they tried to do this by order. In Europe it's happening naturally. If plumbers in London make too much money, enough Polish plumbers will move to London to make plumbing affordable again.'

It's the Polish plumber theory of New Europe, as told by the man who's done as much as any other to make it happen – along with Ryanair's O'Leary, who believes it is his job to 'annoy the w******' who campaign for the environment at the expense of no-frills flights. Boiled down and turned into a slogan, it might translate as: Low-Cost Airlines Make Europe Work.

It's getting stuffy in the tiny easyGroup board room, and I have reached the end of my time with Stelios. We walk along the grey carpet to the circular office. On the way, I ask Stelios if he's ever flown with Ryanair. He replies: 'I avoid Ryanair. I don't like them.' It's the first time he's sounded annoyed about anything.

I ask if he's going on the inaugural easyJet flight to Rijeka. 'Which weekend is that?' he asks, still sounding as though he hasn't got the faintest clue where Rijeka is. I can tell there's about as much chance of Stelios swapping Monaco for Rijeka as there is easyJet developing a new version of Concorde.

I shake his paw and he's soon at his round desk, absorbed in emails. I walk past the wall of cuttings, dodge the dodgy skunk men, slip by a stall selling pink T-shirts declaring 'I love porn', say 'no' to the Asian guy who asks again if I want marijuana, and go down the escalator past the '164 arrests' sign into the station.

On the train, I glance at what the man sitting opposite me is reading. It's the *Time Out European Breaks* guide – with an advert for Stansted Express on the front. Yet another Stelios customer. Another digit to add to the low-cost stats. And, if the Stelios theory of budget flights is right, more peace in Europe.

Who could argue with that?

12

SHOREDITCH, LONDON

GREEN GETS MEAN

Of course, quite a few people would take issue with Stelios on the issue of low-cost flights. And one of those is the man wearing a striped shirt, turquoise tie, blue cords and polished black shoes sitting in a tiny corner room in a 1960s block in a quiet back street of Shoreditch.

He looks at me incredulously as I explain Stelios's defence of low-cost flights. He lets out a breath of air in disbelief when I mention the easyJet founder's point that aviation is only responsible for 5.5 per cent of carbon emissions and so should not be targeted for criticism by environmentalists. He gazes at a row of aspidistras on a window ledge and shakes his head at the 'there would be war' theory.

On the walls are several posters with slogans saying, 'Is the Government doing enough about climate change?' with pictures of a red, apocalyptic sky above the Houses of Parliament. There are rows of books on overflowing shelves with titles such as *Eat Less Meat*, *The Ecology of Tomorrow's World*, and *Not on the Label: What Really Goes Into The Food On Your Plate*. Behind me are posters of parrots and a large map of South America showing the continent's rainforests.

If this were a *Through the Keyhole* guessing game about the type of person who used this office, your guess would have to be that this is someone who *cares about the planet*.

Tony Juniper, executive director of Friends of the Earth in England, Wales and Northern Ireland and vice president of Friends of the Earth International, definitely does care about the planet. As the head of the country's biggest environmental concern group, he is, you could say, one of the greenest men in Britain. And as such, he's not the biggest fan of low-cost flights.

He peers at me from under dark eyebrows and a mop of greying brown hair. He may be green and a do-gooder, but he does not fit the stereotypical image of a green do-gooder. He looks no-nonsense and businesslike – as though he would not be out of place on the board of British Airways, to pick the unlikeliest of career moves.

He's soon on the attack. 'Humph!' he says, listening to Stelios's points. 'Simplistic! Facile! Where do I start?'

He leans back in his chair and considers his answer to Stelios's arguments. 'The more efficient and better managed – in other words, full – aircraft with cleaner engines we have, is the better, obviously. But the point is: how much aviation can we have? Is there going to be a demand management policy that's going to be putting signals in the market and into the aviation economy in the years ahead about how many planes are going to be doing those flights over seven hundred miles?'

We're meeting, by chance, on the day an Oxford University report on air travel is published. This report says that, without curbing air travel, the UK will not meet its target of a sixty per cent cut in carbon dioxide emissions by 2050. This is because the proportion of carbon emissions from planes will grow from 5.5 per cent of the UK total now to a quarter in 2050. Much of this growth will come from low-cost planes, with easyJet and Ryanair having big orders for more aircraft.

The authors of the report call on the Government to increase Air Passenger Duty, a charge that is added to all fares, by as much as £25 a year. This would put a stop to a predicted growth in passenger movements at UK airports from 200 million a year at the moment to 470 million in 2030; this figure was just two million in 1950.

The result? No more low-cost flights. Charges would make them high-cost: it would be the end of the no-frills era.

It would also mean that big projects such as the building of an extra terminal, T5, at Heathrow and extra runways at Stansted and Gatwick could become unnecessary, as there would not be enough passengers to make them worthwhile.

The Oxford University report is entitled *Predict and Decide: Aviation, Climate Change and Policy*. The title plays on the Government's current stated policy of 'predict and provide', which has led to the expansion of Heathrow. The authors describe politicians' handling of the growth in air travel alongside its commitments to carbon emission reductions as 'clearly contradictory'.

The consequences of such contradictory policy-making will be, scientists agree, mass flooding, hurricanes, cyclones and droughts: the 'catastrophic mayhem' that comes from the 2°C temperature rise created by greenhouse gases. Indeed, in the worst case scenario, homo sapiens would become extinct. This is after living on Earth for 150,000 years. By comparison, the dinosaurs populated the planet for 160 million years.

Low-cost flights might, on the face of it, have a lot to answer for.

Juniper puts the anti-aviation case. 'The approach we've got at the moment is simply to meet demand rather than to manage demand,' he says, sounding as though this is clearly a short-sighted way of doing things. 'And this is the burden of the argument that comes out in the report today. It's about taking the growth forecast as something to be managed rather than something to be met. So, yes, it's right to have good aircraft, as Stelios suggests. But the question is: how many of them do we want to be making those flights over 700 miles? That's where Stelios and I part company. I agree that the technology and management of planes is important. But it's the number of planes that's the problem.'

But what about the economic importance of low-cost flights? The increase in tourism across Europe, with all the benefits that has to our standard of living? Shouldn't that be considered in the balance when discussing environmental effects?

'Let's look at that one,' says Juniper. 'We [at Friends of the Earth] have discovered a net economic loss for the UK economy in terms of exporting tourist money. So these economic arguments can work backwards and forwards.' I later read a recent Friends of the Earth study saying that for every £1 being spent in the regions of the UK by overseas visitors, £6.40 is being spent by Britons abroad.

'The broad point I'd make is that the economic benefits claimed by the aviation industry in terms of the UK economy are dramatically overstated whether it's in terms of jobs, airports, or whether it's in terms of the money tourists are bringing in. Yes it's good for people to be able to talk to each other and be able to see each other. But maybe economic integration and cultural integration could be achieved in ways that are far less polluting than is the case at the moment.'

So would Juniper ban flights altogether? 'No one's saying "no flights", are they?' he replies. 'We're talking about demand management. We're not saying "ban aeroplanes" and we're not saying "stop flying". What we're saying is "have a policy that can manage the industry at a level that is compatible with long-term climatic stability"'. It's very important to be clear about the messages because people say really stupid things about what the environmental community is saying. I mean: huge taxes. We're not saying huge taxes, we're saying sufficient taxes at a level to manage demand. That's very different to pricing people off the air.'

We talk about a recent comment by David Soskin, who runs a website called cheapflights.co.uk – a directory site for low-cost fares. Soskin accused people who slam no-frills airlines as being 'usually newspaper columnists or green spokespeople. They are reasonably affluent, well-educated and tend to live in places like Islington. They are the kind of people used to taking their holidays in the Dordogne and Tuscany and they don't like the fact that that sort of holiday is now affordable for millions of people whom they find it difficult to relate to. One of the proponents of "eco taxes" is Zac Goldsmith, a scion of one of the richest families in Britain. They are so out of touch with the way ordinary people live. They are snobs.'

Juniper is ready for this. 'If you look at some of the figures that are being produced by the industry claiming that curbing flights will harm the poorer consumers of aviation tickets, the figures simply don't bear that out,' he says calmly. 'In fact if you look at traffic out of Manchester Airport in the early part of this decade you'll find that there's actually a decrease in usage by people from lower income brackets. What's happening is that more middle-class people are travelling. They were the people travelling originally and they're now travelling *more* as a result of these low-cost flights. So again in terms of the equity arguments and where the economic benefits are falling, you can see that again there is a distributional element here which isn't reflected in what the airlines are saying.'

What about the benefits Stelios mentioned that tourism brings to other countries – to the wider wealth of Europe? 'In terms of the benefits to the economies of countries like Slovakia and Slovenia, look at the numbers. I mean, what percentage of GDP growth is delivered by low-cost airlines?' he asks. 'Again the claim is being made there that this is a major factor. But is it a major factor? I don't know. Do we have to have this level of growth in aviation in order to be able to sustain these economies' development and integration into the wider EU? It might be, as we've found in this country, that the effect has been quite dramatically overstated.'

I ask Juniper if he's ever been on a low-cost flight. 'Yeah, yeah. I've been on easyJet – you know – from the point of view of saving our money. When I'm doing business, they're good value. I don't dispute the success of the low-cost business model.'

Isn't that contradictory? 'Well actually in the case of easyJet their aircraft are good, they've got a modern fleet and so if you want to do a flight that's going to be relatively at the good end [of planes causing damage to the environment] then you might as well go on one of their jets.'

How many times do you fly a year? 'The approach we take here [at Friends of the Earth] is to try not to fly. But there are some flights you have to do. At the moment I fly six or seven times a year.'

Wow, that sounds like a lot. 'Well, the short-haul stuff I'm trying to avoid,' he responds. In the past year, he has flown to Malaysia, South Africa, Nigeria and Amsterdam. His flights would have emitted approximately eight tons of carbon dioxide. 'I usually need to be in Amsterdam for a meeting and some of those I just can't do by the ferry or the train because it takes an extra day either side. I'm trying to minimise those. We're trying to video conference for some of these things. But for me the problem I've got is being on the board of Friends of the Earth International [which is based in Amsterdam]. Among the staff here I'm probably the one who flies the most.'

Doesn't that make him realise that it's going to be extremely difficult for us ever to wean ourselves off our flights? I mean, if the head of the country's biggest green group finds it difficult to forego flying, surely it's going to be tough for the rest of us?

He looks a bit tied up by this, but replies: 'We had a recent conference in Nigeria, our most recent international meeting, and you can't really get round a flight. I did actually look at going over land. It would have taken a fortnight or something. It's not practical.'

Do you fly on holiday ever, or is it only for business? 'Very, very rarely,' he says, admitting that he took his family by plane to Slovakia last year. 'We're going on half-term holiday next week. We're going across to Amsterdam and we're going to take the ferry from Harwich and use public transport when we're there. I don't think that's any kind of a sacrifice really. I mean planes are actually quite a lot cheaper. But the ferry I think will be good for the kids. They can stretch their legs, run about and stuff.'

Other family holidays, he says, have included trips to Cornwall, Wales, East Anglia, Scotland, the Isle of Wight, and the New Forest. 'A lot of people are rediscovering the great glories that lie on our doorstep: holidays that you can make inside the UK,' he says. 'We went to Cornwall this summer and we went last year as well. It's absolutely fantastic. And you avoid all the stress of going on an aircraft. We can take everything we wanted with us. We can take pets and everything. It was a real pleasure.'

Whereabouts exactly? 'The north coast, in the countryside near Padstow. It was really gorgeous and I didn't feel as though it was any sacrifice at all not going abroad. There is a kind of a fashion – in some ways people don't feel as though they've had a proper holiday unless they've been out of the UK. I find that to be quite the opposite actually. I do feel doubly exhausted when it involves an aeroplane flight. I drove down there [to Cornwall] and took the car and five people in it.'

So not by train then? What car do you drive, I ask. 'I have a kind-of average thing. It doesn't get driven very much,' Juniper replies vaguely.

What about other areas of life? What about recycling? 'We recycle everything,' he says. 'We do all the stuff at home that you would expect in terms of recycling. Plus we have energy-efficient appliances. And pretty much everything we do in town [he lives in Cambridge] is on bike or foot.' At the Friends of the Earth office all waste is recycled – there are great big recycling bins by the front door – low-energy bulbs have been installed where possible, state of the art double-glazing is about to be introduced, new computers hibernate quickly to prevent waste, and solar panels are being considered to provide electricity.

We switch to the possibility of green planes that use 'clean' fuel. Many have suggested that ethanol or hydrogen could be used as an alternative to normal fuel, which is made from kerosene. Juniper says: 'If we can develop planes that don't produce pollution, then wonderful. But my colleagues tell me that it's going to be a couple of decades before there's going to be a serious technological breakthrough in being able to fly aircraft that are going to be clean.'

Some, though, are sceptical that there will ever be clean planes. The radical thinker and writer George Monbiot recently poured cold water on the likelihood in his book *Heat*, in which he points out that alternative fuels such as bio-diesel actually contribute to global warming. Ethanol is too dangerous to use in planes as it is highly inflammatory; and hydrogen would take up four times as much space in planes, making it impractical. Even if one of these were to be developed successfully, he says, the moist hot air from engines flying over 30,000ft can form trails of cirrus clouds no matter what the fuel. These clouds trap heat in the atmosphere – and help explain why plane emissions are believed to have 2.7 times the effect of mere carbon emissions.

So what can anyone do? Is it all doom and gloom? Are we flying ourselves to extinction? Will low-cost flights have to go?

No, says Juniper. But he believes the world's governments must act. In the UK, he says: 'We're seeking a broad legal framework that will govern the whole of the British Government's effort on climate change emissions reductions over time. What we're looking for is a legal requirement to deliver an economy-wide cut that puts us in line with the most recent climate-change science. And so working back from what the climatologists are now telling us, we think that a three per cent annual reduction [of carbon emissions] across the whole UK economy is what's needed. We need to be minus seventy per cent from where we are now. Possibly even more than that, maybe even ninety per cent.'

Does that mean a green tax on flights then? No more 1 pence fares in the future? 'Yeah, yeah. It's obvious. We took a

Department of Transport aviation growth model and we applied fuel taxes at the same level as you paid to fill up your car. If you do that, you automatically – if you use the model – eliminate all the aviation growth that's predicted. Just by that one measure. You also have a range of other tools in terms of Air Passenger Duty, which is like a charge on the tickets. You have emissions charging, which is another tool which would encourage more efficient aircraft.'

The key point is not imposing extra taxes on consumers but on taxing aviation fuel, which currently isn't taxed. In all, the Friends of the Earth believes that the aviation industry is subsidised to the tune of £9.2 billion a year through not having a tax on fuel. This equates to £300 per person living in the UK.

Flight prices will have to go up, he argues: 'But you don't have to end tourism as a logical consequence of managing demand in aeroplanes, you can still have quite a lot of tourism, doing less of it by plane.'

The Bishop of London recently described flying as being a 'symptom of sin'. But Juniper does not believe it is useful to throw around terms such as 'sin' and 'guilt'. This is because the onus should not be just on individuals to make changes to lifestyles, he says. Instead, it is the responsibility of the Government to act. 'It's for everybody to be thinking about what contribution they can make but I don't think organisations like Friends of the Earth are going to get a lot of support for our aims by making people feel guilty,' he says.

'What we do need to do is give people the information in order to make choices, but also give them some credible ways in which these problems can be solved. Even if people feel guilty, it's not going to solve the problem. Even if they don't take that particular flight, it's not going to solve the problem. It can make a difference and start to create a culture where people think about these things. And that is essential. But it's not going to be able to deal with the wider question until governments intervene.'

So what then can us environmentally damaging travellers do? 'The most important thing that the public can do is to signal to their MPs and the government that they want action,' Juniper replies. 'Then, if there's a rail alternative or a surface transport alternative to planes certainly have a look at it. For a lot of people this isn't necessarily that convenient, so we do need to keep an eye on the bigger policy picture. But certainly if people can do the alternatives in a convenient way, we would encourage them.'

We get on to the subject of carbon offsetting – when you pay for measures to be introduced to cover the carbon dioxide cost of flights. This involves paying for trees to be planted or for solar panels to be installed or low-energy bulbs to be used.

'We're not convinced about those,' says Juniper. 'We're looking at them at the moment to see if they can be a credible way of reducing the environmental impact of flying. But we really don't think they are a good and reliable means to un-do the damage that's caused by an aeroplane flight. For example, tree-planting schemes. There are big issues there about permanence, how long these trees are going to be there, and if the climate changes and they catch fire and burn down then your carbon offsets disappear and there's nothing anyone can do about it.'

Surely signing up to a good scheme would be useful? 'Yes, but even if you have the very best schemes – and we do look at these and hope that something is there that we can advocate – the reality is that the problem is not going to be solved by those schemes.'

I get the feeling he's not a big fan of carbon offsetting schemes.

'BA has a voluntary offset scheme that they've been offering to their passengers recently and it's well under one per cent of people who have been taking it up,' he continues. 'What about the other ninety-nine per cent of travellers? The difficulty with all of this stuff, is that all of these things may have merit indivi-dually, but unless they are actually reducing emissions to the point that's going to be compatible with long-term climate stability, it's not going to work. The scale of cuts needed is such that it's going to require intervention from governments: individual governments, regional governments at the EU level, and globally through the United Nations. To that extent I really think it's important to get people to see the need for political action as well as doing some stuff themselves.'

I later check with BA exactly what percentage of people has signed up to its scheme. 'We don't find it useful to release that information,' said a spokesman.

What does Juniper think of current Government policy? 'They've done nothing, they've done absolutely nothing,' he replies despairingly. 'The one thing they and some of the airlines have been talking about is this emissions trading scheme.' This works through areas of industry with high emissions buying 'carbon credits' from other industries where efficiencies have been introduced. 'But the very first introduction [in aviation] of anything like that is going to be 2012, which is still quite a long way away. Potentially, emissions trading could be a very powerful tool, but only if it's used correctly.'

Juniper believes that there is not only a timescale problem. There are also, he says, too many carbon credits, which mean there's insufficient economic pressure on companies to reduce emissions. 'The other problem with applying aviation to the existing scheme is the likely reaction of some of the other big industrial polluters like the cement, steel and aluminium industries across Europe,' he adds, gazing across his aspidistras. 'They fear quite rightly that sticking aviation into the scheme they're in will lead to a very rapid increase in the price of carbon credit. The aviation sector will buy the lot, which will mean that [those industries] will be disadvantaged compared to Chinese producers of steel, whereas the aviation industry won't be because if you want to take a flights from Stansted to Bucharest, you have to start from Stansted. If you want to buy a bag of cement you can buy it from Beijing just as well as buying it from Bromsgrove.'

Juniper starts to get worked up when I ask about Terminal Five at Heathrow. How can politicians even pretend to be curbing aviation growth if they're giving the go ahead to new terminals? 'Exactly,' he replies. 'And that's what's happening. Politicians talk with a deeply forked tongue on this subject of climate and what needs to be done about it. Aviation is perhaps the most dramatic example of their contradictions because of the speed of the growth, and the impact it has because of the altitude of the emissions. It's a particularly stark contradiction.'

So he's not happy with politicians? 'Yes. Let's not try to bury it. There is a political problem. But that's what governments are for: it's to solve big issues that the public can't solve on their own. I mean nobody would expect people to go off and solve terrorism voluntarily, would they? For people to conduct the war on terror by taking personal action?'

This, I can't help thinking, is a very good point.

'Yet with a far bigger threat – global warming – the implication is: "We're not going to intervene, it's up to the public." And that's just bollocks really,' he continues, with a steely look. 'You're not going to solve these problems by saying: "We can't intervene because it's too controversial." Just look at identity cards, freedom of movement checks at airports and everything else. All this has been happily done because terrorism is such a major problem. Tony Blair himself and his chief scientific advisor tell us that climate change is an even bigger problem and yet the political leadership is absent in terms of taking on tough issues that potentially are going to generate quite negative headlines in the short term. On climate change the not very deeply hidden message is: "Well public, you should sort this out for yourselves." '

*   *   *

After Stelios's spirited defence of no-frills flying – all the
economic arguments and the role of low-cost planes in economic
integration – Juniper is food for (a lot) of thought.

It's clear there are no easy answers when it comes to reconcil-
ing cheap flights and keeping the world green. Juniper admitted
as much himself with his regular easyJet trips to Amsterdam and
his conferences in Nigeria. We're all very used to flying. We like
it. Flying is part of our lifestyles. Flying is part of the head of
Friends of the Earth's lifestyle. There are a hell of a lot of cheap
flights about.

It's something I intend to mull over at my final destination:
Rijeka in Croatia. Maybe a swim in the Adriatic and some time
out relaxing in June sunshine – after a carbon dioxide pumping
easyJet flight – will help bring some conclusions on the subject:
to fly or not to fly (or maybe just not fly quite as much)? Are we
all hypocrites? Are we – homo sapiens – destined to be a blink in
the history of the world compared to the dinosaurs?

But before I get to the Adriatic, I'm staggered by a news report.
Apparently – and I found this hard to believe – flatulent cows are
a bigger cause of gas emissions than the whole aviation industry
put together. There are, I'm informed, 1.4 billion cows worldwide and each produces 500 litres of methane a year. This
accounts for fourteen per cent of all emissions of gases. In a
year, scientists estimate, a single cow releases the equivalent gas
to that created by two return flights from London to Sydney.

So maybe we should just cut down on hamburgers – is *that* the
answer?

Yet more to consider in the Croatian sun.

13

RIJEKA, CROATIA

ON THE BEACH

C roatia may be an increasingly popular place for a break in the sun in the Med, but few people have heard of Rijeka. It's the newest easyJet destination and even Stelios, as he revealed in Camden, doesn't know much about his flights there – clearly a classic example of a little known low-cost flight destination: another overlooked spot that's just a few quid away.

The guidebooks do not exactly sing the praises of Croatia's third biggest city. 'A down to earth industrial city . . . far from beautiful . . . the northern Adriatic's only true metropolis . . . mustering a reasonable number of attractions,' is the *Rough Guide*'s description.

Lonely Planet is equally unimpressed: 'Rijeka . . . a place to leave as fast as possible.'

In other words, it's absolutely perfect for me.

It's also a fitting finale. I've decided that this is going to be my last trip, and it's also a bit of a reunion. I'm here with three of the Polish people I met in Szczecin – Wojciech, from the Radisson SAS, and his friends Anna (of knee-high boots fame) and Elvi (curly hair, hazel eyes). They took me out for a night on the town, nearly half a year ago now; we drank slightly too much, had a good time, and kept in touch.

I'd told him about Rijeka; how I was looking forward to getting some sun, taking it easy, possibly going to a beach or two. Before I knew it, Wojciech, Anna and Elvi were coming to Croatia too, along with Danny, my friend and fellow-traveller in Haugesund.

Which is how we've found ourselves in Rijeka, sitting at a pizzeria overlooking the docks, on a sunny Saturday afternoon in July. It's just the four of us – Danny will be coming by train from Slovenia this evening. Wooden fishing boats with old-fashioned riggings and blue and white buoys tied to the sides are gliding about the harbour. A large blue ferry has just docked, its engine purring across the water. Seagulls are swooping above. Youthful locals in sunglasses are walking towards a row of shops near our hotel. A row of cargo cranes is silhouetted on the horizon, looking like a family of large insects. In the distance, mountainous coastlines loom through the afternoon haze.

And it's really, we've already decided, not so bad. Rijeka is a decent spot for a weekend break. It's so laid back. We have got to be the only tourists here. It's not the dead end the *Rough Guide* described, but a quiet and not uncharming working port. We are staying at its best hotel, the Grand Bonavia, a concrete and tinted glass structure in the centre of town. We have balconies overlooking terracotta rooftops of venerable nineteenth-century houses on to the harbour. Not bad considering the rooms cost £60 a night, after our £67 easyJet tickets.

We've come on the inaugural easyJet flight, and the hotel staff seems bemused to have no-frills holidaymakers bounding in to stay for the weekend. The receptionist said that most guests are either 'business people or just passing through'. She's also told us that Tom Selleck, Goran Ivanisevic, Kurt Douglas and Natasha Kinski have stayed at the hotel – which seemed a little unlikely.

Wojciech looks like a holidaying footballer, with tan trousers, sandals and a short back and sides. Elvi is wearing jeans with trendy turn-ups and a cute purple top, and has flowers painted on her fingernails. Anna is in a lime-green blouse with tight jeans. We arrived at midnight last night, but Elvi and Anna went straight out to check out the local bars, and ended up in three different clubs, not coming back til 5.00 or 5.30 – they can't remember which. They seem very impressed by Rijeka's clubs.

Apparently people were dancing 'on the stairs, dancing on the chairs, dancing on the tables,' according to Elvi. Anna adds: 'Everyone was trying to meet us. They knew so much about Poland. It was fun!' The girls estimate that they were chatted up 'ten to fifteen times', which they seem very happy about. They want to go the clubs again tonight to be chatted up some more.

We tuck into large pepperonis – and the Poles have a debate about whether to stay in Poland or go abroad to find a job. It's the kind of talk I've heard time and again over the past few months; and it just doesn't seem to go away.

Wojciech, who has ordered two pizzas as he's famished, is in favour of Poles staying in Poland. 'There are a lot of young successful people in Szczecin,' he says. 'If we want the city to improve we need young people to do it.'

Anna says she wouldn't mind working abroad, possibly in the UK, after she's finished her part-time degree while employed at Szczecin's airport. 'Yes, but come on,' she says, responding to Wojciech. 'If you are a scientist or a doctor what's stopping you going abroad? The laboratories are better. The pay is better.' She turns to me. 'It is just a fact that most well qualified people now at least think about going to work in another country.'

'And these people always say they will bring back money after they have been away a few years, but do they? No!'

'Humph! Many people come back. Many, many,' Anna retorts. They munch their pizzas.

A horn sounds on the ferry and a thoughtful air descends. I can tell each is considering moving west. Will they go abroad soon? Can they face leaving home? Is that what the future holds?

After lunch we go for a city tour with Sandra, who is sporting a big smile and even bigger Gucci glasses. We stroll down the Corso, the main, pedestrianised shopping street There's a deep blue sky. Cafés line both sides of the street. 'People drink coffee here all day long,' says Sandra. 'We are great coffees drinkers.

We drink when it's sunny. We drink when it rains. We just drink a whole lot of coffee.'

We pass the long row of cafés, and Sandra tells us some very odd local history. In the aftermath of the First World War, she says, there was uncertainty about who exactly ought to control Rijeka. Italy and the Serbs, the Croats and the Slovenes all had claims. There were international meetings in Paris to discuss the matter. Yet they came to nothing because a rather mad-sounding Italian poet called Gabriele D'Annunzio had other ideas.

On 12 September 1919, after raising a ragbag mini 'army', D'Annunzio seized Rijeka and offered the port to Italy in the way mad poets do for their country. Italian officials, concerned that D'Annunzio had overstepped the mark, declined his offer. So he set up his own state. He wrote a constitution that included ten different strata of society – ranging from agricultural workers to seafarers to teachers to civil servants to 'heroes, poets, prophets and supermen'.

D'Annunzio declared that music was to be a founding principle of the state and there should be regular musical state events. He also brought in a black-shirt police force and introduced the practice of dousing opponents in castor oil to humiliate them (when he was feeling generous) or kill them (when he wasn't).

Simply stated, D'Annunzio was a fascist. Many believe him to have created the world's first fascist state, which lasted up to December 1920, when he was eventually driven out by Italian forces.

His actions caught the eye of another Italian: Benito Mussolini, who some consider to have been partly inspired by D'Annunzio. Just two years later, Mussolini was ruler of Italy, and he gave D'Annunzio a seat in the senate, and later, a state funeral.

Sandra says: 'He is a part of Rijeka's history that has been hidden in the past, especially during the socialist time. During my education we never heard about him or that Rijeka was the first fascist state in the world.' Is there a museum about his life? 'No, no. D'Annunzio took everything – objects of art, documents, photographs – with him to Lake Garda in Italy and there is a museum dedicated to him there. Here there is no museum nor even a tiny room dedicated to D'Annunzio. It is as if as he was never here.'

We scoot about the sites, including St Vitus's church, which has a cannonball lodged in a wall by the entrance. Apparently this was fired by the British when they were attacking Napoleonic forces, although the assault was stopped short when a pretty local woman called Karolina 'used all her feminine side', as Sandra puts it, to persuade the Brits to cease fire. Karolina has become a local hero and there are now bars and cafés named after her.

The subject of the 1991–95 civil war in Croatia crops up. Sandra says, 'In other cities there was fighting. There were hard feelings in those cities. There was not fighting here. We were living and working as usual and trying to forget the other areas.' The Serbian population at the time was around ten per cent in Rijeka. Now it is much lower.

'Most left, though some stayed and fought with the Croatian army,' she says. 'I was working at a school at the time. Sometimes kids would just disappear overnight. They would not turn up for classes. Nothing would have been said. It was just presumed that they had left [for Serbia].'

Most industry collapsed in Rijeka during the war – including the closure of a massive paper mill. 'The second largest in the world,' according to Sandra. Now it is a cultural centre, but once it provided as much as half of the cigarette papers used by Marlboro.

The economy, however, has improved rapidly in the past few years, mainly on the back of renewed confidence after the initial hangover created by the war. 'Since 2000 we are finding our identity again. We make the city more vivid.' You mean lively? 'Yes. Lively. Vivid. Up to 1996, this was a dead town. Life is much better now than it was fifteen years ago,' says Sandra. 'Friends who used to live here but now have lives abroad come back here, from Trieste, Milan, wherever, and they say how much better it is.'

Sandra shows us the fruit and veg, meat and fish markets. The air is heavy with smells of melons, strawberries, cherries and nectarines one moment, and pungent and salty with fish the next. The markets are down by the docks where thousands of emigrants left for the US in the nineteenth and early twentieth centuries – including Fiorello LaGuardia, the future mayor of New York City who gave his name to one of New York's airports.

By Trsat Castle on the top of a hill looking down on the city centre there are grand Austro-Hungarian era houses. The Poles have their picture taken next to a statue of Pope John Paul II – like all good Polish people would. The former Pope visited Rijeka a few years back.

The city is spread out below, its harbour full of boats and cranes, the acres of terracotta roofs and its string of Tito-era housing blocks on the slope of the hill. I'm so used to seeing blocks like this in Central and Eastern Europe now, that I hardly find them unusual. Could they be considered architecturally important in a modernist, functionalist or other '-ist' way? I ask Sandra what she thinks: 'No! They are ugly! We think they are ugly!' But they won't be pulled down, as they provide important housing.

Sandra tells us that Bernie Ecclestone's wife is from Rijeka. 'We are hoping that maybe he will bring the Formula One to us.' Somehow I can't help feeling that might be a long shot.

Later, I learn that the Port of Rijeka was recently proclaimed a 'cultural monument' by the World Bank, which is contributing £107 million to a project to build a marina, redevelop the port, add new hotels and restore old buildings. Much of this is meant to be ready by 2008, although when I mention this to one local, their reaction was along the lines of: 'And pigs might fly!'

But when I speak to the head of the local tourist board, Petar, I find that he's a believer. He says: 'The city in the past has just been a transport hub – a big industrial place. Now the city has an opportunity to go in a touristic way. We get 100,000 people coming through Rijeka a year. It is not so many. We want more. We hope to become a touristic centre. We have museums. We have nightlife. We have shopping. Cruise ships will be able to visit the new marina. Things will change for us.'

It's a far cry from places elsewhere on the Mediterranean. Most places in the Med are crawling with tourists. Here there are hardly any to speak of. Yet there are big plans for the future. Petar shows me a map of the region as he talks about the new marina and the future. And suddenly I notice something: Trieste is just twenty-five miles to the north-west, across the Istrian peninsula, in Italy. On my first weekend, way back in Szczecin, I came across the old Churchill quote about an 'Iron Curtain [descending] across the continent' from 'Stettin in the Baltic to Trieste in the Adriatic'.

Having started at one end of the 'curtain', I'm ending up at the other. And I've seen quite a bit of what's in between as well.

In the early evening, Danny arrives in time for us all to watch England play Portugal in the World Cup quarter-finals. England loses during penalties – what Elvi calls 'the kicks' – and we go out for a meal to cheer ourselves up.

Outside, few people are about. The fish restaurant we'd had our eye on is closed. At the Opium Buddha Lunch Bar, we sit outside and eat grilled chicken and chips, watching the sun set over Rijeka's docks.

Afterwards, we go to a succession of bars and clubs for A Very Long Time. Anna and Elvi start ordering Red Bulls and vodkas and get chatted up by people – all of whom seem to have been to Krakow and want to tell them everything about Krakow, and don't stop telling them about Krakow till 4 a.m.

My recollections get a little hazy here, All I will say, is: it is very lively in Rijeka. If you're after good nightlife, you'll find it in Croatia's largest port. People apparently come from miles around to go to the clubs near our hotel. You'll probably be the only tourists there.

And you'll probably have a very good time too.

Croatia has more than 1,100 islands. Most people who visit Croatia go to the islands, but many are hardly touched by tourism, almost unbelievably so, given how naturally beautiful they are and how most of the Mediterranean is overflowing with tourists. One of the reasons for this is simply that there are so many islands. But the recent wars have also had a big effect.

In the 1980s about 500,000 Britons visited the country each year. It looked like Croatia could go the way of Greece and Turkey, where tourism was also booming at the time as people moved on from Spain and France to explore other parts of the Med. But tourism collapsed after the 1991 civil war, during which the Serb minority and the Yugoslav army fought Croats over their decision to become independent. This was followed in 1999 by the start of the Kosovo war, which hit tourism even though Croatia was not involved. Visitor levels from the UK dropped to 68,000 in 2000 and many in the travel industry despaired that Britons would never return in large numbers.

Tourism has picked up in recent trouble-free years. But it's still way down on what's been going on in Greece and Turkey. About 255,000 people visited from the UK last year. And this means many parts – especially the islands – are lovely and quiet.

Cres, a short drive and a ferry from Rijeka, is no exception. Cres is about forty miles long and five miles wide – the largest island in the Adriatic Sea. It is also one of the quietest with 2,900 inhabitants living in tiny villages in its mountainous interior, most making a living from sheep farming, olive growing, bee keeping, fishing and, of late, renting rooms in small buildings for tourists to stay.

Danny and I catch the ferry to Cres and drive through tiny mountain roads in bright sunshine past scrub-like vegetation to meet Vulture Man.

Goran Susic is based here on a tiny eco centre on a hilltop in a village called Beli. From a crumbling old school house that was occupied by Italian forces under Mussolini, Susic runs an operation that helps conserve a surprisingly large local population of griffin vultures. These have become a tourist attraction since he set up his centre in 1993, bringing a trickle of visitors (and tourist cash) to his out of the way operation.

Goran greets us enthusiastically when we arrive. 'You have arrived!' he exclaims. 'You have come to see our biodiversity! I will show you the biodiversity of the vultures!'

He loves his vultures. 'It is the poetry of their flight!' he says, leading us past a group of Italian children who are visiting to help repair stone walls and clear pathways on a series of nature walks. We enter a room with a large stuffed griffin vulture hanging gruesomely from the ceiling. We are informed that the vultures can weigh 8–15 kilograms and have wingspans of 240–280 centimetres. 'They can starve for up to three weeks and lose half their body weight, but then they must eat,' says Goran. They eat birds, sheep and the odd donkey – and there are seventy-five pairs on the island. This is up from twenty-five pairs in 1993. Vulture couples stay together for sixty to seventy years.

Displays in this room explain how the Parsee people believe in leaving dead bodies out in the open to be devoured by nature, often by vultures. 'Yes, vultures are still eating dead humans,' he says. 'The Parsee people are still using this. They are not allowed to bury or burn or put bodies in the river. The only way is to give to nature. Then the soul goes to heaven, they believe.' Another display shows that griffin vultures were the symbol of Upper Egypt in the days of the pharaohs.

Outside, two large black vultures with shiny pink heads are lurking in a green cage. They have injured their wings and are doomed to life in captivity. They hop from one perch to another with great swoops of black feathers as Goran explains how his eco centre works. 'You see, I decided to protect this island, to protect this species, to protect the ecosystem.' There are about 20,000 sheep on Cres, but Goran has convinced shepherds to allow the sheep to live organically. This means they are not treated with medicines, resulting in ten per cent dying naturally in the open each year.

He says: 'The vultures eat these to survive and the farmers are able to sell top-quality organic lamb at a good price. There are 375 plant species on the island. So the sheep have plenty to munch on. And the farmers are happy.'

Do the vultures get on with humans? 'Yes, yes, on the whole,' Goran says. 'But a man on the other side of the island said that one of the vultures tried to take his sandwich once. I'm not so sure about this.'

Goran believes that his kind of nature tourism is the way forward. 'There are not many people on this island. So the villages are small. I know the people in the villages. They live in a traditional way. But they can also benefit from tourism. And they see people coming to visit our centre, so they are happy.' About 14,000 people come to help at his centre each year, staying in dorms at the old yellow school house. 'This is why we are not going for the Coca-Cola and the McDonald's way of living. The local politicians can see that we are attracting people without that. Anyway tourists like that are not tourists at all. They are destroyers. You see it on the Spanish and the Greek islands. You see it everywhere: planes coming every thirty minutes; "*damen*" and "*herren*" written on the toilet doors; German music in all these huge hotels. The traditional way of life is destroyed.'

Past fig and olive trees and along a small pathway, there are sweeping views across a bay. In the distance we can see Rijeka;

the tower blocks just visible. On the pathway there are abstract sculptures by a local artist. These are dotted around eighty kilometres of trails throughout Cres. Apparently, it takes about three days to do the full loop. The sun is bearing down and not far away two enormous black birds are swooping on thermals near the shore – vultures looking for a sheep lunch, no doubt. 'Aren't they just wonderful?' says Goran, staring at them dreamingly. 'Poetry, I tell you, simply poetry.'

Wojciech, Elvi and Anna are raring to go – to the beach. We drive to Baska, a lovely pebble beach on Krk, another island just to the south of Cres and reached via a long bridge.

The water is clear, calm and warm. Rows of yellow sunshades line the narrow strip of pebbles. It is busy. We splash about in the sea. This is more like it. After the winter months in Poland, Slovakia and Finland, it's absolutely great to feel some heat. We lie on the pebbles and soak in the sun. Maybe there are other overseas tourists around, but it's difficult to tell. Most people look like locals: tall, tanned and fit. In other words: not very British at all. I don't think Baska is in danger of doing a Benidorm – as Goran fears some parts of Croatia will.

Way back in freezing Szczecin half a year ago, I did not really know what I was letting myself in for, I reflect, lying back on the pebbles. I had liked the idea of visiting the places no one else wants to visit. I liked the idea of 'seeing the unspellables'. There was a big sense of adventure when I stepped off the plane last December in Poland. Very few people go on holiday in Poprad or Paderborn. These were (largely) uncharted tourist waters.

So it was the adventure that led the way, and the adventure that sustained my interest. As did the people I met on my long weekends away. I saw at first hand – especially in Szczecin, Poprad and Brno – the pressures on people to move to the West. Characters like Hubert, on my first flight, are the bread and butter customers, it seems, for Europe's low-cost flights.

But there is a lot of uncertainty. If they do move abroad, is it for ever? Most of those I've met appear unsure. Mirko, the art historian, and Natalia, the DJ and translator, both left Slovakia in something close to despair. Both told me they didn't feel like they fit in.

'I feel different,' Natalia told me. 'I want to have a faster way of life. I am not like other people round here.' Little-known places in Eastern Europe may be getting brand names like Tesco, but a few brand names do not transform an economy. Almost every mall or shopping precinct I've seen has been quiet: lots of shops, very few people shopping. All you've got to do is look at the GDP figures to see that there's a long way to go. This creates a sense of impatience among the young. Maybe it's exacerbated because people can see western lifestyles on television and on the Internet. Now they can jump on low-cost flights for 1 pence each way and give western lifestyles a go.

Low-cost aircraft are crucial to this vast movement. Almost every flight has been, I'd guess, ninety per cent full of locals. No-frills planes are clearly the commuter buses of Eastern Europe. Hubert in Szczecin was just the first of many. How long the Huberts will stay no one knows. How many there are, no one exactly knows. Politicians in the UK are back-pedalling and creating tougher immigration rules for newer EU countries such as Bulgaria and Romania. After previous underestimates, they're getting heavy. Travelling on Ryanair, Wizz Air, SkyEurope and easyJet to these little-known spots, I've seen this exodus from the frontline. Without the convenience of no-frills flights, immigration would surely be a fraction of levels today.

I've also witnessed the movement to the East of all the British property speculators and stag and hen parties. The statistic that fifteen per cent of people in Europe now have second homes is amazing but – it's clear from taking these low-cost flights – probably true. Programmes such as *A Place in the Sun* are selling the get-rich-quick Eastern European dream. Buy in Bulgaria –

and watch you investment rise forty per cent in value every year. You may never need to work again! Clearly some of the sales pitches are OTT: reports are starting to come back from the likes of Bulgaria about major rip-offs and hopelessly unrealistic sales promises. But people are bound to keep going for them. Property prices are just too high back home. Many feel it's a better bet becoming an Eastern European property speculator. But as I saw, there is a nasty side to the business – the racism, the 'them and us' suspicions of being cheated, and the ugly sense of making a quick buck on the back of a poorer country.

Meanwhile the stag and hen groups just keep on coming. In Tallinn I saw just how much money can be made from stag-party tourism. And yes, much of the behaviour is unedifying. There were fights, people were hopelessly drunk, and there is a sex industry side to stag tourism. Andrus from Skype's comments about his girlfriend being hassled as he walks through town struck home. As did a feeling that we are definitely flaunting our wealth and that this is all quite unpleasant. Sure, it's fun shooting guns in the Estonian woods and letting your hair down once in a while – plus the local economy prospers. I must admit I enjoyed it. Yet the people of Tallinn seemed so naturally reserved – one of the reasons E-Stonia loves its emails – that it seemed a shame to have hordes of Brits descending on its compact medieval city centre.

Then, of course, there have been some straight up surprises: like the joys of North Sea fishing in Haugesund, the perhaps not so joyous cold water plunges of Tampere and the squaddies of Paderborn. This random, 'experimental tourism' aspect of flying on a low-cost plane to a place you've never heard of is exciting. Really, when it comes down to it, you're not quite sure how things will work out when the aeroplane nose lifts off the runway at Stansted. But *that's* the whole fun of going.

You discover all sorts of historical stories you'd never expect. Just now in Rijeka, D'Annunzio, the writer, daredevil and prototype fascist. In Tampere, the meeting of Lenin and Stalin. In Szczecin, Solidarity's forgotten man. In Brno, the work of Ludwig Mies van der Rohe at Villa Tugendhat. In Paderborn, Himmler's spooky castle. In lovely Ljubljana, Plecnik's wonderful architecture.

You come across characters aplenty – some more likeable than others: the mayor of Poprad with all his secretaries; Vidar and his fascinating facts on Haugesund; Stephen Toms and his vegetarian food shop in Tampere; X and her views on Gypsies and the Vietnamese in Brno; our vulture man Goran in Rijeka; Miglena, the world's sweetest estate agent, in Bourgas; the Dark Industrialists of Ljubljana; Anet and her strippers and lethal green vodkas in Tallinn.

All of this has made me begin to think differently about travel. Of course, going to so many no-name destinations seemed like madness at first. Many of these are the places that the guidebooks have written off. Yet I was constantly surprised by the places I chose. It was that element of surprise that made me feel like I was being a real traveller. There was a definite sense of travelling into the unknown. Okay, I'm missing the Eiffel Tower and Rome's Trevi Fountain, but I don't mind. On each visit I felt like I was opening a metaphorical travel present. Here was another mysterious place to discover. I stepped off every no-frills journey with a real sense of excitement.

Who says the age of 'real travel' is dead? Yes, we're all jetting away to Machu Picchu and the pyramids in our weeks off. But I think there's plenty still to explore. It's just a matter of knowing where to look.

There was also a feeling of exclusivity. Most of these places are completely off the beaten track. Go and there won't be many others around; just like on Baska beach, you'll probably be the only tourists. Why go with the flow? Why not try something different? You're much more likely to meet other people if you're thrown into the tourist deep end. Locals are curious: who is this madman who's come to see us in the middle of our Eastern European winter?

And the flights are cheap. Never forget the flights are dirt cheap. On average I worked out, they cost £48.36 return – pretty amazing when many train journeys in the UK are more than this. The tickets are, quite simply, fantastic bargains. If you combine them with cheap accommodation, as I did in Ljubljana, you can easily do a three-night break for around £150, spending money included.

But what about the environmental cost? I listened to Stelios's views on flying being key to bringing economic and cultural integration in the EU. He's right. Yes, maybe there should, as *The Economist* suggested, be a square named after him and Ryanair's O'Leary in Brussels. But even though the low-cost fleets are new and 'cleaner' than many traditional carriers – with many more seats – there is no getting round the carbon emissions impact. Low-cost planes are damaging the world. There is no question about this.

Yet you might argue that it is better to fly to the fjords in Norway than it is to fly to the fjords in New Zealand. You might also argue that it's less polluting to fly to the Bulgarian Black Sea than it is to fly to Mauritius. How about a city break in Ljubljana instead of New York? Or what about a trip to Estonia's little-visited islands in the summer instead of the Caribbean? The temperature is warm, the islands are beautiful – as my sister reported after a trip last summer. The point is that there are an awful lot of interesting places that are a short-haul flight away.

I've also listened to Tony Juniper's arguments on flying, though, and it's clear we ought to cut down. The occasional trip is fun, but I know that I will never again be able to fly around Europe so frequently without thinking twice. Yet I also agreed with Juniper's point that it is the Government that must act to increase taxes so that planes are taxed at the same level as cars – to me that's common sense. Individuals should not be made to feel guilty for flying – it's human nature to want to see new places and to take advantage of these bargains.

It is probably only a matter of time before taxes and charges increase, so perhaps we are living through a golden age of cheap, no-frills flights. Whether the Government or individuals decide it, it clearly can't go on for ever. But it's been wonderful to be able to go. Despite the odd misadventure – I try not to think about Brno too much – I'm definitely going to miss these trips.

Our weekend is over, and we're at the airport. The evening easyJet flight is late. We are sitting on an open-air concrete balcony, drinking coffees and mineral waters. Rows of pink and white flowers (possibly azaleas) are below. There's a half-moon hanging low and a tangerine sunset speckled with inky clouds over the hills towards the port.

Wojciech has just told me how he intends to set up a website called healthandrelax.pl offering dental, spa and plastic surgery tourism – 'any kind of tourism: get your teeth white tourism!' – in Poland. He wants to know whether it would do well with UK travellers? Probably, if it's cheap enough, I reply.

He explains his investment plans and an idea to have an advertising campaign on the Tube. 'Do you know that the average Tube journey is thirteen minutes? We could get those little adverts they have by the Tube maps. £15 each they cost, I've researched it. We'd need a lot of them . . .' Wojciech is full of tourist ideas for Szczecin.

Danny is jokingly grumpy: 'I'm never flying easyJet again. I'd rather pay more for BA. B*******. I'm mean look at the conditions. Perfect ******* conditions! They should be fined every time they're late. Fined!'

We look across at the tangerine sunset, watching as our plane glides down to Rijeka. It's a mild evening, and all is very peaceful. There's not another plane at the airport, and not much we can do about this flight being late. Danny suddenly has a moment of inspiration: 'Let's have a beer.'

As the easyJet boarding queues form, we raise our bottles of Beck's. The sun sinks over the darkening hills in the distance.

It's two hours' back to Luton . . . and a whole world away.

Acknowledgements

Many people shared their time both overseas and in the UK, without whom I would have found myself very lost in little known parts of Eastern Europe. I am especially indebited to Ewa Binkin, Wojciech Liszka, Eric Wiltshire, Natalia Balajova, Sarah Dean, Rita Leinan, Linda Borchert, Neil Taylor, Riitta Balzar, Jo Gaukrodger, Katie Keenan, Mary Stuart-Miller, Jaka Terpinc, Steve Roman, Tiina Randviir and Julia Berg. I would also like to say a special thanks to Tom Otley for his support, enthusiasm and commissions, as well as to Nick Davies and Nicola Doherty for steering me along at Hodder & Stoughton, and to Lucy Luck for getting the ball rolling. Friends including John Kiddle, Julian Sykes, Les Webb, Mary Gold, Danny Kelly, Rupert Wright, Zsuzsa Simko, Tara Munro and Nicki Glancey have given me great encouragement, for which I am very grateful.